To OBTAIN:

Drucker — Practice of Mgt.
Chandler — Strategy & Structure
Andrews — Strategic Planning

The New Management
LINE EXECUTIVE AND STAFF PROFESSIONAL IN THE FUTURE FIRM

WILLIAM H. GRUBER
Sloan School of Management
Massachusetts Institute of Technology

JOHN S. NILES
Office of Budget and Management Systems
Government of the District of Columbia

McGraw-Hill Book Company
New York   St. Louis   San Francisco   Auckland   Düsseldorf
Johannesburg   Kuala Lumpur   London   Mexico   Montreal
New Delhi   Panama   Paris   São Paulo   Singapore
Sydney   Tokyo   Toronto

Library of Congress Cataloging in Publication Data

Gruber, William H, date.
  The new management.
  Includes bibliographical references.
  1. Management. 2. Industrial management. I. Niles,
John S., joint author. II. Title.
HD31.G767   658.4   76-5414
ISBN 0-07-025073-1

Copyright © 1976 by McGraw-Hill, Inc. All rights reserved.
Printed in the United States of America. No part of this
publication may be reproduced, stored in a retrieval system,
or transmitted, in any form or by any means, electronic,
mechanical, photocopying, recording, or otherwise, without
the prior written permission of the publisher.

1234567890 KPKP 785432109876

The editors for this book were Robert A. Rosenbaum and Ruth L. Weine,
the designer was Naomi Auerbach, and the production supervisor
was Frank P. Bellantoni. It was set in VIP Baskerville
by University Graphics, Inc.

Printed and bound by The Kingsport Press.

To Lucretia and Libby, with thanks for being patient during our many evenings and weekends of work on this book

Contents

Foreword vii
Preface ix
Acknowledgments xiii

ONE *The Challenge of Management Performance* 1
    Research and Experience in Management   2
    The Evolution of Management   5
    Prior, Present, and Future Firm   6
    Performance Based on Management Innovation   16
    Preview of the Book   17

TWO *Investment in Management* 21
    A Company President's Discovery   21
    Finding Management Problems is Easy   22
    The Management-Investment Ratio   24
    The Big Losses   27
    Thin Management   29
    Good Management and High Profits   30
    Investment in Management at General Electric   32
    How Much Is Enough?   35

THREE *New Resources for Management* *38*

    Availability of Management Knowledge   39
    Education of Business Graduates   42
    Computers   44
    Supply Push and Demand Pull   49

FOUR *The Failure of Management Science/Operations Research (MS/OR)* *55*

    The Rise and Fall of Quantitative Management   55
    From Science to Practice in Management   63

FIVE *Research and Experience in Management* *67*

    Experience in Management   67
    Two Views of Management   70
    Shifting Pattern of Management   73
    Research-Responsive Management   75
    Everyone a Specialist   77
    Cognitive and Emotional Factors   79
    Conclusion   80

SIX *The Management of M.B.A.'s* *82*

    The Corporate M.B.A. Strategy   84
    Differences Among M.B.A.'s   85
    M.B.A. Means High Cost   87
    Return on the Investment of M.B.A.'s   90
    Factors Affecting M.B.A. Retention   91
    Summary   94

SEVEN *Specialization and Integration in the New Management* *96*

    Kinds of Specialists   100
    Practice on the Specialist Problem   102
    Integration of Specialists   104
    Inventory of Integration Techniques   107
    The Job of the Integrator   112
    The Michelin Strategy   113
    Conclusion   114

EIGHT *Specialization, Integration, and Performance* *117*

    Integration in Six Plastic Firms   118
    Integrating EDP in Banks   120
    Computer Utilization in One Bank   122
    Integration of the R&D Function   125
    Innovation Based on Research   127

NINE Information Is Powerful 129
The Crisis in Corporate Information   129
Data and Information   134
From Information to Models   136
The Failure of Accountants   139
Corporate Information Strategy   143

TEN How to Innovate in Management 146
Factors in a Successful Innovation Effort   147
Strategy for the Management-Innovation Effort   152
Stages in a Management-Innovation Program   155

ELEVEN Management of a Management-Innovation Project 163
Flowchart of a Project Cycle   164
Summary   174

TWELVE Task-Force Management 177
Background for this Chapter   178
Basic Task-Force Strategy   179
Case Studies of Task-Force Management   181
Task Forces or a Program of Innovation in Management?   183
Usefulness of Research-Based Management   184

THIRTEEN Environmental Forces in the Development of Future Firm 187
Limits to Growth   188
A More Difficult Business Environment   190
Reduced Economic Performance   205
Business Ineptness   207
Future Firm Management   209

FOURTEEN Management Innovation in Future Firm 213
From Present Firm to Future Firm   214
From Practice to Science   221
Future Firm Performance   225
A Final Word   232

Index   235

Foreword

The most serious barrier to the utilization of computer-based information systems to support managerial decision making and the control of operations is the implementation problem. The extraordinary rate of technological progress during this last two decades has provided the computer hardware and software capabilities to meet most of the serious needs of management for improved information systems. In addition, the supply of well-educated specialists in the computer sciences has been significantly increased in the last decade.

Thus the technical problems that have been experienced in the development of computer-based information systems either have been largely solved or are being actively worked on. The implementation problem continues to baffle specialists in computer-based systems and the line executives who need improved information to cope with the more difficult business environment that they are experiencing. The Gruber and Niles book, which focuses on a strategy for the utilization of specialized knowledge in the practice of management, provides needed and timely answers to some of the problems which have reduced the usefulness of computer-based information systems. This reduction is such that only a small fraction of the potential contribution for the improvement in the effectiveness of management is now available as a result of the technical progress achieved in the last two decades. Gruber and Niles provide solutions to help overcome this failure to fully utilize the available potential that has been developed in such diverse areas of specialized knowledge as computer-based information systems, management science, and organizational development.

Many professors of management have historically allocated much of their research effort to the development of ever more sophisticated and powerful management techniques. There has been relatively little attention in schools of management to what is now called "the implementation problem" and the "utilization lag." This tendency for faculty members to concentrate so heavily on the development of *new* knowledge is questioned by Gruber and Niles in their book which focuses on the utilization of *existing knowledge* now readily available to increase the effectiveness of management. The thorough research of Gruber and Niles in documenting the disparity between the rate of improvement in the technical resources for the New Management and the actual utilization of these new capabilities in the practice of management provides an important reference for line executives, staff professionals, and professors of management who are concerned about this problem.

The Center for Information System Research was established at the M.I.T. Sloan School of Management to define, research, and report potential solutions to significant managerial problems in the utilization of computer-based information systems. In the Statement of Purpose for the Center for Information System Research, we noted this disparity between the opportunity and the actual utilization of computer-based information systems, and proposed an interdisciplinary research program as a strategy for developing answers to implementation and the problems which have retarded the utilization of the potential power of computer-based information systems. A multidisciplinary approach which brings together hardware/software, planning and control, management science, and organizational behavior was the obvious strategy for the management of the Center for Information Systems Research, given the great complexity of the problems that are experienced in the utilization of computer-based information systems. Dr. Gruber, who is on the Sloan School faculty, and John Niles have written an interdisciplinary book which will be useful for professionals in all the specialized areas of business and for the line executives who utilize the specialized knowledge of their staff professionals.

MICHAEL S. SCOTT MORTON
*Professor of Management and Director,
Center for Information Systems Research
Alfred P. Sloan School of Management
Massachusetts Institute of Technology*

Preface

The myth of immortality is very comforting. Somehow people tend to believe in a future for their country, their business, and themselves. This assumption of survival and continuity, a belief in the future, requires the adaptation of our organizations and institutions to new conditions.

This book is about evolution and revolution in the practice of management in American business. Evolution generally implies a long time horizon. But in a period of great discontinuity, such as the 1960s and 1970s, there is not enough time for evolution. A revolutionary rate of improvement in the practice of management must be achieved if there is to be an adequate adaptation to changes in technological, economic, and social conditions. Rapid adaptation is occurring in some companies. We document the impressive improvements in the practice of management in a small number of leading companies, and then extrapolate to the level of management competence which appears to be possible in the best-managed companies in the 1980s. These leading companies we call "Future Firms."

Given the problems in the 1970s, it is difficult to imagine the effective management of corporations, governments, and other organizations with the procedures that were adequate in the 1950s. We forecast a dramatic increase in the implementation of the new management techniques described in this book.

Today the most critical skill for improving the practice of management is the ability to use the readily available specialized knowledge of staff professionals. A bridge which spans the communication gap between line managers and specialized staff professionals is needed if decisions are to be based on research and knowledge rather than intuition and experience. We agree with Peter Drucker's observation that in an age of discontinuity, experience becomes less useful.

The New Management, as we define the concept, is a blend of new and old knowledge whose sum results in the quality of staff work which is required to make decisions and monitor progress during a period of wildly fluctuating and discontinuous environmental conditions. There are the newer areas of specialized knowledge such as computer-based information systems, strategic planning, management science, and organizational development. And there are the older areas of specialized knowledge such as law, accounting, and R&D. Management in Future Firm will effectively integrate the experience and intuition of line executives with the specialized knowledge of staff professionals. In Future Firm, the effectiveness of management practices will be scored as an important test of performance. Good management means more than bottom-line performance this year, because short-run profits are too often purchased with a deterioration of the longer-term viability of a company. We demonstrate in this book that it is possible to measure the competence of management by the effectiveness with which new management techniques are utilized.

The evolution of progress in the practice of management is analyzed in order to place the current surge in the utilization of new management techniques in historical perspective. This book was greatly influenced by our research and consulting on R&D problems. We see the acceptance of new-management practices as resulting from the demand pull and supply push factors which are often used in technology forecasts for new products and processes. A large number of examples are provided to illustrate the high performance which can be achieved through the utilization of what we call the New Management. Our forecast of a rapid improvement in the effectiveness of management is not mere speculation, but an extrapolation of readily observable trends and case studies of company experiences.

We document in this book a small number of important and interrelated ideas:

- The problems confronting leaders in business, government, universities, and other organizations have increased in seriousness at a sobering rate during this last decade, and there is strong evidence that a still further decrease in the ability of government, business, and other organizations to cope will continue during this next decade.

- An extraordinary increase in the usefulness of new-management techniques has been achieved in the last twenty years. There has been a revolution in the new knowledge for management and the supply (in both quantity and quality) of business school graduates with this new knowledge. This new knowledge has been made more cost-effective as a result of the improvements in the quantity and quality of powerful computer hardware and software that is useful in the practice of management.

- There is a serious communications problem between the experience-based older line executives, who make decisions, and the younger, research-based staff professionals, who understand the usefulness of new management techniques. The younger staff professionals tend not to have the intuition and experience of the older line executives, who, in turn, tend not to know how to manage these highly educated young staff professionals.

- The most critical problem in management today is the shortage of people who can bridge this communications gap between line managers and staff professionals. In many large companies there is now an adequate supply of staff professionals with good new-management skills. What is missing in most companies are the line managers who know how to utilize the New Management and the staff professionals who know how to translate their new-management skills into a language which can be understood by line management.

Problems experienced in efforts to utilize the New Management are being solved in many companies. A major objective in writing this book was to present the state of the art in the management of specialized knowledge. We document the fact that management increasingly involves the utilization of specialized knowledge.

Some of the ideas presented in this book were developed over a decade ago, and thus there has been a long history of working with colleagues and clients. Parts of the book have been published in fourteen journals and the comments of editors and reviewers of these journals have been of great assistance in sharpening our concepts and our writing skills.

From the many sources of assistance that we would like to acknowledge, we have selected but a small number of people who have greatly influenced our understanding of the New Management and the related problems of specialization. About ten years ago, Dr. Gruber taught a seminar at M.I.T. on the Management of R&D Interface Problems for senior-level R&D executives. As a class assignment in the seminar, one of the participating executives, Gerald D. Laubach (then vice president-research of Pfizer, Inc., now president of that firm), developed a questionnaire to measure the quality of R&D interface conditions. We have used this technique first developed by Dr. Laubach many times in our research and consulting on interface problems, and findings from these experiences are presented in this book. Note that interface problems which exist among specialized staff professionals and line executives are probably the greatest barrier to the utilization of specialized skills to improve the effectiveness of management.

During Dr. Gruber's consulting assignments at Pfizer, he worked with Dr. Laubach and the director of systems, Dr. G. M. K. Hughes (now vice president and general manager of Pfizer Medical Systems, Inc.). The experience in working with Drs. Laubach and Hughes in their efforts to increase the effectiveness of management at Pfizer provided an extraordinary opportunity over a large number of years for Dr. Gruber to observe and participate in a program of innovation in the practice of management. One of the underlying themes in the book is that the process of increasing the effectiveness of management is similar to R&D for new products. This idea was conceived during the decade of working with Drs. Laubach and Hughes, who began their careers as research chemists.

It is impossible to identify all of the many client experiences which are the source of our recommended strategies for increasing the effectiveness of management. We do want to note our particular thanks for the ideas and performance of William R. Synnott, senior vice president, EDP Services Division, The First National Bank of Boston, which had a profound influence on our thinking. Ideas and support from a number of professors in the M.I.T. Sloan School of Management were important in the writing of this book. Assistance from the late Donald G. Marquis, David Sarnoff Professor of Management, was of particular importance in the conceptualization stage. Our understanding of the interface factor in the utilization of new technology was greatly enhanced by Dr. Gruber's study of international differences in R&D management which was supported by a National Science Foundation grant to the Harvard Business School.

Behind many authors patiently sits an editor, busily improving the quality of their writing. We were very fortunate to have Helen Webber as our editor. Her assistance and the advice and support of a large number of clients, friends, and secretaries are acknowledged with appreciation. The final product, this book, is the sole responsibility of the authors and does not represent the positions of any of the organizations with which we have been affiliated.

W.H.G.
J.F.N.
March 1, 1976

Acknowledgments

The authors first presented many of the findings in this book in fourteen journals published by professional associations and universities. We acknowledge with appreciation permissions to use these materials that were received from the editors of the following journals and listed below by chapter in our book:

CHAPTER 1. THE CHALLENGE OF MANAGEMENT PERFORMANCE: *Organizational Dynamics,* Spring 1974, a journal of the American Management Associations, and *Financial Executive,* April 1971, a journal of the Financial Executives Institute.

CHAPTER 4. THE FAILURE OF MANAGEMENT SCIENCE/OPERATIONS RESEARCH: *Management Science,* April 1975, and *Interfaces,* November 1971, journals of The Institute of Management Sciences.

CHAPTER 5. RESEARCH AND EXPERIENCE IN MANAGEMENT: *Business Horizons,* August 1973, a journal of the Graduate School of Business, Indiana University.

CHAPTER 6. THE MANAGEMENT OF M.B.A.'S: *Management of Personnel Quarterly,* Fall 1971, a journal of the Graduate School of Business, University of Michigan.

CHAPTER 7. SPECIALIZATION AND INTEGRATION IN THE NEW MANAGEMENT: *Industrial Management Review,* Fall 1967, a journal of the Sloan School of Management, Massachusetts Institute of Technology.

CHAPTER 8. SPECIALIZATION, INTEGRATION, AND PERFORMANCE: *Research Management,* November 1973, a journal of the Industrial Research Institute, and *R&D Management,* Summer 1974, (co-authored with Otto H. Poensgen and Frits Prakke).

CHAPTER 9. INFORMATION IS POWERFUL: *Journal of Accountancy,* May 1971, a journal of the American Institute of Certified Public Accountants, (co-authored with Louis L. Logan).

CHAPTER 10. HOW TO INNOVATE IN MANAGEMENT: *Organizational Dynamics,* Fall 1974, a journal of the American Management Associations, and *Management Adviser,* March–April 1972, a journal of the American Institute of Certified Public Accountants.

CHAPTER 12. TASK-FORCE MANAGEMENT: *The Utilization of Specialists by Company Presidents,* Presidents Association, Special Study No. 60, American Management Associations, 1975.

CHAPTER 14. MANAGEMENT INNOVATION IN FUTURE FIRM: *California Management Review,* Summer 1972, a journal of the University of California.

We would also like to acknowledge quotations used with permission from the following original sources of publication:

Murray L. Weidenbaum, *Government-Mandated Price Increases,* 1975, American Enterprise Institute

Robert N. Anthony, *Planning and Control,* 1965, Division of Sponsored Research, Harvard Business School

"A Price Monitor Keeps the Dough Rising," *Business Week,* December 7, 1974

Robert Ball, "The Michelin Man Rolls into Akron's Back Yard," *Fortune,* December 1974

Fred G. Withington, "Five Generations of Computers," *Harvard Business Review,* July–August 1974

W. N. Conrady, "Accounting Education for What Purpose?," *The Journal of Contemporary Business,* Winter 1972

Russell L. Ackoff, "Management Misinformation Systems," *Management Science,* December 1967

Leonard Sayles, *Managerial Behavior,* 1964, McGraw-Hill Book Company

David B. Hertz, *New Power for Management,* 1969, McGraw-Hill Book Company

Russell L. Ackoff and James R. Emshoff, "Advertising Effectiveness at Anheuser-Busch, Inc. (1956–68)," *Sloan Management Review,* Winter 1975

Kenneth Bacon and Mitchell Lynch, "Ford Administration May Really Be Serious About Antitrust Drive," © *The Wall Street Journal,* November 16, 1974

ONE

The Challenge of Management Performance

Revolutionary challenges to the practice of management have occurred since World War II. Discontinuities in the business environment have made the achievement of acceptable levels of corporate performance a far more difficult task.

Think about the peaceful days of the Eisenhower administration. There was little foreign competition. Computers were just beginning to emerge as a replacement for tabulating and bookkeeping machines. Wage-price controls were never considered seriously. Pollution, equal employment, consumerism, and other such concerns of the 1970s were of little consequence in the 1950s. Business schools, according to the respected Ford and Carnegie Foundation studies published in 1959,[1] taught little that was useful, but this did not matter because it was a stable world in which experience was an adequate background for a career in management.

Now less than twenty years later, there is a revolution in the environment of business. It is no longer possible to predict that the future will be similar to the present. Consider these disturbing factors in the present environment of business:

    1. A rate of inflation three times greater than that experienced between 1955 and 1972

    2. A volatile stock market much more demanding of corporate profits and sales growth performance

    3. Questioning of previously accepted national activity—for example, of the prevalence of private automobiles over mass transit

4. The energy crisis
5. Pollution and other environmental problems
6. Consumerism (defined as higher standards of consumer protection on a wide range of products and services)
7. A significant decline in the international competitive position of many United States industries
8. Shortages of many materials
9. Increase in the required disclosure of corporate performance and accounting practices
10. An academic environment increasingly critical of business

Clearly, business people have greater worries today than the rigors of competition. Management in the 1970s is faced with problems never before imagined. An environment in which experience provides little guidance in the design of corporate strategy and the conduct of business operations is the challenge of the 1970s for corporate management. Old ways of managing have limited provisions for handling the new problems in the business environment.

In order to understand the revolution which is occurring in the practice of management, it is first necessary to accept the fact that the severe discontinuities in the environment of business—abrupt changes from what has happened in the past—have made obsolete the experience-based intuitive style of management that was very effective through the 1950s and even into the early 1960s.

Experience-based management means the utilization of skills that are learned from experience on the job. Business has historically been managed by executives who have learned how to manage from the lessons of work-based experience. Today, *research-based* staff work, systematically researching the business environment, gathering and summarizing information, and making analytical studies, is necessary to support the experience-based, seat-of-the-pants manager. As Robert Charpie, president of Cabot Corporation observed, "A decision that may be correct when the rate of inflation is two percent a year may be totally inappropriate during a double digit rate of inflation. It is necessary to take a much harder look at assumptions when making decisions during a period of volatile business conditions."[2]

RESEARCH AND EXPERIENCE IN MANAGEMENT

The long history of management has been a record of practice built on past experience. Managers learned not from books, but rather from their observations of successes and failures—their own as well as other managers'. We expect a physician, lawyer, or engineer to have a degree in his or her field of specialization; we do not expect this of a manager. Some of today's most successful business executives have never had a course in management; some have never graduated from college.

Managers of almost any activity make decisions about such varied problems as prices or equipment purchases or personnel motivation using very little systematically applied knowledge. Experienced managers making pricing decisions may, if they have been in finance, take projected unit volume as a given and push for higher prices. If they have been in sales, they may urge lower prices to gain more customers and hence higher unit volumes. These issues would probably be resolved in discussions with other managers who have experience or at least an opinion to add. Pricing decisions are frequently made without reference to organized information about the impact of previous pricing decisions or analyses of market segments which were most price elastic. The probable effect of a pricing decision on unit volume is often not estimated, and thus a learning experience is made more difficult because it was not possible to observe feedback from actual versus projected performance.

An experience-based manager who is assisted by research-based staff professionals, on the other hand, would reach pricing decisions on the grounds of information supplied by such procedures as analysis of historical relationships between price and quantity purchased, creation of a market test area, consumer surveys, and an analysis of competitive actions.

The training of a research-based professional allows him or her to determine what facts are needed to solve a given problem. The critical knowledge of such a professional is an understanding of the process of problem finding which is then linked to problem solving through the *use of such research-based technologies as strategic planning, econometrics, systems analysis, organization development, and computer-based management information systems.* Expertise in structuring procedures for the search effort and for processing information enables the research-based professional to create relevance out of unanalyzed data.

Research-based management requires the time, as well as the educational background, to do research on problems related to management decisions and practices. This work usually depends on knowledge that is learned in courses in management. Partial freedom from the urgency of line operations is also needed, because research-based management takes more time than is available to line executives, who tend to be overwhelmed with the details of managing daily activities.

It is useful to regard research-based people as those who understand what is happening around them to such an extent that changes in the environment do not upset their ability to solve problems. C. West Churchman illustrates this concept with an example from sales forecasting:

Often in companies we find that men with years of experience have arrived at methods of managing operations which cannot be matched by analysis. For example, a vice-president of sales of a large company would forecast sales of the company's products based on reports received from the field, economic data, and other types of information, coupled with his own judgment. He seemed to have an uncanny way of coming up with accurate estimates that we could not duplicate by any statistical methods known to us. In this case the company could be said to have arrived at the correct action, but again I doubt if we would want to say that the company had knowledge of forecasting. If the vice-president were to leave, the environment would be changed and the company would have no obvious way to adapt to the change. Thus, our statistical methods, though perhaps slightly inferior to those of the vice-president under current conditions, constituted something more like knowledge than the vice-president's intuitively-based decisions.[3]

Churchman reported on the effectiveness in forecasting of the experience-based vice president of sales in 1964, a time of relative stability compared with the volatile conditions of the 1970s. Our experience in working with clients indicates that even experience-based executives with good track records have been less effective in making decisions in the uncertain times of the 1970s. The senior management in one large bank recently began a program of staff studies and a greater involvement of senior officers in research on the serious problems that were afflicting the banking industry. The chief executive officer of this bank recognized that senior management just had inadequate knowledge about how the bank would be affected by what James Smith, comptroller of the currency, has called a "general disquiet in the financial markets." *The Wall Street Journal* story "Currency Comptroller Has Job of Restoring Trust in Bank System" notes: "Effects of the Federal Reserve Board's stringent monetary policies, sky-high interest rates, intense competition for investor funds, feverish foreign-exchange speculation and seething world-wide inflation are all spawning doubts about the strength of the nation's financial system."[4]

The response to these difficulties by the senior executives in a number of banks and by the chief financial officers of many corporations has been to increase the resources allocated for the development of research-based management techniques which collect the data and provide analysis of the probable impact on their operations of the volatile financial conditions. In banking and in the financial management of business, environmental conditions have forced experience-based executives to seek professional staff assistance in order to improve their capabilities to manage during a period of serious volatility in the financial markets. Experience without research-based management as a basis for making decisions in this new environment has proved to be totally inadequate in the environment of the 1970s. This inadequacy of experience-based management was not as observable in the environments of the 1950s and early 1960s. We are finding with increasing frequency that experience-based line executives are seeking the assistance of research-based staff professionals. The final decision is still made by the experience-based line executive, but this decision is now based on the organized information produced in the research of staff professionals as well as on the intuition and judgment of the experience-based line executive.

THE EVOLUTION OF MANAGEMENT

Alfred D. Chandler, in *Strategy and Structure*,[5] surveying the growth of American enterprise, reveals the overall evolution of business through stages of development. As business confronted new problems during the growth of the American economy, three stages of corporate structure resulted from the process of adaptation. A review of Chandler's three stages will provide a basis for understanding a fourth stage of corporate structure which appears to be emerging in response to the new challenges in the environment of business. This fourth stage provides for the synthesis of experience and knowledge needed for management in an "age of discontinuity."

Stages of Business Organization

Entrepreneurial activity The first stage of business organization was the activity of the entrepreneur, recognizing and meeting a market demand with the aid of a small, informal organization. This was the case for practically all businesses before 1850; large, stable, well-organized firms did not exist.

Centralized formal organizations The second stage involved the creation of an organization to administer the business after it became too large for informal control. After the Civil War, large railroads developed administrative structures characterized by functional departments linked to a central office which monitored the enterprise as a whole. In the last half of the nineteenth century, management structures became increasingly the concern of the industrial empire builders. A failure to adapt organization structures to the new economic environment was found to be the cause of poor performance in fourteen unsuccessful combinations and consolidations formed around 1900. In these fourteen companies, overreliance on personal contact and individual ability was the major cause of business failure.[6]

In this second stage—the creation of managing organizations—a separation of personnel into line and staff was developed to distinguish between those who made decisions about basic operations and those who provided support. The Pennsylvania Railroad pioneered in this organizational hierarchy before the 1880s. However, as firms became larger and moved into different product lines and different geographical territories, even the second-stage structure proved to be inadequate.

Decentralization The third stage was the decentralized, divisionalized structure—an organizational innovation which began to appear around 1920. Introduced in such firms as General Motors and Du Pont, the divisionalized structure, now widely employed by large firms, permits line managers to concentrate on the problems associated with a particular market segment or product, while corporate officers coordinate the activities of the enterprise as a whole. Decentralization moved the point of decision making lower in the hierarchy.

An organization structure in harmony with the economic environment and corporate objectives is a major determinant of successful corporate performance. When product lines are narrowly defined and markets are regional, centralized management is sufficient for meeting objectives. As companies increase the number of their products and widen the geographical scope of their markets, decentralization permits greater flexibility by giving authority for decision making to managers in closer contact with the economic environment. In an important study, Fouraker and Stopford found that firms with a decentralized organization structure were more successful in establishing multinational operations.[7] Thus, organization structure first developed to cope with domestic problems also facilitated corporate expansion in international markets.

Chandler's third stage of organization structure was sufficient for the business environment of the 1950s, but it is now apparent that a fourth stage of business response to the environment is necessary. We suggest that the development of organizational arrangements to utilize research-based staffs is the most appropriate business response to today's environment. The historic process of adapting the corporate structure to environmental forces, diagramed in Figure 1.1, includes a fourth stage, research-based management.

PRIOR, PRESENT, AND FUTURE FIRM

Today, most companies maintain some research-based management activities in support of line executives. Five years ago, there was far less of this research-based activity, while ten years ago the quantity was minimal. Business executives have a need to know how well they are doing relative to their competitors. When there is a rapid rate of change in technology, such as in the computer and office copier industries, management must forecast trends in the improvement of products. There is a similar interest

Structure	Individual entrepreneur	Formal management structure & centralization	Decentralization	Research-based management
Time	Before 1850	1850–1920	1920–1970	Beyond 1970
New problems arising toward end of period	Size and operational complexity; informal management not sufficient for control	Expanding markets and product lines; centralized management not responsive to diversity	Environmental complexity and growth of knowledge; experience not sufficient to cope with discontinuities	

FIG. 1.1 *Stages of corporate structure in response to problems.* (Based on the description of the evolution of American business in Alfred D. Chandler, *Strategy and Structure*, Garden City, New York, Doubleday, Anchor Books ed., 1966.)

in monitoring competitive marketing practices. Despite the rapid improvement in the practice of management, we have not observed an equal interest in monitoring competitive management practices. One reason for this disparity in the interest in monitoring competitive performance is that improvement in the practice of management is not as easy to monitor.

Improvement in the practice of management does not appear to have as direct an impact on short-run financial performance as a lead in a new product or a successful new marketing strategy. What is usually lost in comparisons of relative competitive performance in marketing and R&D for new products is that improvements in the practice of management are frequently the underlying cause of the marketing and R&D results which are visible to competitors.

In a number of industries, such as banking, we have observed very wide disparities in the effectiveness with which research-based management techniques are utilized.[8] These observed disparities in the effectiveness of management and the speed of improvement in the utilization of research-based management techniques have provided the information for developing a continuum of management competence.

There is a range of possible estimates of the rate of improvement in the utilization of research-based techniques. Readers are invited to reflect upon the practice of management in 1960, 1970, and 1975. Our own evaluation of the rate of improvement in the utilization of research-based management techniques is based on observations of the practices in a large number of companies. Based on these observations, it is our estimate that if we scored as 100 the level of research-based management activity in practice today, we would probably discover that the average utilization of these techniques five years ago might rate a score of 25 and ten years ago a score of 5 to 10. Firms increasingly are competing in the utilization of research-based management techniques, just as twenty years ago they began to compete more intensively in R&D for new products. Because both the utilization and the effectiveness of these techniques are increasing at such a rapid rate, it is useful for executives to keep score of their progress.

To provide a qualitative system for scoring progress in the evolution toward the utilization of research-based management, we have identified three levels of management competence, which we have labeled Prior Firm, Present Firm, and Future Firm. The level of utilization of research-based management in the typical firm in the early 1970s is called Present Firm. There is no question that the Present Firm is much better managed than the average firm in the early 1960s, which we have labeled Prior Firm. The Present Firm has a more effective staff of research-based professionals with responsibilities for activities such as the development of management information systems and strategic plans. And the line executives in the Present Firm are more sophisticated users of research-based techniques than were the line executives in the Prior Firm.

Present Firm managers have come a long way, but our work with those managers indicates that much corporate activity continues to be out of control. Difficulties created by new sources of competition, more complex government regulation, and environmental concerns have resulted in a need for research-based capabilities that exceeds the progress achieved in the transition from Prior to Present Firm. The ability to cope with this level of difficulty will have been greatly increased through the development of research-based capabilities that will be in common use in Future Firm, which we define as a firm with *average management* in the 1990s. The *best-managed* firms in 1980 will have a Future Firm level of new-management capability—they will achieve a level of management competence that will be the average level of competence in the mid 1990s.

The lags which have been experienced in the utilization of new technology provide a useful analogy to what has been experienced in the rate of adoption of research-based management techniques. The findings of Edwin Mansfield's study of the rate of diffusion among the large firms competing in the bituminous coal, iron and steel, brewing, and railroad industries are presented in Table 1.1.[9] Note that a lag of almost eight years was experienced between the time when the first company innovated with an important new technology and the time when one-half of the leading companies had initiated the lead of the innovators.

TABLE 1.1 Time Lag between First Successful Application and 50 Percent Diffusion (among Major Firms) of Several Major Innovations in the Bituminous Coal, Iron and Steel, Brewing, and Railroad Industries

Innovation	Number of years until 50% diffusion
Bituminous coal industry:	
Shuttle car	7
Trackless mobile loader	7
Continuous mining machine	4
Iron and steel industry:	
By-product coke oven	15
Continuous wide-strip mill	8
Continuous annealing	18
Brewing industry:	
Tin containers	1
Pallet-loading machine	7
High-speed bottle filler	9
Railroad industry:	
Diesel locomotive	11
Car retarder	15
Centralized traffic control	15
Average	7.8

SOURCE: E. Mansfield, "Technical Change and the Rate of Innovation," *Econometrica*, October 1961, pp. 287–288.

Similar lags appear in the adoption of research-based management techniques. Because the range of management competence will have broadened between 1975 and 1980, the high performers will be much further ahead of the low performers than they are now. Just to remain at an average level of management competence, the average 1975 firm will have to step up its utilization of research-based techniques during the 1975–1980 period.

In Figure 1.2 we have diagramed the distribution of firms measured by level of utilization of new-management techniques as estimated for 1975 and 1980. Our research on the speed of innovation in the utilization of new-management techniques indicates that there will be significant shift toward a Future Firm level of management competence during the interval from 1975 to 1980.

Note that as of 1975 we find no firms that can be ranked at a full Future Firm competence. By 1980, however, a small percentage of firms in the *Fortune* 500 list of large corporations (and related lists of the largest 50 commercial banks, insurance companies, etc.) will have achieved a Future Firm level of management.

10 / *The New Management*

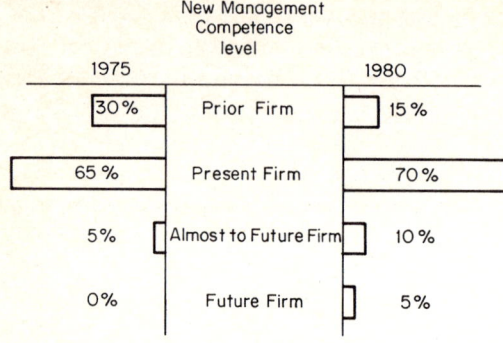

FIG. 1.2 *Profile of new-management competence in 1975 and 1980.*

Future Firm management has been defined as a level of competence that will be achieved by a small number of leading companies by 1980. It is not an unchanging standard of performance. Progress will continue in the first companies to achieve a Future Firm level of management. Thus our Future Firm level of management is but a milestone on a path that leads to ever more effective levels of management competence.

Example of Prior, Present, and Future Firms

The three kinds of management can be identified and illustrated in the progress achieved in one of our client companies.

Prior Firm management The management capability of this firm at the time of the selection of a new company president can be assigned a Prior Firm rating. Little attention had been allocated to internal management practices during the decade preceding the promotion of the new president. The firm had grown rapidly as a result of new, patented inventions from its research division. Price pressure from competition had not been severe, profit margins were good, and demand was very strong. Top management of this company was thin relative to the size of operations which had been built in such a short spurt of growth. Here was the typical Prior Firm. It had a management doing a good job inventing, manufacturing, and selling products in fields where there was historical operating experience.

Staff support was not available in such basic areas as management information systems, long-range planning, production cost controls, market forecasting, acquisitions, and government relations. (Most technologically advanced firms had severe regulatory problems even five years ago, although this was not as publicly recognized then as it is today.) The computer was used as a big adding machine. The most elementary management information was largely unavailable.

Sales forecasts were an arbitrary extrapolation of trends. Sales quotas by product and territory were determined on the basis of inadequate information. The positive effect of the sales quota on performance of the sales force was assumed without any effort to examine feedback with a sales-quota/performance analysis. Millions of dollars were spent on advertising without any reason to believe that such expenditures were useful. Very little effort was given to linking sales forecasts with production scheduling. Sales were subject to severe seasonal and cyclical forces, and arbitrary sales forecasts for an entire year would have been of little assistance to manufacturing even if an effort had been made to link sales forecasts and manufacturing schedules.

Control of manufacturing costs was not even considered by the top management of this company. Plant accountants were responsible for setting cost standards. There was evidence that standards were set to minimize variances rather than provide a basis for efficient manufacturing cost controls. The production reports produced by the plant accountants were accepted without analysis or reservations by top management, and there was very little interaction between top management and the manufacturing activity, which was located in plants separated geographically from corporate headquarters.

Present Firm management   The new company president was able to bring the firm from a Prior to a Present Firm management capability in less than three years after assuming the new position. Almost every facet of management activity from forecasting sales to planning for workforce requirements was improved in this short period of time.

Although there were a large number of management innovations during the first three years of this effort, only eight will be described. These examples were selected to illustrate the breadth of management activity that was improved.

1. *Computer-based corporate planning capability* provided a basis for evaluating future activity (for example, sales by product line) under various assumptions. This capability made planning easier, and it increased the commitment to planning of a large number of the corporate executives. In addition, the budgeting for the next year was made more efficient because this new computer capability produced alternative budgets quickly with relatively little clerical effort. One result of this increase in the utilization of information for planning was the questioning of previously accepted expense/sales ratios. This computer-based planning capability facilitated analyses of the effect on corporate sales and profits of changes in discretionary expenses such as advertising and sales force levels.

2. *Monthly sales forecasts by product* adjusted longer-run trends by

seasonal and cyclical factors. These forecasts were used for sales quotas, marketing strategies, and production scheduling. Responsibility for profit-center management by product line became a reality when sales performance was evaluated against expectations calculated with trend, seasonal, and cyclical effects identified.

3. *Product cost control system* identified expenses which could be controlled at the product line level. Allocated costs to product lines which could not be controlled by product line management were separated from the controllable costs, thereby increasing the visibility of the product line performance effect on corporate profitability.[10]

4. *Marketing customer control system* identified and maintained a record of activity for each customer. Sales people were given instructions for each customer, and better communication to and from sales people was achieved. Systems analysis of the marketing information used prior to this new capability revealed that sales people were reporting customer activity which was incorrect. A huge marketing information system had been in use which did not have interactive capability. Sales people had been flooded with useless information. Sales reports were completed but never used. This large mass of information which had been passing back and forth between marketing management and the sales force was terminated, and the new system, which created a dialogue between the marketing data base and the sales force, was substituted in its place. Thus a little-used static system was replaced by a dynamic information system which created a capability to absorb new information and thus enrich the customer data base as a result of the experience reported by the sales force.

5. *Programming software capability* allowed managers who were inexperienced with computers to ask questions of the system. The involvement of line management with new computer-based management information system was an objective given high priority by the director of management systems. His staff were instructed to encourage line executives to work directly with the computer-based MIS (management information system) that had been developed. Software was developed permitting executives who were inexperienced in the use of computers to achieve useful MIS outputs with a relatively small investment in time allocated to learn how to ask questions of the computer system. Terminals were located close to the offices of the line executives.

6. *Share of market budgeting system* provided a more realistic set of objectives for product line managers. It had been the practice to calculate the budget for one year in November and December of the previous year. Seasonal and cyclical factors soon made this budget irrelevant, and yet each month variances from this static budget were calculated and "explained." Under the new system, product line managers were held

responsible for a share of market, and actual performance was compared with a sales budget calculated each month from estimates of total market activity by product line.

7. *Variance budgeting systems* predicted year-end variance based on year-to-date results compared with budget. Total market volume estimates were calculated for the year on a monthly basis. Thus all levels of management received a report of the estimated potential by product. The actual year-to-date performance was compared with estimated yearly performance on a monthly basis in order to give management an approximation of what was needed to fulfill the contribution of each product line to budgeted corporate performance.

8. *On-line production and inventory planning system* replaced a slow and labor-intensive system. This gave more detailed information by kind of item within a product line and provided an estimate of production costs under various volumes and product mixes (such as forecasted cost of goods sold).

The progress described in this company involved management innovation in the utilization of information. The development of information systems does appear to be a primary source of improvement in the effectiveness of management. As we will describe in Chapter 2, companies tend to be out of control for a number of reasons. Many firms have increased in size by ten and twenty times over the last two decades. There just has not been the management depth and experience to maintain control over companies that are expanding rapidly during a period of volatile economic conditions. Computer-based management information systems provide at least potentially the most cost-effective strategy for gaining control of operations. However, the development of management information systems is not all there is to the improvement of management. Organization changes are of critical importance. Who receives the reports produced by the new MIS? How well do managers know how to ask questions of and utilize the reports that can be produced by the new information systems? Then there is the question of management development. How are good managers discovered, developed, and motivated? How is job rotation utilized to provide breadth and balance in line managers and members of the professional staffs? Although the major thrust of the effort to improve the effectiveness of management in this company was in the development of information systems, senior management was aware of these organizational development issues, and progress in human resources was also achieved.

This brief overview of the major systems innovations implemented in just a few years shows what can be accomplished with a small MIS staff that understands the information needs of management. The information required as data inputs to the new systems was readily available. The computer programming was not difficult. These new capabilities were developed quickly because of the quality of the MIS–line-management relationships and the high quality of the MIS director and his staff.[11]

Future Firm management Despite progress in reaching an improved level of management competence, this Present Firm company and all other large corporations continue to be out of control. By this strong statement, we mean that management is not yet prepared to respond adequately to the more difficult environment of the 1970s. Major decisions are made with inadequate information. Serious problems have been increasing faster than line management and staff resources. In a volatile business environment, company managements will probably always jump from one crisis to another. In that sense, if the discontinuities in the environment of business continue to occur at the rate experienced in the last ten years, it may be that the management of companies will always be somewhat out of control. However, in the innovations in management that are now in the development stage in Present Firm a superior standard of management competence is beginning to be observable. This higher level of management competence will be referred to as Future Firm management. One can predict that in this decade there will emerge a small number of corporations in which control is achieved over the practices of management. The procedures used to gain this control will be described in this book. For example, case studies of task-force management described in Chapter 12 provide examples of effective responses to difficult problems. Future Firm management will have a strong environment-scanning capability. Serious problems will be anticipated. Resources will be allocated to the improvement of conditions before there is a crisis which threatens the viability of a company. The executives of these Future Firm corporations will allocate management resources in harmony with business problems and opportunities.

The performance of Sears Roebuck, a leader in management innovation, provides an example of what one company can achieve. Consider the complexity of managing 23,000 suppliers, 200,000 items, and 41,800 retail merchandising departments; Sears has increased its sales from $5 billion in 1963 to $11 billion in 1973, yet it is difficult to recall even a single major management error similar in magnitude to those experienced by so many other giant companies. The appointment of Arthur M. Wood, a lawyer rather than merchandiser, as president and chairman of Sears reflects the trend in retailing toward recognition of the importance of general management, rather than marketing skills. *Business Week* observed in an interview with Wood:

Today's merchant must have a broader grasp of government regulations and laws, finance, labor unions, real estate investments, consumerism, and the host of other complex elements that populate today's retail environment. At Sears, Wood can call on what he describes as "specialists in depth" for merchandising, finance and other areas. "We rely on them in critical decisions. Staff work shows the way."[12]

The extraordinary progress achieved by some executives in the utilization of research-based management techniques provides a strong refutation of the critics of management science who do not distinguish between the frequent uselessness of sophisticated models as compared with the tremendous power of other kinds of new-management techniques, such as computer-based management information systems, in which staff work shows the way. The evolution of the Sears computer capability is a case in point. In 1963 Sears began the development of regional computer centers for the processing of crediting, accounting, and ordering activities. The next stage of the Sears computer effort was program innovations to provide accounting and management information for merchandising and inventory management. Today, Sears is in the process of implementing point-of-sale cash register computer terminals for the input of inventory and sales data.

The consistent leadership of Sears in profitability has been a challenge to competitors. Its profits as a percent of sales were 5.1 percent in 1972, compared with 2.9 percent for J. C. Penney, 0.5 percent for Marcor, 4.1 percent for Federated Stores, and 1.9 percent for Allied Stores. A direct relationship between the utilization of computer-based management information systems and corporatewide performance is difficult to determine, but imitation by competitors may be a good indication of the usefulness of computers. For example, in a report on the resurgence of Montgomery Ward, *Business Week* emphasized the usefulness of computers as a management resource:

> Items in the catalogue itself have been programmed into a computer that categorizes each by cost, merchandise return, catalogue expense, and other factors. With the data, a "sensitivity analysis" can be obtained that projects sales and profit if the various elements are changed. A hand-held power saw, for example, that previously had been given small display space on a page of the catalogue was featured on a page of its own, in color, and with its price reduced $1. Sales jumped immediately from $40,000 or $50,000 a year to $500,000. Overall, enthuses Allred [Vice-president—catalogue sales], an increase of 43 percent in "tonnage" pages that feature single items has brought about an increase of 128 percent in the item's volume.[13]

PERFORMANCE BASED ON MANAGEMENT INNOVATION

Corporate performance is increasingly determined by a company's position in the race to build a research-based management capability. Our surveys (see Chapter 8) on the speed with which companies have introduced new-management techniques provide the basis for ranking corporate performance along a Prior–Present–Future Firm scale. It has been our experience that executives are able to evaluate their corporate performance on this scale, given some guidance about the definition of each level of management competence.

Our research on the speed of innovation in the utilization of new-management techniques indicates that there will be a significant shift toward a Future Firm level of management competence. By 1980, we estimate that 5 percent of all large firms will have achieved a Future Firm level of management. That would mean that twenty-five (plus or minus perhaps five to ten firms) on the *Fortune* 500 list will achieve a Future Firm level of management competence by 1980. Those numbers of firms in different classes of management competence that we present in Figure 1.2 represent estimates of the response of company executives to the problems and opportunities that we analyze in this book. Some consultants and researchers on the practice of management may reach other estimates of the numbers of companies in different categories of management competence. The volatility of conditions and the speed of change in the practice of management in many companies preclude estimates with great precision. The primary importance of the changes in management competence that are predicted in Figure 1.2 is that the wide range of competence existing in 1975 is expected to increase by 1980.

Note that our range of management competence is for large firms on the *Fortune* 500 list. Smaller firms will lag in the application of new-management techniques for several reasons. First, research-based management techniques are a kind of investment, and it is more efficient to spread the cost of this investment over a large volume of activity. Second, research-based management techniques are more necessary in large firms because (1) problems in the planning and coordination of activity do not appear to be as serious in smaller firms, (2) informal sources of information for the control of operations are more useful in smaller firms, and (3) the diversity of operations is a less-serious problem in smaller firms. For these reasons, we limited our study to firms in the *Fortune* 500 range.

We also project a rapid movement of firms from Prior Firm classification into a Present Firm classification and a movement of firms now in the Present Firm category into the almost-to-Future Firm category. We expect very little leapfrogging from Prior Firm to Future Firm status. Progress in the development of the capability to use the techniques of the New Management requires time if improvement is to be achieved at an acceptable level of return on investment.

There are several reasons for this forecast of extraordinary improvement. One of the most important is competitive pressure. For example, Sears will, we think, be one of the first firms to achieve a Future Firm level of new-management capability. As we have noted, a result of the management capabilities developed at Sears has been that its profitability and sales growth have set a standard of performance for others in its field. When one firm in an industry leaps ahead toward a Future Firm capability, its competitors will be forced to improve their rate of innovation in management capabilities or risk a progressively uncertain future. This imitation of the leading company in an industry has also occurred in baking, where competitors of Campbell Taggart are copying its control systems, and in banking, where the financial planning and control system innovated by the North Carolina National Bank has been recognized as a major contributor to the historically superior performance of this bank. Competitive pressure will be an important factor causing the whole distribution of firms by management capability level to shift toward the Future Firm level. A second reason for the rapid shift toward Future Firm status is the improvement in the human and technical resources upon which New Management rests. We shall consider that in some detail in Chapter 3. The difference between Present Firm and Future Firm is a question of the relative importance of research-based management techniques. It has been our experience that the research-based knowledge and the human resources are available to improve management problems. There is not a need to attempt high-risk projects. Research-based management techniques are now contributing to the growth of sales and profits in a large number of companies. Progress from a Present to a Future Firm level of competence involves the greater utilization of what is now working in many companies.

PREVIEW OF THE BOOK

The New Management (that is, research-based management) consists basically of good staff work that in turn leads to changes in the way line managers do their work. Figure 1.3 lists some inputs and outputs of research-based management. The inputs are problem-solving methodologies, such as operations research, and knowledge disciplines, such as law. The outputs are systems and procedures that management evaluates as useful and incorporates into its pattern of decision making. It is vital to understand that, by and large, most of the new-management inputs should make a contribution to any given new-management output. But in

Inputs	Outputs
Operations research	Computerized information systems
Organization development	Planning procedures
Systems analysis	ROI (cost-benefit) analysis
Computer programming	Usable models
Institutional specialties	Task monitoring
(law, public affairs, accounting, and so on)	Organizational designs

FIG. 1.3 *Inputs and outputs of the New Management.*

practice the synthesis of new-management inputs in the creation of new output is often incomplete, and the output suffers accordingly.

When this synthesis of new-management resources fails to occur, it may be because staff professionals suffer from the myopia that results from a specialized education and limited work experience, and yet are assigned responsibility for projects that are broader than their background. Examples of this disparity between ability and responsibility are commonly seen in management information systems. The failure of systems specialists to understand the implementation problems inherent in the systems they design is legendary. But when behavioral considerations from organization development staff work *do* make an impact on the design of the management information system, the result is often a significant increase in the effectiveness of management.

Note that the list of inputs includes new areas of specialization, such as organization development and systems analysis, and old areas of specialization, such as law and accounting. Given a business environment that is increasingly regulated, it is critical that new-management project teams include professionals in both the old and new areas of specialization. For example, the systems staff can develop the procedures to assist management in complying with new regulations such as the requirements of the wage-price guideposts, SEC and FTC disclosure, and equal employment if there is assistance from specialists in law, accounting, and public relations. The meshing of staff specialists is difficult, but some executives have developed the skills required to knit together specialized professionals to find solutions to the complex problems confronting management today.

Effective utilization of the new techniques is a major force that is reshaping the practice of management. Why is the revolution in the practice of management occurring now? What delayed this revolution? How can an executive keep current during this period of discontinuity? What evidence is there that these innovations make a difference—that properly applied, they make a company more effective and profitable?

How can a company lead in this new kind of competitive effort? These questions will be answered in the chapters that follow.

In this book we describe research-based management techniques and analyze the forces which have retarded acceptance of these new-management techniques. We develop a strategy for the management of research-based techniques, and then we analyze the factors that will force business executives to adopt the new techniques which are now so underutilized. We forecast the practice of management in 1980 in order to illustrate the consequences for executives of the new power which is even today available to improve the efficiency of management.

We have attempted to write a book that will lead to an improvement in the ability of (1) line executives to use the New Management, (2) staff professionals to assist line executives, and (3) educators to prepare students in schools of business in such a way as to reduce the seriousness of the problem that has been created by the disparity of attitudes and knowledge between older, experience-based line executives and younger, research-based staff professionals.

The ability of corporate executives in some firms to make rapid progress in management innovation has improved impressively during this last decade. The rate of progress in the adoption of research-based management techniques has been accelerating. In the concluding chapter, "Management Innovation in Future Firm," we predict the level of management competence in the corporations that are the leaders in utilizing new-management techniques; this chapter can be used as a standard for evaluating current management practices. Gaps between the level of management competence to be experienced in leading firms in 1980 and present practice in a company can be used as the basis for specifying the goals of the corporate long-range plan for building an improved level of management competence.

NOTES AND REFERENCES

1. See Frank C. Pierson, et al., *The Education of American Businessmen*, New York: McGraw-Hill, 1959; and Robert A. Gordon and James E. Howell, *Education for Business*, New York: Columbia, 1959.
2. Personal communication with Dr. Gruber.
3. Churchman, C. West: "Managerial Acceptance of Scientific Recommendations," *California Management Review*, Fall 1964, pp. 32–33.
4. Schellhardt, Timothy D.: "Currency Comptroller Has Job of Restoring Trust in Bank System," *The Wall Street Journal*, Oct. 10, 1974, p. 1.
5. Chandler, Alfred D.: *Strategy and Structure*, Garden City, N.Y.: Doubleday Anchor, 1966.
6. Ibid., p. 44.
7. Fouraker, Lawrence E., and John M. Stopford: "Organizational Structure and the Multinational Strategy," *Administrative Science Quarterly*, vol. 13, no. 1, June 1968.

8. See Chapter 8 for some examples.
9. Mansfield, Edwin: "Technical Change and the Rate of Innovation," *Econometrica,* October 1961, pp. 287–288.
10. We will make frequent references to the problems created by specialists. Accountants are a class of specialists who tend to practice "full" costing in which the direct or marginal costs relevant for decision making are lost. *Business Week* ("Airline Takes the Marginal Route," Apr. 20, 1963, p. 111) quotes Sidney Alexander, former economist for CBS and now a professor at the M.I.T. Sloan School of Management, to the effect that "the economist who understands marginal analysis has a 'full-time job in undoing the work of the accountant.'" That is so, Alexander holds, "because the practices of accountants—and of most businesses—are permeated with cost allocation directed at average, rather than marginal costs." This problem was corrected in the product costs system developed at Continental Airlines.
11. The management strategy used to achieve these innovations will be described in Chapters 10 and 11.
12. *Business Week,* Dec. 10, 1972, p. 53.
13. *Business Week,* Jan. 19, 1974, p. 39.

TWO

Investment in Management

Research-based management costs money. Strategy planning, management information systems, and organizational development are all activities which involve investments of corporate resources. During a recession it is tempting for corporate management to think about cutbacks in planning, management information systems, and other research-based activities. After all, if company management does not survive the year, what does it matter if it did not plan for the next year or for the next five years?

We do not buy this short-run view of corporate performance. For most large companies in the United States, profits fall during a recession, but the survival of the firm is never in doubt. It has been our experience that funds for improving the effectiveness of management have a higher rate of return than the other uses of corporate funds. Failures to invest adequately in management affect the return from other corporate expenditures, as the following experience in a client company indicates.

A COMPANY PRESIDENT'S DISCOVERY

One day a company president asked his vice president of marketing how the sales force made decisions about which potential buyers to see. The problem, as perceived by the company president, was that the sales force was just too small to see all the possible users of the products of this company. How were decisions made for the allocation of sales-force time? The vice president of marketing referred the question to the sales manager, who reported that the individual sales representatives made the decisions about which potential buyers to visit. How did the sales representatives make these decisions? What information about the sales potential of each customer in a territory was given to a sales representative?

A company president asking a simple question led to the discovery that sales representatives who were given very little guidance from management made the critical decisions on how $15 million in sales-force expenditures were used. This initial discovery resulted in a decision to do an analysis of how the sales representatives allocated their time. In this analysis it was discovered that many high-potential customers were not seen at all, and many low-potential customers were seen all too frequently.

This discovery about the nonmanagement of sales-force decisions is not an extreme case of unusually bad management. We see this kind of nonmanagement in the inventories of management practice we have performed in a number of client companies. In Prior Firm and emergent Present Firm companies, the management depth required to solve problems is just not available.

FINDING MANAGEMENT PROBLEMS IS EASY

The problem-solving capabilities in the majority of all companies can be summarized by three statements:

1. Finding serious problems in management is relatively easy.
2. Conceptualizing the solution for these problems is not perceived to be difficult by those closest to the problems.
3. Serious management problems rarely get solved until several years or longer after they have been recognized.

Some typical corporate problems which have festered for years are listed below.

> They [production and marketing] won't give us time to invent anything. A beer company line goes down and my whole research team leaves the lab. (From a director of R&D in the canning industry.)

> The plant accountants set standards to minimize variances. We do not know how our standard costs reflect potential production productivity. (From a vice president of finance.)

> Our computer costs are now $16 million a year. I am not sure why we need so much computer capacity, but I suppose it must be doing some good. (From a corporate controller.)

We spent over $100 million last year in advertising. I have no idea of whether this is effective—whether we should be spending more or less. (From a vice president of administration.)

There may be some executives who are thinking that our remarks are addressed to executives in *other* companies. Are there companies in which there are *not* serious problems that have been recognized for several years? In your company, are there problems on which little action has been taken? We invite our readers to take a survey in their firms of serious problems which have been recognized and on which little progress has been made.

We have asked many executives whether our three-statement summary of the current status of management was accurate. The vast majority of those interviewed agreed quite readily with the first statement that finding serious management problems is easy. A few senior executives did not accept this statement as accurate. Those who rejected the first statement were asked a series of questions such as:

1. How much market research is used in the allocation of the R&D budget, and how are R&D scientists and engineers kept informed about marketing and production problems?

2. How easily can you get EDP and systems to produce the management information reports that you need at a reasonable cost in time lag and money?

3. How is sales forecasting linked to production scheduling?

4. How is your return on advertising calculated?

5. How are sales-force quotas set? How effective is your sales-force management information system?

6. How are manufacturing cost standards set?

A serious management problem is usually admitted within four questions. The questions that we ask vary by position of the corporate executive who has disagreed with our statement that serious problems are easy to find. An executive of marketing might be asked questions about the allocation of the promotion budget. An executive in finance would be asked about the cost, control, and productivity of the computer facility.

The second statement that the problems are conceptually easy is accepted by a smaller percentage of executives than the percentage of those who agree with the first statement. This unwillingness to accept the ease with which a given problem can be solved can usually be overcome by a comparison of the resources required to improve the unsatisfactory condition with the benefits to be achieved from such an improvement. One of the most important reasons for investing in a research-based management capability is to provide the resources for solving the serious problems which today are recognized, but unsolved. Procedures for improving imbalances between investments in management and levels of corporate expenditures are not difficult to implement, as we shall demonstrate in later chapters. Little progress toward the implementation of these procedures can be achieved, however, until this basic concept of investment in management becomes part of the thinking of managers.

THE MANAGEMENT-INVESTMENT RATIO

Improvements in the effectiveness of management require investments which are similar in many ways to investments in new plants and equipment or expenditures for marketing, manufacturing, or R&D. A proposed investment in management should be evaluated by the same standards that are applied to other cash outflows: the benefits should be greater than the costs.

In order to understand what is meant by investment in management, it is necessary to consider the ratio

$$\frac{\text{Cost of management}}{\text{Level of expenditures}} = \text{management-investment ratio}$$

The denominator of this ratio is any category of expenditure (for example, marketing, R&D, a product line, or a division of a company). The numerator is the level of investment in the management of these expenditures.

Consider, for example, a company with twenty product lines and marketing expenses of over $100 million a year. These marketing expenses are controlled by twenty product managers. If the salaries and related expenses of the product managers were the only marketing management costs, then the ratio of management to expenditures would be

$$\frac{\text{Salary and expenses of 20 product managers}}{\$100 \text{ million}} = \text{management-investment ratio}$$

This is clearly a simplified example. Additionally there are group managers, a vice president of marketing, marketing research, and other such expenditures, which will increase the numerator of the management-investment ratio.

Investment in management means a conscious effort to relate the competence of management (defined in terms of quality and quantity) to the importance or magnitude of what is to be managed. Sometimes more managers are required. Sometimes less are needed, but with a different mix of management skills. Other times what is needed for effective management is a more comprehensively skilled research-based staff to back up the line managers. Management is a resource with qualitative and quantitative dimensions.

Consider the return-on-investment (ROI) calculations in new plant and equipment decisions, in acquisition decisions, or in measuring the performance of an operating division. Why are such return-on-investment calculations made? The basic reason for ROI calculations is that capital (that is, what is invested) has a cost and is a scarce resource. Therefore, the allocation of this scarce resource for a given use must pass the test of whether the return on the investment is high enough to justify the use of funds. An important test of performance of an operating division is the rate of return on the corporate investment in that division.

The resources in shortest supply in most companies are high-quality line managers and staff professionals. Whether or not there will be a good return from a corporate investment in an operating division is largely determined by the quality of line management and staff professionals who are assigned to achieve that high rate of return.

Good management of a division involves three kinds of people: (1) the line management in the division; (2) the research-based staff at both the corporate and divisional levels involved in such activities as strategic planning, management information systems, and organization development; and (3) senior corporate officers, with the assistance of their research-based staffs, who have ultimate responsibility for divisional performance.

A people investment decision should not be very different from the decision to invest dollars in plant and equipment. An article called "Put People on Your Balance Sheet" affirms this point of view:

> Employees should be considered as assets. Furthermore, if a company is to develop its full potential, the top managerial, commercial and technical skills must be considered as assets. This means the company should assess its needs for these skills, invest in their expansion and maintenance, and allocate its limited supply of these skills to the most promising divisions and projects. No organization which handles its employees as expense items can make as wise plans or as rational allocation decisions as the one which recognizes explicitly the asset characteristics of its human resources.[1]

An investment in management means more than the selection of a superstar. As we have observed in Chapter 1, the days of management by experience are over. Good management today means the development of a team of able, experience-based line executives who are supported by a strong staff of research-based professionals. The analyses of the research-based staff professionals are used by both divisional and corporate management. Communications between levels in the organization are made more effective by the work of the research-based staffs. Senior corporate management is surprised less frequently because of the effective planning and monitoring of divisional activities which are performed by research-based staffs. Organization-development professionals contribute to the quality of tomorrow's management.

Management resources should be invested in proportion to the expected return on investment from the utilization of a given level of management competence in a given activity of the business. There is little information in most companies about what management costs or what can be expected from investments in management. To correct this void, a formal system for investment in management that is comparable to the return-on-investment systems used for other kinds of corporate expenditures can be developed by the same research-based staffs which carry out traditional rate-of-return calculations on investments in plant and equipment, or on new product lines. A primary reason why so many corporations have experienced large losses on investments is that there has not been a return on investments in managements system which augments traditional investment calculations.

All this management costs money! And so does advertising, selling, manufacturing, R&D for new products, and a host of other activities. The cost of management includes the line executives who authorize expenditures and the utilization of research-based management techniques which increase the rate of return on expenditures associated with the introduction of a new product line, sales-force advertising, and other promotional activities, acquisitions, and investments in plant and equipment. If good management costs (say) 3 percent of operating expenses and inadequate management costs 2 percent, what increase in the effectiveness of the 97 percent nonmanagement portion of total operational expenses is necessary before there is an extraordinary return on the increase in management expenditures from 2 to 3 percent?

Return-on-Investment Calculation

As an example of a return-on-investment calculation for the allocation of management resources, let us return to the company with a $100 million marketing budget that produces sales of over $700 million a year. What management actions can be taken to increase the sales produced from that $100 million in marketing expenditures? Let us look a little deeper. Marketing costs are distributed among classes of the following expenses: space and TV advertising, sales force, exhibits, customer technical assistance, market research, direct mail, brochures, displays, and other such costs. As might be expected, an analysis at the divisional level reveals that marketing costs are distributed among the expense categories in different ways. A deeper analysis indicates that within a division, the distribution of the marketing budget among the expense categories varies from one product to another—even when the products appear to have similar market characteristics.

Interviews with the managers responsible for spending this $100 million marketing budget indicate that there has been only a minimal effort to obtain feedback on the returns on the marketing expenditures. There is not a company-level system for scoring results of promotional campaigns. A successful promotion for one product does not lead to similar efforts for other products. There is little communication or coordination among the managers responsible for spending this $100 million in marketing expenses.

Given these marketing expenses, it is possible to develop a program for investing in management in order to increase the return on the marketing expenditures. The basis for a return-on-investment calculation is to estimate the ratio of better performance achieved to the cost of the management actions which generates the superior performance.

Improvements in this $100 million in marketing expenditures result from such actions as a better selection of media, a transfer of funds from the less effective to the more effective categories of marketing expense, and an increase in the efficacy of the sales force. When over $100 million a year is spent on advertising and sales-force activities with very little research-based management effort to evaluate the return on this large investment in promotion, it is not difficult to justify $100,000 to $500,000 in efforts to increase the effectiveness with which the $100 million is expended. A 5 percent increase in the effectiveness of a $100 million promotion budget represents an increase in profits of $5 million. From this return on the expenditures on research-based management, it is necessary to deduct the costs of achieving better promotional activity in order to obtain the net return on the management effort.

Consider two alternative expenditures of an additional $500,000 in a company that is already investing $100 million in promotion. Will sales and profits be greater if the company expends $100,500,000 in promotion that is allocated by experience-based managers who have neither the time or the training to evaluate the effectiveness of alternative promotion strategies? Or will the return be greater if the company spends $100 million on promotion and $500,000 on research-based management techniques to increase the effectiveness of the $100 million base in promotional costs?

THE BIG LOSSES

We see the problems created by a failure to invest in management when we do inventories within a company or when we give management workshops. Newspaper accounts of large losses are another source of information about the cost of inadequate management.

Company executives each year invest fortunes in new plants and equipment, R&D for new products and processes, advertising to increase market penetration, and acquisitions to absorb other companies. Each of these activities is very risky, and each year there are stories of huge losses occurring because of management errors. We are all familiar with many of the stories of large company losses such as the estimated $400 million loss by RCA in an abortive effort to enter the computer industry, the close to $100 million loss by Du Pont as a result of the Corfam synthetic leather effort, and the $39 million write-off by General Foods of its Burger Chef and Rix fast-food chains. These famous losses are but the tip of the iceberg. Many companies hang on to divisions that are performing badly, and the total loss is never disclosed. For example, it appears that Continental Corporation has a total investment and loss experience in Diners Club of over $200 million. How likely is it that Continental will experience some recovery from this investment? How much further investment will be required to "save" Diners Club?

Executives who are willing to spend millions for new plants and equipment, R&D for new products, acquisition, and other investments have been unwilling to invest in the management activities required to give some assurance that the other kinds of investments will be profitable. Company-financed R&D for new products and processes totalled over $13 billion in 1974.[2] In the light of this figure, how much should companies invest in efforts to improve the efficiency and effectiveness of management, to achieve management innovations? If RCA can afford to lose over $400 million in its efforts to develop a computer division, how much should it invest in the management of how serious decisions, such as whether to enter the computer industry, are made? It appears that the abruptness with which RCA shut down the computer division was the result of top management not knowing how badly the division was doing until a management audit was undertaken. It was the shock of learning about conditions far worse than expected that triggered the quick decision to close the division. How much should RCA invest in developing and implementing the management systems required to keep corporation-level management adequately informed of division-level performance?

The RCA experience is similar to the large number of losses experienced in the conglomerate and diversification movements of the 1960s. Large losses at Litton, LTV, General Foods, and W. R. Grace came from unprofitable operations in acquired companies. The long list of companies that have lost large amounts of money in acquisitions raises three important questions. First, what investment in management was made as part of the effort to locate acquisitions? Second, what investment was made to build a strong management in the acquired company? Third, do these investments in management compare with the funds that should have been allocated given the potential and the risks associated with acquisition efforts?

Perhaps more serious than the large losses reported in the press are the losses which are experienced and not publicly acknowledged—or even recognized by senior management! We can think of a number of investments in promotion and manufacturing facilities which were made with totally inadequate analysis prior to expenditures of considerable sums of money. A company that can afford to invest over $100 million a year in promotion can afford the analysis required to achieve a good return on this investment.

THIN MANAGEMENT

When there are difficult problems which must be solved with an insufficient level of management competence (measured in the quality of available line executives and staff professionals), there can be said to exist "thin management." If an investment in an improved management capability can be expected to result in a high rate of return and the funds for investment are available, there exists "unnecessarily thin management."

The difference between "thin" and "unnecessarily thin" management is the availability of resources to invest in better management. Some companies cannot help having thin management. A small firm that is going bankrupt may not be able to invest in the new machine tools required to increase productivity. If a General Motors or a United States Steel did not invest in new machinery which could be justified on the basis of good returns on investment, this would be a case of bad management. A failure to invest in needed management is the same as a failure to invest in profitable machinery. One difference between the two concepts is that the calculation of profitability on investment in machinery is widely utilized, but the idea of investment in management is rarely discussed.

Examples of Unnecessarily Thin Management

The following examples are selected from our experience with large, profitable firms, well able to add whatever management might have been found useful.

1. One of the country's most profitable and fastest-growing corporations experienced a very high stock market price/earnings ratio. Almost all of this company's sales were in one market area, and top management had made the policy decision to diversify. One man was hired to examine acquisitions (which were brought to the attention of this company in large

numbers because of the high price/earnings ratio). This one man could not examine the many acquisition possibilities. Soon a large number of negotiations were backlogged as corporate executives gave this director of acquisitions the companies which were called to their attention. The corporate executives who became excited about some of the possible acquisitions which they discovered began to experience frustration because this director of acquisitions without a staff could not process his backlog. Frustration among the executive staff built up to such a level that several acquisitions were made without an adequate analysis. The price/earnings ratio was so high that money did not seem real. Some of these casual acquisitions soon began to cause management problems, and a large number of corporate executives were transferred from the profitable operations of the parent company to the unprofitable operations of the acquired companies. All this occurred because the importance of an acquisition strategy was not recognized and thus this function was staffed with an unnecessarily thin management.

2. The top management of one company has recognized for over five years that one of its four R&D laboratories was not effectively managed. This company has continued to invest $8 million a year in this research facility because top management of this company has not had the time to correct the problem.

3. A third company spends over $100 million each year in job-shop manufacturing. The top management of this company has recognized for several years that improvements could be made in the production quantity–inventory–marketing set of decisions. Despite an inventory problem which has been creating serious difficulties, top management has not found the time to work on this problem.

What do these three examples have in common? First, a serious problem was created because management resources were not made available to solve a problem. That is, there was a disparity between the importance of a given problem and the quality of management assigned to solve the problem. Second, each of these firms had the profits to invest in the increase in the level of managerial competence required to solve the problem. And third, these firms are considered to be well managed; all three had experienced rapid increases in sales and profits. Yet all three allowed unnecessarily thin management to perpetuate unnecessary problems.

GOOD MANAGEMENT AND HIGH PROFITS

In the short run, it is sometimes possible to generate high profits by taking excessive risks, by a matter of luck, and by other factors which are not related to good management. New York Stock Exchange member firms experienced a decade of rapidly rising volume and profits, protected by the fixed-price system allowed by the Securities and Exchange Commission. This profitability was built on thin management, inadequate capital, and a failure to invest in the management procedures required to cope with the volume of transactions. The high profits of the 1960s evaporated, and several hundred New York Stock Exchange member firms went out of business as a result of a fall in stock market volume and the disarray of accounting records. Were the rapidly increasing profits in the 1960s of these New York Stock Exchange member firms an example of good management? How is it that there was such thin management in an industry that grew and prospered on the slogan "Invest in Growing America"?

A pharmaceutical manufacturer, after the licensing of what appeared to be an unimportant drug invented in France, discovered that this pharmaceutical provided an effective cure for a serious illness. This pharmaceutical company had a decade of high profits based on this one drug, and lagged behind its competition in the introduction of new drugs. The patent on the key drug has now expired, and competitors are now selling this drug at lower prices. Profits of this drug company have recently been falling. Were the high profits during the growing years a mark of good management?

Think about the once high profits at General Motors. Why is it that almost every major technical advance in the last decade was introduced by foreign companies with but a small fraction of the sales and profits of General Motors? As Gruber, Poensgen, and Prakke ask: "Why is it that the major automotive industry inventions such as the Wankel, invented in Germany and utilized first by a Japanese firm, or fuel injection, invented by a parts supplier in the United States and first utilized as standard equipment by a German auto manufacturer, or front wheel drive, or radial tires, or the Honda compound vortex control system to control emissions and so on for almost every major automotive invention in the post World War II period, were made and/or utilized first by non-U.S. automobile manufacturers?"[3]

Auto makers are now paying for the high profits earned through neglect of environmental impact by a myopic management. *Business Week* called its review of the automotive industry "Has Detroit Learned Its Lesson?"[4] The short-run profit maximization of General Motors can be seen in the statistics. Large, heavy cars were once more profitable than small cars. In the twenty years from 1955 to 1975, the full-size Chevrolet went from 3,245 to 4,365 pounds and from 180 to 350 horsepower. The average miles per gallon of 1975 General Motors cars was 13 in contrast to the 25 to 30 miles-per-gallon range of the foreign imports. The *best-performing* General Motors car in gas mileage, the Vega, ranked 22 in miles per gallon in the EPA tests. The General Motors market share dropped from 50 to 41.9 percent since 1965. The General Motors stock market price fell down to a sixteen-year low. As noted by *Business Week,* "After decades of dominating the world auto industry, U.S. auto makers have developed a case of the product blahs. They have moved too slowly and too late to satisfy today's market."[5] One could go further. The auto makers cost the United States billions in foreign exchange by allowing imports rather than producing lower-profit, smaller cars to satisfy an important market segment. They encouraged the purchase of over-powered cars which were guzzlers of gasoline. They built cars causing high air pollution for over a decade after there was absolutely conclusive evidence of the harmful effects of air pollution.[6] *The auto makers caused the unreasonable government regulations which now burden the industry.*

The fall of the United States auto industry is an example of the need for a research-based management capability to anticipate trends in the business environment and to develop the strategic plans needed to assure *future* as well as *present* profits. Profits bought at the expense of the future of a company are not evidence of good management.

Good management, therefore, means more than high short-run profits. It means a performance record across a growing list of activities. This list now includes product innovations, multinational activity, cost control, and responsiveness to environmental and consumer legislation. The list of performance measures as a test of management competence has been increasing, and this has created a need to redefine what we mean by good management. It is increasingly easy for "good management" to become "unnecessarily thin and ineffective management" in a very short period of time.

INVESTMENT IN MANAGEMENT AT GENERAL ELECTRIC

Consider a firm such as General Electric with over 200 operating departments. Each department is responsible for a given product—such as medium steam turbines, small jet engines, light bulbs, or small appliances. A general manager responsible for a department is evaluated according to the potential in that market. In a department serving a rapidly growing industry, such as the market for electric generating equipment, expectations are very high. General Electric should invest more in the management of a department serving a large and rapidly expanding market than in a department serving a small and stagnant market area. The investment in management—the depth in number and quality of the line managers and research-based management staff professionals who are assigned to a given division—should be determined by the potential contribution of this investment in people to the objectives of the corporation.

There is evidence that General Electric has maintained a corporate policy of depth in line management with a strong supporting staff of research-based professionals. In the *Business Week* story about the restructuring of the top management of General Electric by Chairman Reginald H. Jones, credit was given to earlier General Electric efforts to innovate in management.

> Jones' predecessors have each put their own distinctive stamp on GE, and they have done it successfully enough to make the company a pacesetter in management structures and procedures. Ralph Cordiner applied decentralization to GE's operations in the 1950's, an approach copied by company after company. Fred J. Borch, who took over from Cordiner in 1963, created the "office of the president" device in the 1960's. This top-level management structure was designed to spread the president's job among a triumvirate of executives. In the early 1970's, Borch, working closely with Jones, put GE heavily into strategic business planning—a technique that treats the company's vast array of ventures as an investment portfolio, backing the winners and pruning the losers through systematic analysis.[7]

The new General Electric chain of command is presented in Figure 2.1. Note that there are ten executives who report directly to Chairman Jones. Seven of these ten positions are for research-based executives. This General Electric organization chart provides a good example of the kind of work involved in research-based management.

It is obvious from this corporate structure that General Electric is investing in the staff resources required for an adequate level of support for the decisions of experience-based line executives. Each of the seven research-based executives provides the management for a given category of staff problem. There are resources at the corporate level to do the analyses required if funds and key personnel are to be allocated effectively to over 200 product departments.

The General Electric organization structure provides for staff resources at the corporate level to evaluate the billions of dollars which are spent each year in the operating departments. In addition to this corporate-level research-based management capability, the executive officers of the three major operations areas have a research-based staff capability to provide the planning, systems, and staff work needed for the effective management of their operations. General Electric's operations have a hierarchy of control which begins with the vice chairman and executive officer for an area. The operations in an area are divided into groups, the groups are divided into divisions, the divisions are further divided into operating departments, and the operating departments are divided into product

34 / *The New Management*

```
                    ┌─────────────────────────────┐
                    │  Chairman of the Board and  │
                    │   Chief Executive Officer   │
                    └─────────────────────────────┘
```

Vice Chairman of the Board and Executive Officer	Vice Chairman of the Board and Executive Officer	Vice Chairman of the Board and Executive Officer
Consumer products group	Aerospace business group	Components & materials group
Major appliance business group	Aircraft engine business group	Industrial group
Power delivery group	International & Canadian group	Special systems and products group
Power generation business group		

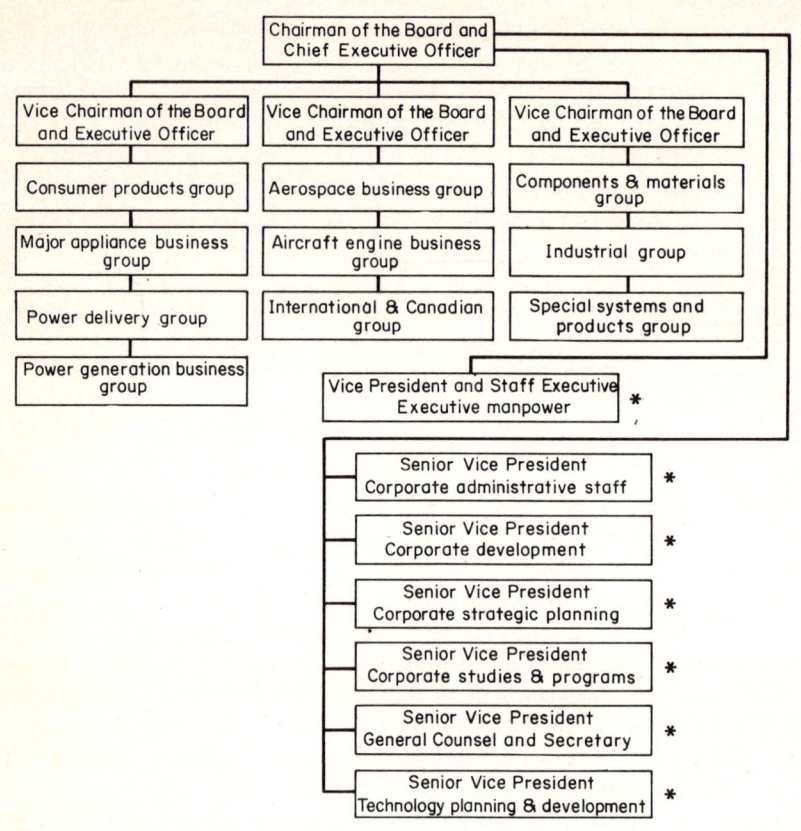

Vice President and Staff Executive Executive manpower	*
Senior Vice President Corporate administrative staff	*
Senior Vice President Corporate development	*
Senior Vice President Corporate strategic planning	*
Senior Vice President Corporate studies & programs	*
Senior Vice President General Counsel and Secretary	*
Senior Vice President Technology planning & development	*

FIG. 2.1 *The organization at General Electric.*[8] *The asterisks* denote research-based management positions.*

lines. There is decentralized responsibility all the way down to the product lines.

Decentralization does not mean that higher levels of management are unaware of the important decisions that are made at lower levels in the organization. There must be a strong research-based corporate-level capability to do strategic planning, monitor performance, allocate resources, set priorities, and otherwise protect the company from the difficulties which have been created by discontinuities in the business environment.

It is relevant to note that the present chief executive officer of General Electric, Reginald Jones, "vaulted to the top of GE by embracing strategic business planning, the approach that led to the spin-off of GE's money-losing computer operation to Honeywell, Inc. in 1970."[9] The orderly sale of the General Electric computer division contrasts sharply with the disarray experienced in the abrupt closing by RCA of its computer division. We expect that General Electric will continue to pioneer in the practice of management and will be one of the first companies to achieve a Future Firm caliber of management competence.

HOW MUCH IS ENOUGH?

Senior management in many companies is now reviewing this problem of management depth and the related question of return on investment in management resources. It has been our experience in working with clients that all companies experience a shortage of good line executives and research-based staff professionals. There will never be "enough" good line executives and new-management staff professionals to fill all the positions which are open. A backlog of management projects with a high potential return on investment exists in all companies.

For some reason corporate executives are perfectly willing to invest huge sums to save a bad decision. Key managers are reassigned. Additional funds are pumped in. When the full story is written, a corporation may invest in a bad acquisition key personnel or funds worth over a thousand times the cost of an adequate acquisitions search and evaluation effort. Where do corporations find enough key people and funds for efforts to save a bad acquisition or to correct losses from new product failures or to reduce manufacturing costs after their production efficiency is no longer competitive? Where do these funds and key people come from? The answer appears to be that the line management and staff resources and the cash for investment are available when there is a crisis—but are frequently not available to provide competent management as a standard of performance.

Occasionally one finds a company that invests "enough" in research-based management techniques. One such company is IBM. As disclosed in the Telex suit, IBM had strategic plans for almost every facet of the computer business. These plans were carefully evaluated by senior executives in meetings of the IBM Management Committee.

Reginald H. Jones, president of General Electric, described his company's research-based management as follows:

> Many companies claim they do strategic planning, but the process may or may not be anything more than intuitive wheeling-and-dealing by the top man.... For large companies the only path to solid, high-quality growth in earnings is through rigorous analysis, entrepreneurial business planning, and selectivity in the allocation of resources. Hard work, frankly. Under Fred Borch's leadership, General Electric instituted a comprehensive system of strategic planning. We've had two years of experience with it at corporate and operating levels. We're learning how to accelerate our growth in earnings, as well as sales, through selection of the right mix of growth businesses and current

money-makers, and withdrawing from business situations where we don't see a feasible strategy for making a profitable contribution.[10]

Note that Jones derided the lack of a serious strategic planning effort in many companies. We find that this attitude of impatience with thin and inadequate management is common in the firms that are leading in the race toward a Future Firm level of management competence. Jones made this presentation in 1972. Apparently a serious strategic planning effort began in General Electric in 1970. Even the *best-managed* companies have had only a relatively small number of years of experience in the use of a strong research-based management capability. How much is enough? Even the leading almost-to-Future Firm companies in research-based management are a long way from a drop-off in opportunities for profit improvement from investment in management resources. Most Present Firm companies are so far away from investing enough, so far from an extraordinary amount of improvement in the effectiveness of management, that this question need not be answered.

One warning, however. An investment in research-based management is similar in many ways to an investment in R&D for new products. It is necessary to know how to manage research-based management. Tossing money into R&D for new products or into research-based management is unlikely to bring a satisfactory level of return. Research-based management must be managed, and we will describe how to achieve this management capability in this book.

NOTES AND REFERENCES

1. Hekimian, J. S., and C. H. Jones: "Put People on Your Balance Sheet," *Harvard Business Review,* January–February 1967, p. 106.
2. National Science Foundation: *National Patterns of R&D Resources, 1953–1974,* Washington, D.C.: U.S. Government Printing Office, 1974, p. 28.
3. Gruber, W. H., O. H. Poensgen, and F. Prakke: "Research on the Interface Factor in the Development and Utilization of New Technology," *R&D Management,* Summer 1974, pp. 157–158.
4. "Has Detroit Learned Its Lesson?" *Business Week,* Oct. 5, 1974, pp. 64ff.
5. Ibid., p. 64.
6. Carbon monoxide emissions by motor vehicles increased from 45 million to over 60 million tons a year between 1960 and 1968. As a result of the Clean Air Act of 1965, which set standards for 1968 cars, and the series of tougher standards that have been established, estimated carbon monoxide emissions in 1980 will be less than half the 1960 level, despite the expected increase in the number of motor vehicles in use. The improvements in emissions began with the Clean Air Act of 1965. Cars manufactured in 1965 caused more air pollutants per car than cars manufactured in 1950, the year Dr. A. Haagen-Smit of the California Institute of Technology reported his discovery that the Los Angeles smog was caused by auto emissions. See *Environmental Quality: The First Annual Report of the*

Council on Environmental Quality, 1970, Washington, D.C., U.S. Government Printing Office, 1970, pp. 61–80.
7. "GE's Jones Restructures His Top Team," *Business Week,* June 30, 1973, pp. 38–39.
8. Ibid., p. 38.
9. Ibid., p. 39.
10. Jones, Reginald H.: "General Electric's Performance and Prospects," address to Investment Analysts Society of Chicago, Nov. 30, 1972.

THREE

New Resources for Management

An investment in management results in one or more people devoting additional time and attention to the management of a particular operation in order to cause changes that will improve business performance. But time and attention are not enough. The rate of return on this investment is also directly dependent on the knowledge and experience and skill of those doing the work.

The raw material out of which a Future Firm is shaped will be research-based knowledge; *it is not simply a matter of experience-based executives trying harder to do things in traditional ways.* Improvements in the practice of management, in the way that decisions are made and performance is monitored, are easy to achieve if managers can understand and take advantage of the process in which knowledge is translated into new-management procedures.

Research is making ever-increasing and more dramatic inroads on management, an activity rarely touched by academicians and scientists until the first few decades of the twentieth century, and only extensively scrutinized since the 1950s.

In fact, knowledge, in the sense of organized ideas and information, has only recently been recognized as a key resource in the economic life of a modern society. Economists began, in the 1950s, to recognize the importance of knowledge for economic growth. Fritz Machlup, in *The Production and Distribution of Knowledge in the United States,*[1] covers chapter by chapter the various aspects of knowledge in the economy: knowledge-producing industries and occupations, education, research and development, communications media, and information machines and services. As the United States undergoes economic recession in the mid 1970s, we see coming true management consultant Peter F. Drucker's prediction that the United States would undergo a major societal "discontinuity" and transform from an economy of goods into a knowledge economy. He predicted in 1969 that by the late 1970s "every other dollar earned and spent in the American economy will be earned by producing and distributing ideas and information, and will be spent on procuring ideas and information."[2] As energy and raw material constraints take hold and as the socioeconomic-legal framework becomes more complex, we are seeing it happen.

Jay Forrester, an electrical engineer turned management researcher and educator, opens his book, *Industrial Dynamics* (published in 1961), by discussing the need for research in management. He observes that, because the significant factors in management problems are so numerous, so complex in their interrelationships, and so subject to change, the manager's tasks are "far more difficult and challenging than the normal tasks of the mathematician, the physicist, or the engineer." The relatively low intellectual status accorded the study and practice of management in the past came about, Forrester argues, "because the intellectual opportunities were not recognized and the problems lay beyond the reach of traditional analysis methods."[3] Today, the successful management of our institutions, including business, has become the central intellectual question of our times.

AVAILABILITY OF MANAGEMENT KNOWLEDGE

Knowledge useful for the management of business has been generated at an ever-increasing rate since World War II. Mathematics, economics, electronic data processing, psychology, and systems analysis are now taught in schools of business administration. Specialists in these disciplines eagerly search the business environment for phenomena to be investigated and explained. Inventory levels, pricing decisions, information flows, group interactions, and communication patterns are fair game for rigorous scrutiny by the analytic mind.

A new language for thinking about management problems developed between 1955 and 1965. Before 1955, a very few academic specialists were involved in research-based management. During the period 1955–1965, second and third-generation computers became available, there was a very rapid diffusion of quantitative techniques, and the teaching in almost every field of management was revolutionized.

Mathematical logic and techniques entered the management disciplines. To illustrate this abrupt discontinuity in the quantitative foundation underlying education, consider the contents of the *Journal of Business*, edited at the University of Chicago Graduate School of Business. This journal has wide academic readership and reflects the main currents of academic thought on business problems. The percentage of articles with mathematical content rose from 9 to 53 percent from 1954 to 1966. The *Harvard Business Review*, edited at the Graduate School of Business, Harvard University, is of much greater interest to managers. The mathematical content there rose from 2 to 8 percent. The greater utilization of quantitative techniques in the *Journal of Business* reflects how research in the universities leads business practice.

Research-based management is heavily dependent on the rigor and the technique of mathematics and statistics. The increasing visibility of these techniques, represented by the increase in mathematical content in such periodicals as the *Journal of Business* and the *Harvard Business Review*, points to a major discontinuity in the education of research-based staff professionals who frequently move into positions of line management. Senior executives return for special programs and attend courses in which research-based techniques are described. Thus, the competence of both research-based staff professionals and line executives to work with analytical techniques has improved significantly in the last twenty years. Both research-based staff and line management pipelines are experiencing an important shift toward increasing competence with analytical techniques.

The progress in the analytic rigor of research-based management can be seen in the dramatic changes which have occurred in the personnel and planning functions.

Organizational research In the 1950s, personnel administration was a descriptive academic area which focused on union-management relations, labor law, and administrative procedures. Personnel administration was not based on analytic studies. A very narrow view of the personnel function was taught in courses at even the leading schools of business. The scope of personnel administration and the analytic rigor used to research behavioral problems in management have been revolutionized in the last fifteen years.

Personnel administration evolved into "human resources"; next came "organization theory" which evolved to become "organizational behavior" (OB), and later "organizational development" (OD). OD attempts to integrate industrial psychology, industrial sociology, sociology of occupations, and organizational psychology. The research-based professionals in organizational development view their mission as the changing of people and organizations in order to increase performance.[4] This is a very different focus from that of personnel administration of the 1950s, in which the union grievance committee was the kind of problem of dominant concern.

In the mid 1970s, the terminology has shifted back to "human resources." A recent journal article presented five reasons for a surge of management interest in human resources development.

    1. Management countering alienation, boredom, and job dissatisfaction

    2. Management trying to overcome decreasing motivation and increasing counterproductive behavior

    3. The impact of rising expectations and declining institutions

    4. Entry into a postindustrial age of antimechanism

    5. Management acceptance of the idea that human resources development provides a low-cost and low-risk return on investment in people

As the author of the article points out, the more valid the first four reasons, the stronger the reason for management to focus on the fifth.[5]

Business planning As another example of the knowledge buildup in management, consider the subject of business planning. Although mentioned in most books on general management, the subject did not have a book of its own until 1958—David W. Ewing's *Long Range Planning For Management*.[6] Since 1960, there have been many. Robert J. Mackler reviewed thirty book-length studies in the *Harvard Business Review* in 1970.[7] In 1967 two academics published an article, "A Program of Research in Business Planning,"[8] in which they spelled out thirty-four topics for research! Business planning has become a discipline of knowledge in its own right.

Quantitative management A third area of new knowledge for management, which we discuss in greater detail in Chapter 4, is quantitative techniques. The number of business operations which are modeled with mathematical equations has been increasing at an extraordinary rate. The mathematical techniques which can be applied include linear programming, dynamic programming, queuing theory, econometric forecasting, simulation, statistical decision theory, and game theory. These techniques are usually called "management science," or "operations research," although both management science (MS) and operations research (OR) are broader concepts. Management science is the scientific method—which may or may not involve mathematics—applied to management. Operations research is research on operations—which in the real world requires much more than mathematics, as any manager knows.

    What is not fully appreciated about research-based management is that elements of it entered simultaneously into every function of business. A whole new vocabulary was swiftly created. For example, the production function became intertwined with scheduling models and computer control. Sales forecasting models produce inputs for production scheduling systems. Marketing becomes involved with advertising media selection models and the traveling salesperson algorithm. Top management hears continually about management information systems and corporate simulation models. The carriers of this new knowledge for management are the staff professionals trained in the New Management.

In the last ten to fifteen years, there has been a sudden increase in the quantity and quality of staff professionals who are educated and experienced in such specialized areas as computer-based management information systems, management science, and organization development. The new breed is distinguished by an M.B.A. (or M.S.) from a business school or school of management since the benchmark year 1960.

EDUCATION OF BUSINESS GRADUATES

Trends in the availability of new employees with master's degrees in management (M.B.A.'s) and with master's degrees in computer science/systems analysis are presented in Figure 3.1, in which we also present the increase in the value of the installed base of general-purpose computers. Between 1960 and 1970, the number of M.B.A.'s entering the labor force each year increased from less than 5,000 to over 21,000. The United States Office of Education began to maintain a separate count of master's degrees in computer science and systems analysis in 1964. This source of New Management increased from 146 graduates in school year 1964–1965 to 1,459 in school year 1969–1970. These increases in the human resources of the New Management should be factored for improvements in quality.

The extent of improvement in the quality of education for business is difficult to measure. Leonard Silk, in his monograph for the Committee for Economic Development,[9] summarized the studies of the Ford and Carnegie Foundations (published in 1959) on the education of business executives in the 1950s as follows:

- *Low Standards of Most Business Schools.* The two reports found the movement toward greater analytical rigor and higher standards limited to relatively few schools of business. For the most part, according to the authors of these two studies, academic standards were much too low.
- *Low-Caliber Students.* Because admission requirements were too low, many students who did not have either the background or the innate ability to survive a rigorous college program were admitted to the business schools.

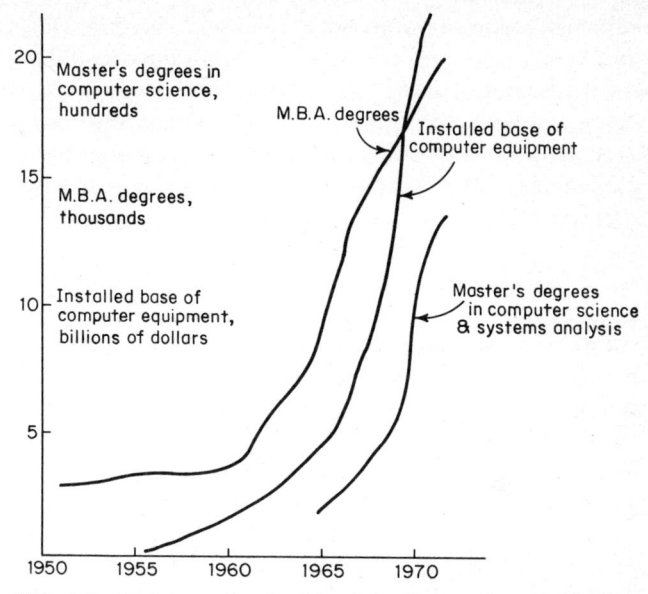

FIG. 3.1 *Resources for the New Management:* **trends in the availability of M.B.A.'s, computer specialists, and computers.**

SOURCES: American Federation of Information Processing Societies, *The State of the Computer Industry in the United States,* Montavale, N.J., 1973, p. 11, for value of installed computer base; U.S. Office of Education, *Earned Degrees Conferred,* for M.B.A. and computer science degrees.

- *Criticism of Teaching Methods.* The teaching methods used in business schools came in for some strong criticism.
- *Low-Caliber Business Faculties.* The reports had some harsh words to say about the overall quality of business faculties.

The quality of both the faculties and the students has been improved in the period since the Ford and Carnegie reports on which Dr. Silk commented. There are still weaknesses in the education of business managers. There may be too much theory and not enough attention to the development of the critical skills which determine the effectiveness of a manager. As Livingston has observed, "One reason why highly educated men fail to build successful careers in management is that they do not learn from their formal education what they need to know to perform their jobs effectively. In fact, the tasks that are the most important in getting results usually are left to be learned on the job, where few managers ever master them simply because no one teaches them how."[10] Another problem is that professors who did not have much to teach have been replaced by superstars who often do not care about teaching. Despite these problems, the recent graduates of business schools have a qualitative advantage over the graduates of the 1950s. However, the new graduates are more difficult to manage, and a new set of skills is required for the experience-based executives to whom the newly recruited research-based types report. The management of research-based graduates of business schools is covered in Chapter 6.

COMPUTERS

Another important trend related to the growth of research-based management is the increase in the value of the installed base of general-purpose computers. In 1955 the value of the installed base of general-purpose computers (not including minicomputers and other such limited-purpose equipment) approximated $130 million; by 1970 the value had increased to about $24 billion, or an increase of about 200 times.

The increase in the utilization of computers has been a necessary precondition for the development of the New Management. A large percentage of all research-based management applications are made more efficient by the availability of modern computers for the storage of data and their transformation into management information. The logic of systems analysis, which is a facet of the development of a new computer program, is also useful for new-management techniques not processed on a computer. Many of the behavioral science findings that are the basis of the organization-development aspects of the New Management have been made possible by the availability of computers to process the research data used to develop the findings. Thus even qualitative and people-centered facets of the New Management are often based on quantitative evidence processed by computers.

The early prophets of research-based management were frequently on the frontier of computer science, and could program the early computers to produce management information and models. These early prophets extrapolated too quickly from their own frontier-level skills. It is true that most of the research-based management techniques in use today could have been processed by the computers which were available over ten years ago. But executives quite correctly were dedicating the early computers to the processing of accounting information. There was an urgent need to automate manual bookkeeping operations. Computers were difficult to use, and the flexibility required by many of the new-management applications represented a level of technology that was simply unavailable in most companies.

The cost of achieving a new-management application on a computer today is but a small percentage of what it would have been just ten years ago. Many management systems which involve the restructuring of large files of data, telecommunications, and interactive time-share processing were just not feasible ten years ago because the computer technology was either too expensive or not available. The professional computer staffs in most companies now are well qualified to program such applications. Executives are more familiar with new-management techniques. The almost 200-fold increase presented in Figure 3.1 in the value of the installed base of general-purpose computers is a good basis on which to forecast the coming of the New Management. Gains in the power and the utilization of computers are presented in Figure 3.2. In an analysis of the history of computer utilization, Withington points out that computers were primarily "paper pushers" during the early years from 1952 to 1966 because computers in this period "were highly practical and oriented to tasks that were well understood. They were designed to support batch processing methods, which were satisfactory to most users because they knew no better way to handle large volumes of transactions; hence these machines were put to a wide variety of uses, appearing everywhere that large quantities of information were to be processed in a routine manner."[11]

It was only in the 1966-1974 period, according to Withington, that computers had the power for communicating with users at remote terminals. The on-line interactive kind of communications which permit the effective utilization of computer power for user dialogues with a computer-based model is a capability less than a decade old. And recently, the remote terminals have become small computers themselves; this is a development which permits changes to be made at remote terminal locations which do not affect the programming of the main central computer.

A model without adequate access to data is often not particularly useful. Note that Withington uses 1974 as the coming of computers as information custodians. He cites (page 103) recent survey data "of 32 large computer-using organizations [which] showed only 7 with application-independent data bases in existence (that is, where a single multipurpose file supports a number of hitherto independent applications). However, 23 more thave definite plans to implement such data bases in the next few years, and the other 2 say they may do so eventually."

One reason that computers have been a source of frustration to management is the problem of "frozen data"—the unavailability of data utilized in one application for use in other applications. This problem is being corrected by the development of companywide data base systems.[12] This frozen-data problem and other similar problems which have seriously reduced the managerial usefulness of computers have been corrected in a small number of firms and are in the process of being

Name	Period	New hardware	New software	New functions	Organizational location	Effect on organization
Gee whiz	1953–1958	Vacuum tubes, magnetic records	None	Initial experimental batch applications	Controller's department	First appearance of technicians (with salary, responsibility, and behavior problems); automation fears among employees
Paper pushers	1958–1966	Transistors, magnetic cores	Compilers, input/output control systems	Full range of applications, inquiry systems	Proliferation in operating departments	EDP group proliferation; some workers and supervisors alienated or displaced; introduction of new rigidity but also new opportunities.
Communicators	1966–1974	Large-scale integrated circuits, interactive terminals	Multifunction operating systems, communications controllers	Network data collection, remote batch processing	Consolidation into centrally controlled regional or corporate centers with remote terminals	Centralization of EDP organization; division data visible to central management; some division managers alienated; response times shortened.
Information custodians	1974–ca 1982	Very large file stores, satellite computers	General-purpose data manipulators, virtual machines	Integration of files, operational dispatching, full transaction processing	Versatile satellites instead of terminals, with control still centralized	Redistribution of management functions with logistic decisions moving to headquarters and

46

Action aids	ca 1982–?	Magnetic bubble and/or laser-holographic technology, distributed systems	Interactive languages, convenient simulators	Private information and simulation systems intercompany linkages	Systems capabilities projected to all parts of organization; networks of different organizations interconnected	tactical decisions moving out; resulting reorganization; field personnel pleased. Semiautomatic operating decisions; plans initiated by many individuals, leading toward flickering authority & management by consensus; greater involvement of people at all levels; central EDP group shrinkage.

FIG. 3.2 *Facets of computer evolution.*

SOURCE: F. G. Withington, "Five Generations of Computers," *Harvard Business Review*, July–August 1974, p. 101.

corrected in a large number of firms. *Thus the historical limitations of computers in the practice of management should not be extrapolated very far into the future.*

This historical experience, however, does explain the continued reports about the uselessness of computers. In a *Business Week* special report on "The Chief Executive Officer," there was a section headed "People contact counts more than computers." The theme of this section can be seen in the following quote:

> Most find the computer a vital business tool but of little value in meeting their own information needs, which frequently have nothing to do with operations or with numbers. Far more useful to most CEO's are the personal approaches to collecting information they have fashioned for themselves. Increasingly, their concerns are "people problems" and for the information to solve them they go to other people.
>
> In fact, far from solving the executive's information problem, the enormous amount of material the computer spews out merely complicates it by turning off the executive who then turns off the computer. "How many executives' offices have you been in lately," asks President Joseph F. Alibrandi of Whittaker Corp., "where there's a big box behind the desk with thick IBM runs that no one has ever looked at?"[13]

The effective utilization of computers as a source of assistance for senior management has been achieved in only a small number of companies. The reasons for progress in management information systems at a rate that has been far below expectations is analyzed in several chapters in this book. Our analysis is directly supported by the commentary of *Business Week:*

> Part of the problem with computerized information systems is undoubtedly that few chief executives really believe they work. The systems tend to be managed by electronic data processing personnel, or, at best, by financial executives who lack the necessary company overview.[14]

We see this dim view of computerized information systems changing in a number of companies. As research-based staffs gain in competence (note that most graduate business schools began to teach research-based management techniques only in the early 1960s) and as the new power of computers begins to be utilized effectively, the resources for the revolution in management will begin to make a much greater impact on corporate performance than has been the experience of the last decade. It is important that executives consider the rate of increase in people and computer resources when they plan for the future of management practice in their companies. Today executives in a small number of companies are aware of the usefulness of these new-management resources. These companies will be the first ones in which a Future Firm management capability will be achieved.

SUPPLY PUSH AND DEMAND PULL

A major factor delaying the coming of the New Management is that the research-based knowledge which makes the New Management possible is of recent vintage, developed since 1955. Twenty years is not a long time for the diffusion of technology in industry, as we saw in Chapter 1. Much management technology—particularly computers and quantitative techniques, but also the consistent application of organizational development skills—is complex and takes sophisticated users.

Another major reason for the delays in the utilization of the New Management is the lack of balance between supply and demand. The strategy we will propose in later chapters for successfully utilizing research-based techniques recognizes that the supply-demand balance problem can be solved in companies by putting the line managers who are the users and the staff who are the suppliers of research-based management skills together on problem-solving teams. But here we want to discuss the same imbalance on a larger scale.

There are two dynamic forces at work in the growth of knowledge for management: supply push and demand pull. Because the various institutions in society believe that the creation of knowledge will *eventually* make a contribution to the solution of problems, resources are allocated to nonmission or basic research. This creates a growing supply of knowledge from nonprofit research institutions such as universities. A large amount of scientific research is carried out ahead of the direct problem-solving need for that research, because of the supply push at work in the basic research communities. Motivated by the prestige and financial incentives that reward discovery and invention, researchers in specialized areas are constantly adding to an inventory of unutilized findings. This inventory provides a ready supply of knowledge which can be developed and applied in response to demand pull, the economic motivation to use science and technology to solve problems through commercial innovations in the market sector of the economy.

Supply and demand factors are listed in Table 3.1.

Science and technology exist in management as well as in the more traditional kinds of technical knowledge, such as chemistry and chemical engineering. Science and technology, whether in management or in chemistry, can be thought of as an inventory of knowledge in the form of books, journals, and technical reports, and more importantly, as part of the knowledge and skills of individuals. A number of studies have ana-

TABLE 3.1 Supply and Demand Factors in the Management Knowledge System

Supply factors	Demand factors
1. Buildup of knowledge; number of scientific papers doubling every ten years	1. Buildup of complexity and speed of change
2. Recognition that elements of the business system are a source of interesting problems; little understanding of management tools needed by managers	2. Recognition that technology may increase effectiveness of management; little understanding of new technology needed
3. Desire among knowledge suppliers to achieve recognition through publication	3. Desire among managers to achieve recognition through economic performance
4. Compartmentalization of knowledge into disciplines	4. Unity of knowledge in operating systems
5. Thinking without action; need for orderly development of findings	5. Action without thinking; need for achievement in the competitive economy

Shared factors

1. Propensity to exploit fads and trends
2. Growth of computer resources
3. Specialization of people

lyzed the factors which determine the development and utilization of new technology.[15] In the literature on technical progress, the concept of demand pull has emerged.

When there is a sufficiently strong demand for a problem to be solved, the work required for solution will be funded. A goal, or mission, is established, and a project is organized. The scientific and technological knowledge needed to complete the mission is pulled out of inventory or developed as a phase of the project effort. In summary, economic demand pulls science and technology into application. This dynamic force is embedded in a market economy. Knowledge is bought to satisfy demands for the solution of problems.

Myers and Marquis collected data on the factors which determined the utilization of 567 industrial innovations in five industries and found:

> Recognition of demand is a more frequent factor in innovation than recognition of technical potential. The idea or concept for an innovation is necessarily a fusion of recognition of both demand and technical potential. In the present study the innovators indicated that the primary factor in undertaking work on the innovation was a recognized market potential or a recognized need in the production process in three-fourths of the cases. In 21 percent of the cases the primary factor was recognition of a technical potential which might be exploited.[16]

When innovations occur as a result of the recognition of a technical capability, this is called *supply push*—which is to be contrasted with *demand pull*. Because the development and utilization of new-management science and technology have become an important factor in determining the rate of improvement in the effectiveness of management, it is useful to review some historical trends.

Business tends to be reluctant to fund research in the sciences. Note in Table 3.2 that only 3.2 percent of industry R&D in 1972 was for "basic research," which generally means "science." Industry just cannot wait the long time required before progress in basic scientific research is translated into technological findings which can be used by engineers in the development of new products and processes. Furthermore, basic research has the serious problem of being very risky relative to engineering or other kinds of development activities. Prediction of a breakthrough in basic scientific research is almost impossible within any acceptable level of cost and time. It is for this reason that basic science resides primarily in academic and nonprofit institutions. Research findings reported by Edwin Mansfield indicated that half of the R&D projects started in his sample of companies had a 50:50 chance of technical success. Mansfield concludes from his review of the literature and his own research findings that "the bulk of the industrial research-findings tend to be relatively safe from the technical point of view."[17]

Management Technologists

Historically, then, new science has been produced in the academic community or in nonprofit institutions, while industry performed the engineering efforts which result in inventions. The industrial effort prior to

TABLE 3.2 Funds for Performance of Industrial Research and Development by Category of Work, 1960 and 1972

	Basic research	Applied research	Development	Total
1960:				
Millions of dollars	376	2,029	8,104	10,509
Percent of total	3.6	19.3	77.1	100.0
1972:				
Millions of dollars	625	3,439	15,457	19,521
Percent of total	3.2	17.6	79.2	100.0

SOURCE: U.S. Department of Commerce, *Statistical Abstract of the United States*, 1974, table 885, p. 534.

the twentieth century, mostly in mechanical and electrical engineering, had a very low science base. Railroads, steel, machine tools, agricultural machinery, and interchangeable parts were invented by individuals with a very low level of science education.

The middle of the twentieth century, in contrast, has been a period in which science became an important source of technological progress. This has been accomplished by giving engineers a very heavy load of science in their education and by creating project teams in which scientists and engineers work together. Engineers have quantitative training and can relate to scientists despite the more theoretical training received in science.

The demand-pull side of innovation in management, however, reminds one of the industrial revolution of the 1800s rather than the twentieth-century science-engineering relationship in R&D. Industry has not had an engineering function in management to absorb the progress in science. There has not been a common set of quantitative skills held by management scientists in universities and by managers in industry because there is no tradition of teaching engineering in the field of management. In other words, the knowledge gap between quantitatively trained professors of management and the managers in corporations has been much wider than the gap between university scientists and the scientists and engineers in industrial research laboratories.

The situation is changing, however. Tremendous management problems surfaced in World War II and created an extraordinary demand pull on both science and technology. The demand pull on technology slacked at the end of the war, but the scientific events continued through supply push. A demand pull on management knowledge finally built up in the 1960s.

This demand pull on management science has now created in business a new category of skilled professionals which we will call *management technologists*. There has been a need for management engineers, professionals who can convert the huge supply of management science into utilized new-management technology. Unfortunately, beginning with the legacy of Taylorism, management engineers and industrial engineering have come to be associated with time-and-motion studies, layout design, and other similar techniques for increasing production efficiency. These methods have a much narrower application when compared with the power of new-management techniques such as strategic planning and computer-based management information systems. Defining a new profession, management technologist, avoids a possible confusion with industrial engineering.

A management technologist is not at the frontier of management science. Instead, a management technologist is usually working to apply management-science knowledge that is over a decade old. A management technologist has a much better understanding of management science than an experience-based executive, yet knows far less about management science than the theoretically educated management scientists. The supply of management technologists has been increasing very rapidly during the last decade, and this is one important reason for the progress that has been experienced in achieving successful applications of new-management techniques.

Applied and Not-Applied Management Knowledge

Knowledge for management is diagramed as an expanding volume in Figure 3.3. Both applied management knowledge and *not*-applied knowledge are expanding, but the latter more than the former.

We now have a basis for analyzing the relationships between demand pull and supply push in the utilization of research-based techniques in management. The supply of management knowledge has been expanding rapidly—and this is what we call supply push. The application of research-based management techniques has been increasing rapidly, but from a very low base. Thus there is a huge inventory of research-based management knowledge which is underutilized. The first applications of research-based management techniques were not as cost-effective as current applications because of the learning experience that had to be achieved. Now a combination of forces is leading to an acceleration of the demand pull for research-based management techniques.

Fortunately, academic researchers, consulting firms, and computer manufacturers have been providing supply push for years and have created a rich backlog of underutilized technology. The management knowledge required to progress from Present Firm to Future Firm is largely available. Results-oriented managers can profit from the last few decades of supply push in new-management techniques.

a = applied knowledge   n = not applied knowledge

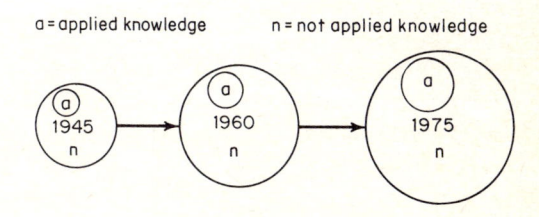

1945   1960   1975

FIG. 3.3 *The expanding volume of management knowledge.*

NOTES AND REFERENCES

1. Machlup, Fritz: *The Production and Distribution of Knowledge in the United States,* Princeton, N.J.: Princeton, 1962.
2. Drucker, Peter F.: *The Age of Discontinuity: Guidelines to Our Changing Society,* New York: Harper & Row, 1969, p. 263.
3. Forrester, Jay W.: *Industrial Dynamics,* Cambridge, Mass.: M.I.T. 1961, p. 1.
4. Strauss, George: "Organizational Behavior and Personnel Relations," *A Review of Industrial Relations Research,* vol. 1, Madison, Wisc.: Industrial Relations Research Association, 1971, pp. 145–206.
5. Mills, Ted: "Human Resources—Why the New Concern?" *Harvard Business Review,* March–April 1975, pp. 120–134.
6. Ewing, David W.: *Long Range Planning for Management,* New York: Harper & Row, 1958.
7. Mackler, Robert J.: "Theory and Practice of Planning," *Harvard Business Review,* March–April 1970.
8. Ansoff, I. H., and R. G. Brandenburg: "A Program of Research in Business Planning," *Management Science,* vol. 13, February 1967, pp. B-219–B-239.
9. Silk, Leonard S.: *The Education of Businessmen,* New York: Committee for Economic Development, Supplementary Paper No. 11, 2d printing, March 1961.
10. Livingston, J. Sterling: "The Myth of the Well-Educated Manager," *Harvard Business Review,* January–February 1971, p. 87.
11. Withington, F. G.: "Five Generations of Computers," *Harvard Business Review,* July–August 1974, p. 100.
12. Nolan, Richard L.: "Computer Data Bases: The Future Is Now," *Harvard Business Review,* September–October 1973, pp. 98–114.
13. "The Chief Executive Officer," *Business Week,* May 4, 1974, pp. 80–81.
14. Ibid., p. 80.
15. For an analysis of the process of technological progress, see Gruber, W. H., and D. G. Marquis (eds.): *Factors in the Transfer of Technology,* Cambridge, Mass.: M.I.T. 1969.
16. Myers, Sumner, and Donald G. Marquis: *Successful Industrial Innovations: A Study of Factors Underlying Innovation in Selected Firms,* Washington, D.C.: National Science Foundation, 1969, p. 60.
17. Mansfield, Edwin, et al.: *Research and Innovation in the Modern Corporation,* New York: Norton, 1971, pp. 20–21,

―――――――――――――――――――――― FOUR

The Failure of Management Science/ Operations Research (MS/OR)

There is a new breed of staff professional trained in mathematical model building—a skill called management science, operations research, or econometrics by the practitioners of this kind of work, and frequently labeled derisively by the experience-based line managers who are the potential users of mathematical models.[1] A management scientist should, by virtue of the name, be simply a person who uses the scientific method to study management. In fact, however, the words have meant and continue to mean one who creates mathematical models which to a greater or lesser degree describe certain business operations: resource allocation, scheduling, distribution, waiting lines, and portfolio selections, to name a few. Actually applying these mathematical models to real-world business situations requires a great deal of skill in the management process of changing the way work is done. We will describe that process in Chapters 10 through 12. In the meantime, however, it is important to understand why MS/OR, quantitative management, has had such vociferous supporters and detractors.

THE RISE AND FALL OF QUANTITATIVE MANAGEMENT

There has been no shortage of optimistic professors and consultants forecasting the coming of a revolution in the practice of management as management-science techniques become utilized. In the late 1950s and early 1960s there was uncritical acclaim for the new developments. Business was about to be saved by the scientifically derived techniques which had helped win World War II. Then it was discovered that the management-science staff professionals were technique-oriented, too theoretically inclined, and frequently not useful to experienced line executives with business problems in a complex organizational setting. A reaction occurred, and the uselessness of these techniques and their protagonists was proclaimed. There was a clash of two cultures, and a poor return on investment was a frequent result of these early efforts.

This led to insufficient demand pull from industry during the pipeline-filling stage in the development of the New Management. It was possible to follow trends in R&D investment, because a threat from competition was readily observable in new products and/or new processes created by R&D. In investments for research-based management, the pattern was more random, seemingly the response to fads and the claims of professors, consultants, and computer manufacturers. What progress does exist in the development of research-based techniques has been produced by a very small number of staff members in a firm. A technically intensive firm might have 500 scientists and engineers in R&D for new products, but a professional staff of 5 at work on quantitative techniques in management.

The failure of management science to live up to expectations has been a great disappointment for business school professors. As Professor Glen Urban of the M.I.T. Sloan School of Management laments, "It seems that little of the vast effort put into MS/OR model building has yet paid off in terms of implementation and the improvement of organization effectiveness."[2]

Some line executives are not as mild in the language they use to describe the failure of management science. Those who call such work "theoretical garbage" and other such names have some justification. There is evidence that research-based management scientists and experience-based managers do not work well together. In fact, there is evidence that management science has been a big disappointment and a great frustration to the executives in many companies.

The Management-Science Utilization Problem

Management-science techniques are underutilized because of the failure by both management scientists and line executives to understand the process in which a new technology is developed and reaches a condition of usefulness. We will examine here the factors which have caused the failure of management science.

The sudden availability of computers was a major cause of the MS/OR utilization problem. First introduced in the early 1950s, computers facilitated quantitative training for management scientists and future managers. Management scientists led a difficult life before computers, since quantitative problems with real-world data had to be solved with mechanical calculators. The solution of a simple regression equation used to examine the relationship of several variables or to extrapolate a trend line might take days or even weeks of laborious work at a desk calculator. By the late 1960s, any college freshman who needed to solve a given equation could type the problem into a time-share terminal and have the university computer calculate an answer within minutes or even seconds. By the mid 1960s one did not even have to know very much about computers or computer programming. In the batch-process days prior to time share (early and middle 1960s) a student could put a few control cards in front of the canned program, add the data deck, and slap on a final card marked "END," and out would come analyses, relationships, and plotted curves—almost everything except an explanation of the assumptions behind the work. Students quickly learned how to produce "findings" that they did not understand.

Nonetheless, computers did make it possible to increase the supply of quantitatively trained graduates of business schools. Management education was expanding rapidly during the 1950s and 1960s. Student enrollment in higher education doubled from 4 million to 8 million between 1961 and 1971.[3] This resulted in a large increase in the number of young professors who needed to publish in order to get tenure and promotion. These young professors had been able to stay in school from undergraduate days through to a Ph.D with little time off for industrial experience. Professors in management schools with a quantitative orientation produced students in their own image. Thus the supply of quantitatively trained professionals educated by quantitatively trained professors who had little real-world experience increased very rapidly in the 1960s.

The first young graduates with new-management skills—from such places as Wharton, M.I.T., and Carnegie—had quantitative training plus knowledge of a large amount of science and very little applicable technology. They learned almost nothing from actual management-technology utilization in business because very little existed. These young and inexperienced new entrants to management were assigned to professional staffs whose missions in the corporation were poorly defined.

Business executives typically were not ready to accept or utilize theoretically trained staff professionals. In an environment where even simple kinds of planning were rarely attempted, management hired young and inexperienced staff professionals trained to build complex mathematical models. Management scientists entered industry conditioned by their professors to push for ever greater levels of sophistication in technique.

Managers did not know how to communicate with, much less manage, such technique-oriented management scientists.

L. Jackson Grayson, Jr., described in a 1973 *Harvard Business Review* article the uselessness of management scientists in his work as chairman of the Phase II Price Commission, and explained this uselessness as a two-cultures problem:

> Managers and management scientists are operating as two separate cultures, each with its own goals, languages, and methods. Effective cooperation—and even communication—between the two is just about minimal. . . . The total impact of management science has been extremely small. Its contributions look even smaller than they are if one compares it to the revolution promised for management offices in the early years. And the wait-until-next-generation theme is wearing thinner and thinner.[4]

The Grayson article was supported by business executives in the letters-to-the-editor section in the next issue of the *Harvard Business Review*. John D. Harper, chairman of the board of Aluminum Company of America, quite properly blamed both the graduate business schools and the business community for the problem:

> I believe that Mr. Grayson's article is thought-provoking and should stimulate interest [among] managers, management scientists, and academics in developing programs that would tend to narrow the gap that currently exists. Mr. Grayson has evidenced a rare insight into the gulf that exists between the theory of management science and its application to practical management problems. His article throws down the gauntlet to the graduate business schools and the business community to rethink in a fundamental way the concepts of business education. The problem cannot be remedied by the schools alone, any more than it can be solved by the business community alone. We need a cooperative interface between the two, so that the movement of young men from the academic to the operative is no longer stepping out of one world into another.[5]

Uneasiness of Management Scientists

The process by which progress in management science is transferred into management operating practices is the cause of widespread uneasiness in the profession. Over the last ten years a large body of proverbial lore has been built up about the "practicality gap" or "interface between MS/OR and management." No overall structuring of the relationship between MS/OR and management as practiced has been accepted, although many intuitively sound suggestions have been put forward. Examples of such proverbs—selected from a very great stock in the literature—are listed in Table 4.1. These examples of management-science utilization problems provide a menu of reasons for the low level of implementation of the new techniques.

The Failure of Management Science/Operations Research (MS/OR) / 59

TABLE 4.1 Examples from the Literature on Problems in the Utilization of Management Science

1. Operations researchers do not emphasize enough human factors, since these factors are hard to model mathematically.
2. The task of explaining new-management applications and convincing the customer to utilize the new techniques should shape the formulation and solution of the problem.
3. Management science must become involved in management as a total process.
4. Management quite often lacks the confidence to use the result that the operations-research group has produced.
5. The inertia of management slows down implementation.
6. Operations-research people should realize that management operates in a real-time, crisis environment,

There has also been an upward trend of concern about the utilization problem as expressed by management-science professionals in their journals, *Management Science* and *Operations Research*. As indicated in Table 4.1, undocumented wisdom has been the first response of the management-science professional community to the problem of low utilization. This is seen another way in Figure 4.1, which shows the amount of

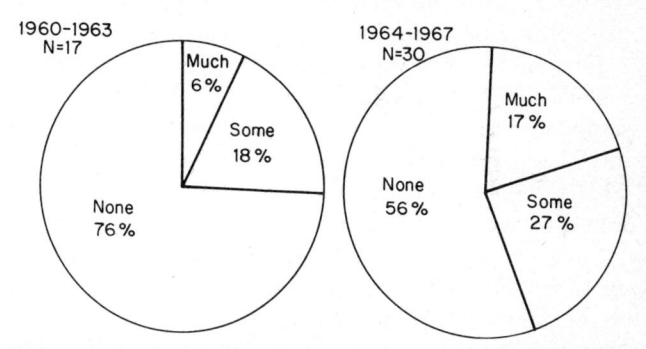

1960–1963 N=17: Much 6%, Some 18%, None 76%

1964–1967 N=30: Much 17%, Some 27%, None 56%

FIG. 4.1 *Level of empirical support given in articles on the management-science utilization problem published in professional MS/OR journals.*

SOURCES: Articles in *Management Science, Operations Research,* and foreign MS/OR journals for the period 1960 to 1967, all discussing the utilization problem, were read and placed in one of three categories: no empirically derived quantitative support (Some): or more than one page describing quantitative support (Much). The 47 articles include all those concerning implementation in *Operations Research* and *Management Science* plus other articles discovered by a search of *Operations Research Quarterly, International Abstracts in Operations Research,* and *Operations Research/Management Science Abstracts* for the years 1960 to 1967.

empirical data used in journal articles on the management-science utilization problem. In the 1960s, articles containing data on this problem were increasing in number. Exhortation was ahead of research, however. In the 1960s, about 40 percent of the presidents of the Institute of Management Sciences (TIMS) and Operations Research Society of America (ORSA) mentioned interface difficulties between management science and management in their annual addresses to the membership. The proportion of actual articles on the subject between 1961 and 1966 in the respective journals, however, ran well under 4 percent. Apparently verbal recognition of the implementation problem was at first sufficient to relieve concern about the utilization objectives of TIMS.

In 1970 the Institute of Management Sciences started a new, very small (compared with their monthly journal), quarterly journal called *Interfaces* with a primary goal of encouraging interactions between managers and management scientists. Many of its articles have been concerned with management-science implementation problems, although it is still clear that most management scientists are not interested in doing empirical research on how to apply MS/OR models. This is because management-science professionals are not trained or encouraged to do empirical research on implementation problems; the failure to do such research is consistent with the meager empirical research on applied management problems close to the point of management practice.

One survey indicates that of the 150 *Management Science: Applications* journal articles from January 1971 to June 1973, only 3 percent represented more than one use of a model or procedure in an organization and but 15 percent were models or procedures that were applied even once.[6] This journal largely describes mathematical models that bear some theoretical relation to management phenomena (prices, sales, inventory, etc.).

Such models are not applicable to management problems without a great amount of further testing and refinement. That models developed at the management-science frontier are of little use in the practice of management is a reason for low implementation that is rarely acknowledged by the authors of management-science literature (who are usually scientists working on frontier problems). Scientific research which produces models of management problems cannot be equated with a body of usable management technology.

The Science-Technology-Utilization Relationship in Management

Two activities are commonly delineated in the management-science literature on the implementation problem: management and management science. The activity of management is defined as the current state of the art of performing various management activities, in other words, what managers do. On the other hand, management science is the activity of those who *study* management or phenomena relevant to management, in other words, what management scientists do. However, it has become clear to us that what is needed is a further differentiation of practice and science in management by way of the explicit recognition of a third class of activity, *management technology,* defined as the development of new techniques for the practice of management. Management technology falls on the continuum between management science and management practice. This activity already exists wherever there are people trying to change the content of management activity. The Institute of Management Sciences defines the management sciences as "scientific knowledge contributing to the understanding and practice of management."[7] Management science is a part of science which is the foundation knowledge for management technology and management practice. Management technology, on the other hand, is manifested by decision-making capabilities implied by models and techniques already implemented in organizations, plus the capabilities implied by models and techniques that *could be* implemented without further use of scientific knowledge.

If management scientists are those who add to the body of scientific knowledge which forms the basis of management technology, then those who actualize the contribution of science to management activity are management technologists. Putting management knowledge into a form which causes change, the management technologist makes possible "mutual understanding"[8] between the manager and the scientist by reducing the abstractness of scientific knowledge to a level that managers can understand. Technologists in management translate a scientific understanding of industrial and organizational phenomena into a means of carrying out managerial functions. Management scientists are concerned with pushing the frontier of knowledge outward, whereas technologists work within this frontier. Technologists are content to push the frontier of application. Managers need only to understand the management technology at a level required to use it. A house painter can use latex-base paint without understanding its chemical properties, and similarly, a manager can understand the input/output requirements and the basic assumptions of a computer model without understanding the mathematical details or even the programmer's flowchart.

An example As an illustration of the flows from science to utilization in management, consider the successful implementation of a media-selection model by John D. C. Little and Leonard M. Lodish. A media-selection model is a series of mathematical equations (usually solved on a computer) which are designed to help a marketing executive decide how much advertising to purchase in various types of television, radio, and magazines. The early stages of the Little-Lodish MEDIAC model for media selection was an effort by a management scientist, John Little, to summarize the available models in a summer course in operations research that he taught at M.I.T. These early models had serious weaknesses, and between 1964 and 1966 Little developed a more powerful model which was a more valid formulation of the problem but still too cumbersome to use. This first Little model was still management science.

Little improved the usefulness of his model in 1966 when he conceived of the feasibility of using an old mathematical technique called the Taylor series as a breakthrough in the efficiency of calculation that had been a serious barrier to the utilization of his model. Little's model is also based on work of a psychologist, Ebbinghaus, who around 1916 developed a precise theory of how people forget things over time. Thus Little, attempting to solve the real-world problem of the need for a more effective decision model for business executives, was able to use the work of Taylor from 1712 and the science of Ebbinghaus from 1916. This science became embodied in management technology when the MEDIAC model was developed into a computer program.

The MEDIAC model was cost-effective in utilization because of the management technology of on-line, interactive computer systems which were just beginning to be useful in industry in the mid 1960s. In order to achieve utilization in the practice of management, Little and Lodish developed the management technology of a system in which "communication [with the model in a time-share computer system] is conversational and largely self-explanatory."[9] Little and Lodish reported on the *science* that they had developed and the *technology and practice* that they had achieved in *Operations Research*. In order to see if their ideas really worked in practice, Little and Lodish started Management Decisions Systems, a consulting firm which offers assistance in the utilization of the models developed by management scientists and technologists. This firm has been successful in translating new science into practice.

Little and Lodish had a heavy academic and scientific interest in the development and utilization of management models. If we studied the translations of theory into practice accomplished by professionals in industry and in the more traditional consulting firms, we would probably find that the majority of the work involves the utilization of well-developed technology. We would find applications involving unsophisticated uses of techniques discovered decades ago rather than the management science produced by John Little and his associates. In fact, we encourage our clients to use "old" management technology which is still years ahead of common practice. Little and Lodish were motivated to try out new-management science "to see if it worked." Most corporations and traditional consulting firms do not have management scientists employed as senior officers. Note, however, that Little and Lodish had to transform management science into an easy-to-use computer program that permitted inexperienced users to work with their model. If the technology of time-share computer systems had not been available, the management science created by Little and Lodish might not have been used in the practice of management.

FROM SCIENCE TO PRACTICE IN MANAGEMENT

Opposed to the above model, which suggests that the results of management science achieve utilization in management practice in a process similar to that which occurs in R&D leading to new products and processes, the assumption often implicit in articles on the management-science utilization problem is that the research of management scientists should be directly applicable to the practice of management.

Churchman and Schainblatt, for example, focus on the interaction of scientists and managers and think that mutual understanding is required. Even John Little has written on what the management scientist should do for the manager. He urges that the models created by management scientists be designed with the interface between the manager-user and the model in mind.[10] The emphasis he places on considering user requirements during model construction is an attempt to shorten the tortuous path between science and utilization in the activity of management.

Approaches focusing on the manager-scientist interaction miss the point that the practitioners and the scientists in any field are going to move further apart when the rate of scientific progress is high. The science behind the activity of engineers and medical doctors has become increasingly complex, but the response to this trend has not been to stifle the development of the science by urging that it conform to the limitations of practice. Instead, there has been a trend toward increasing the science content of engineering and medical education. R&D management has been recognized as a field of research and education. Similarly, more attention to the management of the process by which management science becomes management technology and practice may produce the capability required to achieve utilization of MS/OR models.

The resources of the management-science profession are skewed toward science, that is, toward supply push as discussed in the last chapter. One way to achieve a faster return on an investment in management science is to focus research on applications (that is, work on engineering rather than science). An effort to understand the process in which management accepts the new knowledge may provide higher economic returns than research to increase the elegance of management science which is yielding too much science and not enough improved management practice.

Verbal assurances of interest in the utilization of management science (which necessarily includes its translation into management technology) are insufficient proof to business executives that the academic professionals who publish have more than a secondary interest in utilization. This value judgment in favor of theory is not lost on the research-based professionals whom the professors turn out. Price[11] has noted that scientists write but do not read; technologists read but do not write. There have been too few reports in the literature of successful applications of new managerial techniques. Instead, the *literature available to management technologists has been less helpful than it could be because of its theoretical content, lack of empirical evidence, and lack of feasibility investigation.* These qualities result from the fact that the literature is produced largely by true management scientists with academic affiliations, as indicated by Figure 4.2. The Institute of Management Sciences has two publication series, A for theory and B for applications. Note that Figure 4.2 was calculated from *Management Science,* Series B, which is supposed to be applications.[12] If this is management applications, what is management science?

The magnitude of the investment in scientific research and develop-

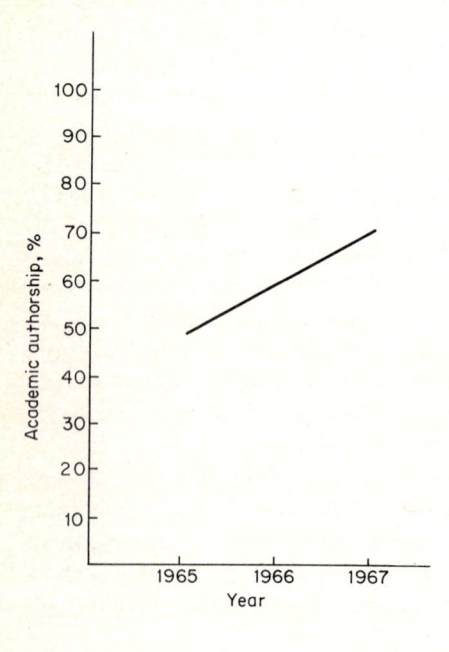

FIG. 4.2 *Management science or management technology? Percentage of academic authorship in the* **Management Science** *applications series.*

ment for new products and processes has aroused an interest in the usefulness of R&D activities. Many conferences and publications on the "transfer of technology," which is the use of technical knowledge in a new way, have recognized that new science and technology have little economic value until an application is made. Until a given advance is actually used in the practice of management, it is difficult to calculate an economic value of the technical progress. This emphasis on translating management science into operations implies the value judgment that management science is not an end in itself, but exists to improve practice. There may be some consumer value in management science for management scientists themselves. However, the justification for the funding of management science is that practice will be improved.

A nonproductive staff function may be tolerated during periods of high profits. The 1969–1970 recession and the rising costs of the mid 1970s provided an incentive for many line executives to reduce sharply the budgets for management-science activities. The easy days of management science for its own sake have left a legacy of disillusioned line executives. In contrast to the experience in the 1969–1970 recession, many companies expanded staff capabilities for such research-based techniques as computer systems, strategic planning, and econometric forecasting in the 1974–1975 recession. It is possible that, at least in the better-managed companies, research-based techniques are becoming an important resource for management during a period of severe volatility in economic and regulatory conditions.

The early employment of management scientists in industry was frequently an act of faith. These pioneer management-science staffs tended to be in separate units in the corporate organizational structure. For example, marketing or production tended not to have their own management-science staffs. These were scientists, not technologists, employed in business a decade ago.

Despite the progress in the employment and utilization of management technologists, there is still the two-cultures problem created by theoretically educated professionals. In some companies, as we will note in the next two chapters, line executives have learned how to utilize young, quantitatively trained staff professionals who have received from their educational experiences an inadequate understanding of the real world of management. Executives in the better-managed companies have discovered that the knowledge learned in schools of business by M.B.A.'s and management scientists will not contribute to corporate performance unless experience-based line executives have a strategy for the effective utilization of these new brainy resource people who are being employed in ever greater numbers.

NOTES AND REFERENCES

1. We will use MS/OR to label this mathematical modeling.
2. Urban, G. L.: "Building Models for Decision Makers," *Interfaces,* May 1974, p. 2.
3. *Social Indicators, 1973,* Washington, D.C.: U.S. Government Printing Office, 1972, p. 106.
4. Grayson, L. J.: "Management Science and Business Practice," *Harvard Business Review,* July–August 1973, pp. 41–44.
5. Harper, J. D.: letter to the editor, *Harvard Business Review,* September–October 1973, p. 42.
6. Urban, op. cit., p. 1.
7. *TIMS 1973-1974 Directory,* Providence, R.I.: The Institute of Management Science, 1974.
8. Churchman, C. W., and A. H. Schainblatt: "The Researcher and the Manager: A Dialectic of Implementation," *Management Science,* vol. 2, no. 4, February 1965, pp. B-69–B-87.
9. Little, J. D. C., and L. M. Lodish: "A Media Planning Calculus," *Operations Research,* January–February 1969, pp. 1–35.
10. Little, John D. C.: "Models and Managers: The Concept of a Decision Calculus," *Management Science,* vol. 16, no. 8, April 1970, pp. B-466–B-485.
11. Price, D. J. de S.: "The Structures of Publication in Science and Technology," in W. H. Gruber and D. G. Marquis (eds.): *Factors in the Transfer of Technology,* Cambridge, Mass.: M.I.T., 1969, p. 96.
12. H. J. Boisseau reports that in a recent twelve-month period of *Management Science,* both Series A and Series B were within 1 percentage point of 71 percent academic authorship. He also reports another survey which showed that 66 percent of TIMS membership was affiliated with industry and consulting. Boisseau, H. J.: "Letter to the Editor - A survey of Management Science Authors," *Management Science,* vol. 15, no. 8, April 1969, pp. B-361–B-364.

FIVE

Research and Experience in Management

Despite the emerging importance of research in what has heretofore been an experience-based activity, there remains the conviction among many that skill in management is inherently experience-based. This conviction is understandable because management is an ongoing activity that has been thriving for centuries.

EXPERIENCE IN MANAGEMENT

There is a natural feeling on the part of managers, past and present, that what they are doing is intuitive, judgmental, and not amenable to improvement through the application of research. This view is reinforced by the fact that the college degree required for admission to the management ladder does not have to be in management or in an area related to management. Bradish[1] discovered in his survey of the education of high-level executives that 63 percent of the degrees held by top executives were in nonmanagement fields, such as engineering, science, liberal arts, or law. The remaining 37 percent were in various management-related subjects. See Table 5.1.

Belief in the value of experience in management was reinforced by the nature of most business education up until a decade ago. As we discussed earlier, the Ford and Carnegie Foundation studies in the late 1950s

TABLE 5.1 Academic Background of Corporate Management (Chairman of Board, President, Executive Vice President)

Background	Percent
Management or management-related fields:	
Management	13.8
Accounting	12.7
Economics	5.3
Marketing	5.0
Engineering and science	28.2
Liberal arts and social science (including economics)	12.6
Law	8.9
Miscellaneous	13.4
Total	100.0

SOURCE: Richard D. Bradish, "Accountants in Top Management," *Journal of Accountancy*, June 1970, p. 51. Survey represents a 57.4 percent return from the 500 largest firms in the country.

revealed that transfer of experience in the form of facts, examples, procedures, and simple rules of thumb made up the bulk of business education in the United States. The most widely known of the business schools, Harvard University Graduate School of Business, implemented the philosophy of experience transfer through the method of case discussions, which was described as follows:

> A case typically is a record of a business issue which actually has been faced by business executives, together with surrounding facts, opinions and prejudices upon which executive decisions had to depend. These real and particularized cases are presented to students for considered analysis, open discussion and final decisions as to the type of action which should be taken. Day by day the number of individual business situations thus brought before the students grows and forms a backlog for observing coherent patterns and drawing out general principles. In other words, students are not given general theories or hypotheses to criticize. Rather, they are given specific facts, the raw materials, out of which decisions have to be reached in life and from which they can realistically and usefully draw conclusions. This opportunity for students to make significant contributions is enhanced by the very nature of business management. Business management is not a technical, but a human matter. It turns upon an understanding of how people—producers, bankers, investors, sellers, consumers—will respond to specific business actions, and the behavior of such groups always is changing, rapidly or slowly.[2]

The method of case discussions is still widely used throughout United

States business schools, even in schools that also present large amounts of material in traditional lectures, readings, and student exercises. This use of case material—unheard of in schools for scientists and engineers, although used in law schools—suggests that the knowledge base for management, as it exists today, is an incomplete basis for educating people who aspire to management careers. And, although skill built through real experience is the vital adjunct to a sound management education, the vicarious experience from debating case material in a classroom cannot provide such an education.

Professor J. Sterling Livingston of the Harvard Business School summarizes several research studies which indicate that "managers are not taught in formal education programs what they most need to know to build successful careers in management."[3] There seems to be no correlation between managerial success and grades in college or business schools. Professor Livingston notes that "men who hold degrees in business administration—especially those with advanced degrees in management—have found it surprisingly difficult to make the transition from academic to business life.... Turnover rates among men with advanced degrees from the leading schools of management appear to be among the highest in the industry.... And this job-hopping often follows a poor performance showing."[4]

The fault with business education, Livingston believes, lies in its emphasis and inherent shortcomings. "Preoccupation with problem-solving and decision-making in formal management education programs tends to distort managerial growth because it overdevelops an individual's analytical ability, but leaves his ability to take action and to get things done underdeveloped."[5] Management education does not produce the capacity to profit from experiences and thus to develop the mixture of style, authority, and empathy which leads to managerial achievement. Unless managers "acquire through their own experience the knowledge and skills that are vital to their effectiveness, they are not likely to advance far up the organizational ladder."[6]

Initially, then, a management school graduate is likely to be well versed in the growing stock of research-based knowledge vital to the understanding of some management problems. However, he or she will be short on the additional experience-based skills about which there is still little to be formally taught, yet which are necessary for achieving managerial effectiveness. Nevertheless, one skill that the graduate should have initially is the ability to do the analysis and study to give a research base to executive decision making. The result of this synthesis of research and experience should yield better business decisions, even before the current generation of business school graduates exercises mature authority.

TWO VIEWS OF MANAGEMENT

The discussion so far has not explained the adamant insistence of some managers that on-the-job experience will never be supplanted by research-based knowledge. Much of the conflict over the relative importance of research and experience can be resolved by examining what management is. The relative increase in the significance of research can then be demonstrated without disparaging the importance of experience. Management can be subdivided in different ways according to differing perspectives. Two of the most useful points of view for dividing managerial activity are the behavioral view and the decision-making view.

Behavioral View of Management

One of the ways of analyzing management would be to examine the behavior of managers. Professor Sayles[7] has thought carefully about how management behavior can be classified. He has observed and recorded such behavior across a wide variety of firms and has noted three broad categories: external work-flow participation, leadership, and monitoring.

Work-flow participation is person-to-person interaction among managers at the same or nearly the same level in the hierarchy in order to accomplish the work of the firm. Most managerial activity is this consultative, participative, bargaining behavior among people of similar organizational rank.

Leadership situations are those in which the manager attempts to get response from a group of people, usually subordinates. In leadership situations, many people have to be reached with the same or similar information, and a one-to-many communication pattern is, of course, most efficient. Note that Sayles's view of leadership puts aside the existence of authority, which need be invoked only when the logic of the work does not determine the hierarchy of activity.

Monitoring is the method or methods used by managers to apprise themselves of how their internal and external relationships are proceeding and to identify stresses and strains that may require their intervention. Intervention which might follow monitoring would occur through interactive or leadership behavior. Monitoring, therefore, is keeping in touch with what is going on. Figures and reports are part of it. Listening and watching are, also. The political content of management—who is getting ahead and why—is an important aspect of a manager's monitoring, and it will never be computerized.

This three-part system of Sayles concentrates on the way a manager gets things done through people. Although what managers do in terms of these kinds of observable behavior is not very distinguishable at different levels of the hierarchy (they all answer telephones, go to meetings, talk with subordinates), the effect on the firm of action at different levels is somewhat different, or at least should be. Note that under the above behavorial scheme there is no discussion of how different levels of management affect the organization. A company president, a division manager, and a department supervisor, all engaging in similar types of behavior in the course of a single day (mostly work-flow participation), would be making different contributions to the company.

Decision-Making View of Management

Another classification scheme, which we will call a decision-making view, distinguishes the effects of decisions according to the position of the manager in the hierarchy. This classification brings in the inputs and the outputs of the decision-making process.

Robert Anthony has proposed a useful framework for the analysis of management activity; he factors the management process into operational control, management control, and strategic planning.[8] He defines each as follows:

> *Strategic planning* is the process of deciding on objectives of the organization, on changes in these objectives, on the resources used to attain these objectives, and on the policies that are to govern the acquisition, use, and disposition of these resources.
>
> *Management control* is the process by which managers assure that resources are obtained and used effectively and efficiently in the accomplishment of organizational objectives.
>
> *Operational control* is the process of assuring that specific tasks are carried out effectively and efficiently.

Each of these three divisions of the management process relates to activities within the organization in a particular way. See Table 5.2 for examples. Strategic planning, which should be the principal form of top-management activity and the form of some of divisional-management activity, builds the road over which the firm will progress through the "total environment" of customers, competitors, government, technology, the economy, and—increasingly—the world. The primary consideration is the contribution of the firm to society and the economy. Management control, which is the province of division managers and functional department managers—that is, managers of managers—keeps the firm on the road determined by the strategic plans. The most important resource in this effort is personnel. Though each manager is responsible for only a part of the organization, the net effect of management control should be to approach the goal of coordinated movement of finance, production, marketing, R&D, and other functions which make up the company. This coordinated movement should tend to maximize the contribution of

TABLE 5.2 Examples of Activities in a Business Organization Included in Major Framework Headings

Strategic planning	Management control	Operational control
Choosing company objectives Planning the organization Setting financial policies	Formulating budgets Planning staff levels Working-capital planning	Controlling hiring Controlling credit extension
Setting marketing policies	Formulating advertising programs	Controlling placement of advertisements
Setting research policies Acquiring a new division	Deciding on research projects Deciding on plant rearrangement Formulating decision rules for operational control	Scheduling production Controlling inventory

SOURCE: Robert N. Anthony, *Planning and Control Systems: A Framework for Analysis*, Boston: Harvard Graduate School of Business Administration, 1965, p. 19. The number of examples is abridged.

resources to the objectives of the firm. Operational control—partly the concern of functional managers, but mostly of lower-level managers and supervisors—is the process of keeping the parts of the firm working smoothly. These parts are the various work groups and relatively limited functions that often can be optimized through the application of computers.

It is not useful to choose between the behavioral and the decision-making views of management, since one is no more correct than the other. The first describes how managers must do their work; the second describes the relationship of the management process to the needs of the firm.[9]

SHIFTING PATTERN OF MANAGEMENT

The notion of management being experience-based seems to be supported by close examination of both the behavioral and decision-making views of management. The work-flow interactions (a behavioral category), which constitute so much of a manager's day, require considerable skill that is impossible to teach formally. Experience is also the prime prerequisite in the work required as one moves up the organizational ladder into the realm of strategic planning (a decision-making category).

In contrast, the behavioral category of monitoring and the decision-making category of operational control are being routinized steadily through work in communications, computer technology, applied mathematics, behavioral science, accounting, and economics. In the two middle categories, there is a vast gray area where experience still dominates research inputs. Although in the behavioral category of leadership and the decision-making category of management control, change resulting from research inputs is much less rapid, inroads have been made here as well. New organizational forms decentralize some decisions to profit-centers, project teams, and task forces; behavioral scientists have developed management by objectives and team-building techniques; the automation of routine management information reporting has been very rapid.

Managers, by definition, are given a good deal of discretion in their work. Managers are not told how to act; they are told to meet objectives within the bounds of corporate policies and the budget. If a job can be described in great detail, then it is not a managerial position but a programmed position suitable for occupation by clerical people or, possibly, a computer. In both the behavioral and decision-making schemes of management activity, some categories are wide open to programming as knowledge about them increases. Other categories are not open to this programming and, in fact, represent areas wherein the experience element is likely to remain paramount.

Furthermore, as monitoring and operational control yield to computerized, systematic approaches, managers can and will turn their attention to the other types of activity. Increasingly, the management process will involve team management, which stresses high interpersonal communications within a peer group, focusing on decisions with strategic implications. In Chapter 12, we will describe the reliance company presidents now place on task forces of specialists to develop and implement recommendations on complex management problems. Task-force management is highly dependent on the contribution of experience-based members of the team. But the continued emphasis on experience-dependent work comes precisely because research is making the former concerns of management nonmanagerial. That is, research inputs are pushing experience-based management activity into new domains of activity.

As research-based knowledge creates understanding in a manager, some managerial tasks will actually become so well understood that they are no longer worth the attention of an executive. In fact, the routine of daily activity carried out by business managers in modern society evolves over time for each particular kind of business. In the electric-power-generating industry, for example, managers have seen their activity change over the past century.

> In an electric utility, boilers and generators are cut in and out and turbines are loaded or shut down as actual and projected loads change from hour to hour, or even from minute to minute. The profitability of a utility company is directly affected by load dispatching decisions. . . .
>
> In the era of the small, local electric utility with a few generators and power units, changes in load were met (or not met) by imprecise adjustments, often after consultation or discussion with management. As systems grew larger and more complex, economic and engineering analysis of the profitability of various kinds of load control became common and the load dispatchers began to assume more and more of the prerogative of deciding how to accommodate the changes. Management simply indicated the objectives, restrictions, and policies that it desired the load dispatchers to meet and follow.
>
> Using tools similar to those of today's management scientists, utility managements soon began to develop means to record and analyze the results of past decisions and to better define the economics—thermal and electrical—of alternative choices in a given situation. The development and codification of these methods suggested that the load dispatcher could be replaced in part by a computer. The result was one of the earliest computerized management applications.
>
> The next step was for the load dispatcher's job to become simply the supplying of the necessary parameters into a computer that, acting on current

operating data, either indicates or actually makes the best load allocations under the circumstances. Management no longer even suggests the parameters. The new, important management task is, of course, to decide whether to buy a bigger and better automatic load analyzer and to tie more units into an integrated network. Such decisions, based on the ability to analyze the pattern of probable demands and evaluate the probable economic and technical effects on a very complex system, are of a higher order than earlier ones.[10]

RESEARCH-RESPONSIVE MANAGEMENT

This pattern of shifting toward higher-order decisions on the part of management has been the result of new-management technology, that is, new ways of doing the manager's job. The change-causing input to managerial activity is research.

Research-responsive management is practiced by executives who are aware of, who change because of, and who use new technology developed out of knowledge in mathematics, economics, behavioral science, systems analysis, and computer applications. Since new knowledge for management is constantly being developed, research-responsive management implies a continuous process of change in the practice of management. When managers first started using telephones or Dictaphones, there was a new type of management. New office products and other new applications of knowledge such as quality-control procedures and market research have continually changed the activity of managers. In this sense, managers have always been research-responsive. Research can reduce a manager's activity to work for a clerk, or for a computer, as Dr. Hertz's example of load dispatching in an electric utility shows. After surveying managerial behavior extensively, Professor Sayles noted that "the manager's job must change as much as that of the skilled worker or the specialized technician. It is almost a cliché to observe that modern industry makes individual skills obsolete at a frightening pace (e.g., the flight engineer). What has not been realized is the extent to which this is true for administrative skills."[11]

The need for change in the manager's job will come because of research-based inputs. These inputs do not define management activity, as Sayles recognizes when he notes that "most management education has little management in it; a steadily increasing proportion of the student's time is devoted to technical subjects."[12] Management, whether in Sayles's behavioral conception or Anthony's decision-making framework, has a breadth not completely defined by a series of technical subjects. The continued use of the case method in management education is an attempt to simulate the breadth required in decision making. However, we do claim that the technical subjects are a valid research input for management, even though they represent very incomplete knowledge.

The curriculum and educational process in business schools often give inexperienced students the impression that management is merely a set of skills in functional and technical areas. In truth, research-developed knowledge is an agent of change in the conduct of experience-based management. New information and concepts pose a challenge to the way things have been done before. Research permits greater productivity for management by allowing the development of refined procedures where once there could be only guesswork and judgment.

When management is falsely equated with various bodies of technical research, problems are created in schools of management, as described here by Sayles:

> The better young professors are probably oriented toward the quantitative-technical-staff fields where there is a reasonable precision and life is not complicated by human problems. These are the fields in which the good business schools "lead" the real world. The messier, more difficult, less quantifiable areas—those we have combined under the title "management"—are neglected, although these are the enduring challenges to the executive. It is not unusual to find the more sophisticated executives in business knowing more about essentials of management than the professors. This is not true of the best professors in other professional fields such as law, medicine and engineering.
>
> The absence of a research base is revealed in student attitudes. One of the few persisting criticisms of the products turned out by schools of administration is their excessive cocksureness. . . . Where there is no tradition of constant inquiry, criticism, and reformulation of concepts and ideas, the student thinks he is getting the final word. He is all set to be a president.[13]

With the kind of attitude described by Sayles prevalent in many business school graduates, the potential of the technical knowledge that does apply to management can be easily lost unless experience-based managers learn how to use the new specialized training of the young graduates of business schools. Experienced management has to learn how to profitably employ M.B.A.'s and their research-based techniques which have been developed with inadequate attention to the needs of managers in the real world. Management will therefore require increased experience and ability in the evaluation and use of the research output of analysts. Experienced managers must translate analytically derived processes and solutions into language which takes into account personalities, politics, deadlines, risks, and interfunctional considerations—factors about which the analyst is likely to be naïve.

EVERYONE A SPECIALIST

We prefer to make the distinction between research-based and experience-based people, rather than the often-mentioned dichotomy of specialists and generalists. To us, everybody is a specialist; we are all defined by our jobs as specialists. Vice presidents of marketing may think that they have a global view of their job; in fact, they think very differently from vice presidents of manufacturing. A product-line manager in ethical pharmaceuticals sees a very different world than a product-line manager in the machine tool industry. We may not think of *ourselves* as myopic specialists, even though it is easy to spot the narrow and distorted view of lawyers, accountants, and management scientists (who are research-based and bent out of shape by their education) or sales and manufacturing managers (who are experience-based and owe their peculiar views to the functional content of their work).

In a rapidly changing business environment in which new knowledge becomes available at a dizzying rate, it has become necessary to specialize in some way in order to maintain one's level of in-depth awareness of current activity in one's own area of job responsibility. Experience-based line executives are becoming more specialized by industry and by function owing to the rapid rate of change in business conditions and the greater complexity of the business environment. There has been an extraordinary increase in the amount of knowledge needed to do a good job in almost every facet of line and staff activity. As William Dougherty, Jr., president of the NCNB Corporation observed, "Our four-man senior executive team provides the resources for getting with the details of operations. Banking is just moving too rapidly and it is just getting too complex for one man to know all facets of banking. Within our four-man senior management team, we specialize in order to understand the activity in our areas of individual responsibility."[14]

Each of the research-based fields of knowledge is now subdivided into smaller areas of specialization, and a manager must go deep enough into the specialty to get a problem solved. A "lawyer" is not needed when there is a problem with the Equal Employment Opportunity Commission (EEOC)—a specialist in equal employment regulations must be consulted. Even within the equal employment area of specialization, it may be wise to seek an expert on employment of minorities, women, or older workers.

A common error is for experience-based management to be unaware of the kinds of research-based specialists that are needed. For example it is incorrect to assume that because someone is an experienced data processing professional, this person is an expert in computer room operations, telecommunications, data base management, or the large number of other areas of specialization within the field of data processing.

So, if everyone is a specialist, then what is a generalist?

A generalist is a specialist who works in several fields of knowledge. The knowledge of a generalist does not have to be at a level of operational detail. Rather, a generalist has sufficient knowledge to utilize the greater depth of understanding which has been achieved by other research-based or experience-based specialists; the key skill of a generalist is the ability to utilize the knowledge and experience of certain but not other specialists. This in itself requires specialized talent and skill. Generalists usually have to specialize by industry and can change easily only to similar industries. The universal manager-generalist is nonexistent, although talented senior managers can adapt very well to a range of new organizations in the same or similar industries.

The specialization that is built on experience in a given industry was cited by Allen H. Seed, III, as the first reason for the high rate of failures (estimated at between 30 and 50 percent) of corporate acquisitions. As Seed notes, "The trouble comes when someone in one field acquires a company in another field and tries to run it like the parent. Many skills are transferable, but there is no substitute for the capabilities that are developed from spending a lifetime in an industry."[15] Almost all senior executives in business today are experienced-based managers. The reality of the specialization that is caused by experience is perhaps best demonstrated in the miserable acquisitions track record of so many companies.

Research-based professionals tend to have an easier transition when moving from one company or one industry to another. For example, a Ph.D. in operations research who had been working for a major airline moved to a large chemical company. Within a month this research-based professional was effectively developing new computer-based management information systems which were designed to improve the practice of management in the chemical company. In contrast with research-based management, experience-based management involves the learning of a large number of details. When an experience-based manager moves to another company or another industry, it becomes necessary to create a whole new inventory of details. In a move between companies or industries this problem of detail discovery is less severe for research-based professionals than for experience-based line executives. An experience-based executive moving from one industry to another is closely comparable to a research-based professional changing fields of specialization.

Part of the task of management is to understand the process in which research-based professionals and line executives become specialized. In the acquisitions problem cited by Seed, research-based professionals can be very useful in assisting experience-based executives to learn the details which are the foundation of effective management of an acquired company in an unfamiliar industry.

COGNITIVE AND EMOTIONAL FACTORS

Research on the thinking processes of experience-based line managers and research-based professionals indicates that there are significant cognitive and emotional differences among the individuals who excel in these two kinds of activity. McKenney and Keen analyzed the abilities of managers and research-based professionals and typed four kinds of thinkers:[16]

Systematic thinkers tend to:
- Look for a method and make a plan for solving a problem
- Be very conscious of their approach
- Defend the quality of a solution largely in terms of the method
- Define the specific constraints of the problem early in the process
- Discard alternatives quickly
- Move through a process of increasing refinement of analysis
- Conduct an ordered search for additional information
- Complete any discrete step in analysis that they begin

Intuitive thinkers tend to:
- Keep the overall problem continuously in mind
- Redefine the problem frequently as they proceed
- Rely on unverbalized cues, even hunches
- Defend a solution in terms of fit
- Consider a number of alternatives and options simultaneously
- Jump from one step in analysis or search to another and back again
- Explore and abandon alternatives very quickly

Receptive thinkers tend to:
- Suspend judgment and avoid preconceptions
- Be attentive to detail and to the exact attributes of data
- Insist on a complete examination of a data set before deriving conclusions

Preceptive thinkers tend to:
- Look for cues in a data set
- Focus on relationships
- Jump from one section of a data set to another, building a set of explanatory precepts

As progress in management shifts to a greater reliance on the inputs of research-based professionals, it is important that individuals contribute to tasks in ways which reflect their thinking and emotional capabilities.

Greater specialization should be recognized and encouraged as beneficial to organizational performance. A strategy for the effective utilization of personnel with different cognitive and emotional characteristics is now an important requirement for good management. Such a strategy exists in only a few companies, although our work in client companies indicates that it is possible to implement an effective strategy for the recognition and utilization of the unique cognitive and emotional characteristics of company personnel. A personnel evaluation system and computer-based skills inventory provide the structure within which to build a strategy for the identification and recognition of important characteristics of line management and staff professionals. The development and implementation of such a system provide a primary resource for the solution of the problems created by the need to encourage specialization in the practice of management.

CONCLUSION

Experience-based executives receiving assistance from research-based staff professionals is the essence of the New Management. However, line executives are likely to receive only mediocre staff assistance unless they learn a new set of skills. The executives in only a small number of companies have learned how to utilize their staffs of research-based professionals, and skill in managing research-based professional staffs is the critical determinant of progress in the practice of management. The skills to manage such professionals stem from the realization that knowledge for management must be integrated into the firm through specific management activities; the skills of the specialist do not become cost-effective simply by the fact of his or her being hired. Management must organize its research-based staffs into problem-solving teams that bring all the relevant inputs—from quantitative, behavioral, and institutional specialists—to bear on whatever problems need solving. Planning for the solution of the executives' problems should be the activity that lends coherence and mission-orientation to the skills of specialists.

Line executives should be involved with the specialists on a project as team members. Regardless of educational background, a line executive is often the most valuable member of a new-management project team. He or she will frequently contribute an understanding of what the problem really is, and, perhaps even more important, an understanding of how a proposed solution can be implemented. The time for line executives to see a proposed solution is not after a project team has completed its work and produced a report containing recommendations. Line-executive participation vastly increases the probability that research-based work will be relevant. Line management must be personally aware of the strengths and weaknesses of the staff specialists on project teams. Involvement with research-based staff specialists is an important new responsibility of experience-based line executives.

NOTES AND REFERENCES

1. Bradish, Richard D.: "Accountants in Top Management," *Journal of Accountancy,* June 1970, p. 51.
2. Gregg, Charles I.: "Because Wisdom Can't Be Told," in Malcolm McNair (ed.), *The Case Method at the Harvard Business School,* New York: McGraw-Hill, 1954, pp. 6–7. See also Robert A. Gordon and James E. Howell, *Higher Education for Business,* New York: Columbia, 1959, The Ford Foundation Study; and Frank Pierson et al., *The Education of American Businessmen,* New York: McGraw-Hill, 1959, Carnegie Foundation Study.
3. Livingston, J. Sterling: "Myth of the Well-Educated Manager," *Harvard Business Review,* January–February 1971, p. 79.
4. Ibid.: pp. 81–82.
5. Ibid.: p. 82.
6. Ibid.: p. 76.
7. Sayles, Leonard R.: *Managerial Behavior: Administration in Complex Organizations,* New York: McGraw-Hill, 1964.
8. Anthony, Robert N.: *Planning and Control Systems: A Framework for Analysis,* Boston: Harvard Graduate School of Business Administration, 1965, pp. 16–18.
9. Emery, James C.: *Organizational Planning and Control Systems,* New York: Macmillan, 1969, provides a useful additional reference on the decision-making or information view of management. See also Jay Galbraith, *Designing Complex Organizations,* Reading, Mass.: Addison-Wesley, 1973, for this focus on management. A good program of action in the use of the behaviorial view of management is provided in Richard Beckhard, *Organization Development: Strategies and Models,* Reading, Mass.: Addison-Wesley, 1969.
10. Hertz, David B.: *New Power for Management: Computer Systems and Management Science,* New York: McGraw-Hill, 1969, pp. 16–17.
11. Sayles: op. cit., p. 203.
12. Sayles, Leonard R.: "Whatever Happened to Management?" *Business Horizons,* April 1970, p. 25.
13. Ibid.: p. 32.
14. Personal communication with W. H. Gruber, Oct. 11, 1974.
15. Seed, Allen H., III: "Why Corporate Marriages Fail," *Financial Executive,* December 1974, p. 57.
16. McKenny, James L., and Peter G. W. Keen: "How Managers' Minds Work," *Harvard Business Review,* May–June 1974, pp. 79–90.

———————————————————————————— SIX

The Management of M.B.A.'s

In the allegedly good old days, someone could become successful in business without even graduating from high school or after majoring in history or Greek in college. Most senior executives in business today who are fifty years of age or older have not received a graduate degree in management. Education for a career in business was not needed thirty or forty years ago. As we indicated in Chapter 3, during the last fifteen years there has been an extraordinary increase in the quality of education for management, and the number of M.B.A.'s graduated each year increased from less than 5,000 to over 20,000 (see Figure 3.1). Today, a graduate degree in business has become a very important source of qualification for joining the ladder leading to higher levels of management in many companies.

Research-based management requires the selection and utilization of employees who have been formally educated (in contrast to learning from experience) for their job responsibilities. An M.B.A. is one category of this kind of employee. Our analysis of the management problems experienced in the selection and utilization of M.B.A.'s applies to other categories of employee with qualifications based on educational experiences.

The importance of M.B.A.'s to business can be seen from their employability in the 1974–1975 recession. *Business Week* noted that "MBA's are finding jobs in the current recession when almost no one else can."[1]

Companies compete for top M.B.A.'s as they fight for customers. The recognition of the need for higher levels of formal education appears to be particularly strong in industries such as commercial banking which are changing dynamically. *Business Week* reported:

> One New York bank sent 20 recruiters to Harvard, where they interviewed one-third of a graduating class of 800. "Chase Manhattan and First National City Bank were pushing hard," says the placement director at another B-school. "They seem to be in direct competition for people, too." Citibank recruited a total of 261 from colleges last year, 155 of whom were MBA's, and plans to hire a similar number this year. Chase hired 43 MBA's in 1974 and has already signed up 52 this year—with still some offers outstanding.[2]

The rush to employ new M.B.A.'s is not a new phenomenon. Several years ago we dramatized the experience as follows:

> Buy the addresses of this year's graduating MBA students and mail them personalized invitations to your reception for them in a downtown hotel. Dispatch your best line managers to graduate schools of business to impress the MBA's that you are serious about wanting them. Fly them to your plant sites. Don't give them tests, or long forms to fill out, and above all don't talk down. Raise salary offers $2,000 over the bid price for last year. Really disrupt the company salary structure in order to be in the race. When you have managed to hire a few, give them responsible positions; let them learn in a job which they have too little experience to handle successfully.
>
> About when these MBA's have gained sufficient experience to achieve results for your corporation, watch them leave for a better job in another company. Hire even more next year, if you can, to compensate for this turnover.[3]

Some of our clients have slowed their employment of M.B.A's and other specialized professionals. The need for research-based management technology to aid experience-based executives to cope with changing demand, regulation, and consumerism is greater than ever, and we are urging our clients to recognize the imperatives of maintaining a minimum-level investment in research-based management through selective hiring. Salary expectations of M.B.A.'s are heavily moderated in a period of economic uncertainty, and many firms have reduced recruiting substantially, so the opportunity exists for an aggressive firm to pick up top-flight talent at last year's prices.

In any event, graduate education in management provides corporations with the New Management that some firms will use to reach Future Firm status. As described in an earlier chapter, the M.B.A.'s of the 1970s are very different from the product of the 1950s. Today, M.B.A.'s at the top schools[4] are no longer taught what a business executive already knows; they have learned what the executives of the future will need to know.

The new knowledge for management described in Chapter 3 is laced throughout the curriculum. Industrial relations for the new M.B.A. means behavioral science and organization theory. The student of accounting is taught statistics and computer applications. Problems in finance, production, and marketing are solved by an M.B.A. with mathematical models implemented on computers.

THE CORPORATE M.B.A. STRATEGY

The employment of personnel with graduate degrees in management has been a painful and high-cost activity for many corporations. The utilization of research-based resources involves a new set of management skills, which have been lacking in these corporations. Senior executives in many companies have been disappointed with their efforts to profitably employ M.B.A.'s. Yet some have had great effectiveness in the utilization of M.B.A.'s. Hiring of M.B.A.'s for these firms is a critical source of new managers and new members of professional staffs. In some companies, M.B.A.'s are first employed on professional staffs and then promoted into line management. In contrast to companies with a well-conceived strategy for the utilization of M.B.A.'s, there are other companies without an awareness of what determines the usefulness of M.B.A.'s. The employment of M.B.A.'s in some companies can best be defined as merely the participation in an expensive fad. Some firms hire widely; others only at certain schools; others not at all. Prejudice abounds; meaningful understanding is scarce.

The employment of M.B.A.'s can be dangerous. We were impressed with this fact when we learned during one of our consulting assignments how it was that credit cards were introduced in the two largest banks in what must be an unnamed city. It seems that senior management in each of these banks had made the decision not to introduce credit cards. These were the early days of bank credit cards, and the huge investment required for the development of this new service did not appear to have an adequate payback.

By strange chance, one of these two banks employed more M.B.A.'s during the annual recruitment drive than there were job slots. To resolve the embarrassment of what to do with an extra M.B.A., a decision was made to have this M.B.A. do research on the kinds of customer services that this bank was not then offering. Given this assignment, the M.B.A. began to research the bank credit card market and sent out questionnaires (market research through questionnaires is one of the skills which many M.B.A.'s learn while in graduate school). The president of the competing bank learned of this survey effort and created a crash program to get his bank first into the credit card service. The president of the bank that had hired too many M.B.A.'s learned of the crash program of his competitor and he rushed his bank into the race to be the first bank in the city with a bank credit card. The race to be first with a bank credit card was just about a tie. Within three years, the combined losses in these two banks on their credit cards was over $100 million.

Does the unhappiness of many experienced executives with people trained in research-based management refute the theme of this book? This is one possible conclusion from the horror stories about bad experiences with a brash M.B.A. who has spent weeks producing a useless computer output or a worthless management-science model. An alternative conclusion to be reached from the history of unsatisfactory experiences from attempts to use those trained in research-based management is that *corporate executives must learn how to use these resources more effectively.*

The primary usefulness of M.B.A.'s is in the knowledge they can bring to the firm. The new M.B.A.'s believe that their knowledge of new-management skills is important and want to use those skills. They tend to underestimate the value of experience, a misconception matched only by the disdain of experienced personnel with whom they must work. Management awareness of and response to the friction created by the interaction of research-based and experience-based people are necessary for the strategy of M.B.A. utilization. A successful corporation in the present environment needs a fusion of research skills *and* experience on the management team. The new M.B.A. should be encouraged to assist the experienced managers in their understanding of new techniques. Likewise, the established managers should share their experience of the company business. A complementary relationship is possible and should be cultivated.

The methods of achieving innovation in management described in Chapters 10 and 11 constitute our major recommendations of how to profitably organize new M.B.A.'s and other research-based staff. At this point, however, we want to focus on the peculiar problems associated with hiring and retaining M.B.A.'s.

DIFFERENCES AMONG M.B.A.'S

M.B.A.'s vary widely in quality and in knowledge. It is possible to receive an M.B.A. from some schools and learn little that was not taught ten years ago. Just as companies vary widely in the level of management competence on our Prior–Present–Future–Firm continuum, graduate schools of management also vary in the quality of the students accepted and the quality and focus of the education received by students. M.B.A.'s from many schools receive little research-based education and do not differ significantly from students with no business majors in their ability to apply

TABLE 6.1 Percent of M.B.A.'s by Field of Specialization in Four Major Graduate Schools of Business Administration

	Harvard	M.I.T.	Chicago	Stanford
General management	35	25	1	8
Finance	34	14	46	37
Accounting	2	2	2	1
Mathematical methods	2	15	17	6
Other fields of specialization	27	44	34	48

SOURCE: Calculated from data reported by M.B.A. Enterprises, Inc.—*MBA Recruitment, 1968,* New York, 1968, Table 10, and *MBA Recruitment, 1969,* New York, 1969, Table 10.

research-based techniques. This chapter is about M.B.A.'s who have been educated in schools with at least moderate capabilities to educate in the research-based techniques.

It is important to recognize that the personnel produced by graduate schools of business have skills which vary according to the student characteristics and faculty interests of each school. It can be seen, for example, in Table 6.1 that the largest proportion of Harvard graduates in 1968–1969 specialized in general management. M.I.T. requires far more work in quantitative methods for all students than is required of Harvard M.B.A.'s, and a far larger proportion of M.I.T. management graduates specialize in mathematical methods.

The substance covered in an M.B.A. program varies from almost pure analysis and discussion of cases (such as described for Harvard in the preceding chapter) to a very heavy concentration in the research disciplines described in Chapter 3. What effect does the difference in educational strategies listed in Table 6.2 have on the usefulness of the M.B.A.'s produced in these schools? Should the company M.B.A. strategy recognize this difference in educational experience? A reasonable hypothesis is

TABLE 6.2 Educational Experience of M.B.A.'s in Three Leading Graduate Schools of Business Administration

School	Experience
Harvard	Almost pure case method; relatively little quantitative methods required
Stanford	Combination case method and discipline education
M.I.T.	Essentially discipline-based education

that M.B.A.'s educational environment during their management training *will* affect their output of work once they are on board with an employer. This would be particularly true for the M.B.A. graduate with limited prior work experience. An initial survey of each incoming M.B.A.'s course work will allow a personnel department to correlate academic background with job success. A better understanding of the education of the M.B.A.'s in the company will lead to future success in hiring, placement, and utilization. Even within a given school, there is no question that a student who has majored in behavioral science will have a completely different set of attitudes and capabilities than a student who has majored in quantitative methods. A finance major at Harvard Business School will probably be strong on knowledge about the institutions, customers, and regulations in the field of finance. A finance major from M.I.T. is much more likely to be a good economist and econometrician with very little understanding of daily activities in the real world of finance.

In an environment of selectivity in hiring, companies want the best possible attitude characteristics in newly hired M.B.A.'s. A substantial proportion of business school graduates are "mature" as indicated by marital status, military experience, and work experience. This is particularly true of those who are obtaining these degrees on a part-time basis. However, many M.B.A.'s earn their graduate degree with full-time study just two years after their bachelor's degree. The values of the two groups can be assumed to be substantially different. For example, men who have children, military experience, or more than two years of work experience tend to deemphasize the importance of social responsibility for business.[5]

Differences in work experience prior to the M.B.A. should be considered from another angle. The 1970 M.B.A. Enterprises survey of M.B.A.'s reported that M.B.A.'s with one to four years of work experience were more likely to change employers quickly than M.B.A.'s who became graduate students without a break after undergraduate education.[6] Each company should maintain a record of its own experience in the staying power of M.B.A.'s with and without work experience. A company may not want to trade an M.B.A.'s early departure for the higher performance and maturity that often accompany prior work experience.

M.B.A. MEANS HIGH COST

Though the usefulness of newly graduated M.B.A.'s is sometimes debated, there is no doubt that they are expensive on all counts. To begin with, recruitment costs are often relatively high, since graduate schools of business are geographically dispersed. Furthermore, new M.B.A.'s have come to expect a level of treatment that is expensive.

- They expect high-caliber recruiters to interview them, preferably line managers who are familiar with positions available to M.B.A.'s. An uninformed recruiter is viewed as worse than none at all.
- When given plant trips, new M.B.A.'s expect well-organized tours and contact with line managers. The plant trips are taken at the M.B.A.'s convenience, not at the convenience of the firm.
- In general, students prefer personal and high-quality attention to their needs. They want personalized letters, meals in executive dining rooms or the best restaurants, personalized itineraries, and the time of high-level executives.

The fact that some firms give this treatment means that those which do not are at a serious disadvantage. The following favorable comments from University of Chicago M.B.A.'s on recruiting practices are typical:

- I liked companies that sent me personal letters which were truly personal, i.e., not form letters.
- The company was liberal on expenses. I don't mean wasteful but I dislike limits put on hotel expenses and meals.
- I met the Chairman of the Board and many other very high executives.[7]

There are also unfavorable comments:

- Telegrams or letters sent to the masses that sounded as though you were the "greatest guy on earth."
- The placing of an unreasonable limit on my expenses.
- The personnel officers were not representative of the executive staff.[8]

M.B.A. students compare notes very closely during the recruitment season. Firms which are clearly economizing on recruiting costs through impersonal techniques become well known. Students know if the letters sent to their classmates were the same as the letter sent to them. The M.B.A. population at a given school is usually close-knit, since the structured curriculum of an M.B.A. program means students take many classes together. The emphasis on group projects at many business schools also implies a high level of intercommunication.

The most apparent high cost associated with the new M.B.A. is the salary required to bring him or her on board. The trend has been upward through the class of 1974 and only in the current recession is leveling off. The median salary received by the graduates of the M.I.T. Sloan School of Management Masters Degree Program increased from $16,000 in 1972 to $17,500 in 1974.

We have observed that the content and quality of education, the attitudes and conditioning received by students, and the quality and background of students vary from one graduate school of business to another, which affects salaries. An M.I.T. Sloan School of Management or Harvard Business School (H.B.S.) graduate has a degree which is valued at a much higher price than that for a degree from the average graduate school of business. This halo effect is lasting. Alan Wolfley, H.B.S. 1949, now executive vice president of Cerro, observes that for the first five to ten years of business "the trademark is the single most important thing. And it reads 'H.B.S.' right across your forehead."[9]

In a survey of the performance of the Harvard Business School Class of 1949, it was reported that the class median earnings in 1972 were $53,561. Of all men of similar age and years of education as the H.B.S. graduates of 1949, only 27 percent were making $25,000 or more. The H.B.S. graduates of 1949 found 53 percent with earnings of $50,000 or more and 18 percent with $100,000 or more. In the year after graduation, the median earnings for them was $5,200.[10]

It is interesting to note that the M.I.T. management students tend to be younger and have less work experience than the students enrolled in the Harvard Business School program. The average starting salaries of M.I.T. graduates, however, have been higher than those offered to the Harvard Business School graduates. This differential appears to result from the stronger technical background of the M.I.T. graduates. An undergraduate in chemistry who receives a master's degree from the M.I.T. Sloan School of Management tends to command a higher starting salary than an undergraduate history major who earns an M.B.A. degree at the Harvard Business School.

M.B.A. students often regard salary as the first screening criterion in making their choice of where to work. Salary, in other words, is a necessary condition for joining a company. If salary is acceptable, *then* the new M.B.A. will consider a company further in terms of job characteristics, coworkers, and advancement opportunity. Companies have to make a substantial offer (determined by market factors) just to survive the M.B.A.'s initial screening of offers.

Salaries for M.B.A.'s can seriously damage a firm's salary structure. Although the hiring of young graduates from professional schools often creates a telescoping of the salary structure, the problem is particularly difficult in the case of M.B.A.'s. The impact on the total company management payroll must be considered. The whole salary structure may be raised to permit bidding for new M.B.A.'s. If the salary structure is not raised and new M.B.A.'s are paid a salary which rewards them more than commensurately with the value of more experienced employees, the older employees may seek other employment, or decrease their productivity, or initiate interpersonal friction with the new M.B.A.'s.

Management activity in which some M.B.A.'s participate has traditionally been experience-based and still seems to be so to the older management personnel. The work of the M.B.A. can involve a great deal of interaction with experienced personnel, thus making the difference between knowledge and experience particularly evident. The high salary of a visible M.B.A. management trainee provokes more comment than high salaries paid R&D scientists and engineers, whose activity involves far less interaction with experience-based people.

RETURN ON THE INVESTMENT OF M.B.A.'S

Consider the hiring of a new M.B.A. as an investment. During an initial period the contribution to company performance produced by the new M.B.A. will be lower than the salary and training-assimilation costs related to his or her employment. As M.B.A.'s gain in experience, their revenue-producing capability will increase more rapidly than their salary. Training-assimilation costs will decrease as a function of the time they have been employed in the firm.

Company experience with net profitability in the employment of a new M.B.A. is diagramed in Figure 6.1. It will be observed that a firm experiences a net loss on its investment in a new M.B.A. for a period in the early stages of career activity until revenues attributable to this professional rise

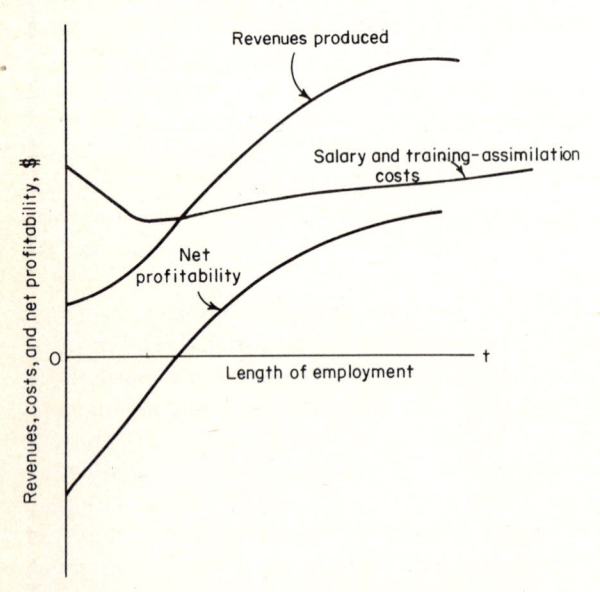

FIG. 6.1 *Company experience in the employment of a new M.B.A.: revenue produced minus salary and training-assimilation costs related to length of employment.*

above costs. The shape of this company experience will vary according to the success of the company strategy in hiring, using, and keeping new M.B.A.'s. Companies that lose a significant proportion of new M.B.A.'s will experience a far lower return than companies able to maintain the employment relationship.

The propensity of new M.B.A.'s to leave the firm has a cost in lower company morale. Coupled with the high start-up costs of new personnel and the low initial productivity of new M.B.A.'s in particular, a high rate of early attrition can make the hiring of a particular M.B.A. a risky investment.

Albrook in a review of research on the mobility of executives concludes that the propensity of M.B.A.'s to change jobs is part of a trend in which there is a "growing 'professional' detachment of their executive corps, the erosion of corporate loyalties that once spelled security. . . . What worries some companies most is that their losses are highest among younger college-trained men—whose restlessness shows every sign of being endemic."[11]

The trend toward a decrease in the usefulness of experience in the practice of management may be one of the factors which has encouraged the greater mobility of executives. Albrook cited findings by professors Schein at M.I.T. and Harrell at Stanford, who reported that there was a high rate of job switching by graduates of these schools. This greater mobility may be associated with the attitudes and visibility which result from the achievement of a graduate degree in management. Albrook concluded that "More and more of tomorrow's middle management and top executives, it appears, are going to have a lifelong [mobility] itch." This greater propensity to leave a company should be a matter of serious concern because surveys have shown that "the men who leave are also better men."[12] As Albrook notes, "When a valued man cleans out his desk and heads for the door, most corporations find his departure hard to face. He has in effect 'fired' his employer. Others often are inspired to follow his lead. The corporate ego is directly challenged."[13] If M.B.A.'s assimilate knowledge of crucial corporate processes and plans, their departure could be costly. And a resignation for a better job raises the expectation of the other employees.

FACTORS AFFECTING M.B.A. RETENTION

There are short-term and long-term factors affecting a company's ability to keep M.B.A.'s on its payroll after they have been hired. In the short term, there will be a few M.B.A.'s who cannot be assimilated into the organization because of unwillingness to learn and do what the established personnel believe to be necessary. Beyond one year or so, the problem becomes more a matter of the M.B.A.'s choices in the face of dissatisfaction and other alternatives.

Short-Term Losses: Failure of Organizational Socialization

Edgar Schein ties the failure of firms to retain new graduates of business to the process of organizational socialization, which he defines as "the process of 'learning the ropes,' the process of being indoctrinated and trained, the process of being taught what is important in an organization or some subunit thereof."[14] He notes several responses of an individual to organizational socialization; one of these, rebellion, defined as the rejection of organizational values and norms,[15] concerns us here. Schein summarizes the conflict that can lead to rebellion and withdrawal from an organization.

> On the one hand, the organization via its recruiters and senior people tells the graduate that it is counting on him to bring fresh points of view and new techniques to bear on its problem. On the other hand, the man's first boss and peers try to socialize him into their traditional mold.[16]

Organizational socialization must occur every time M.B.A.'s enter a new organization, such as when they are transferred to a new division of their company. But no later socialization will be as difficult for them as the one that marks the transition from business school to business. We can postulate that the failure of business school graduates to be socialized would mean that they are not promotable in the organization. Thus, in addition to the frustration of being incompatible, the nonsocialized M.B.A. feels restrained on the career ladder. Quitting the organization follows naturally.

Long-Term Losses: Failure to Maintain Balance[17]

The ability of a corporation to keep an M.B.A. on its payroll in the long run can be thought of as a two-part problem of balance. First, do the M.B.A.'s feel that they are getting more out of the corporation than they are putting in? Second, if the balance is not in their favor, what are their possibilities of doing something about it? Considerations of the first kind we will put under the heading "Desirability of Quitting." Considerations of the second kind we will discuss as "Ease of Quitting."

Desirability of quitting Of paramount importance here is job satisfaction. Is the M.B.A. satisfied with his or her position in the company? The question has three components.

First, the M.B.A.'s jobs must reinforce their image of themselves. For example, although many specific readings, papers, and exams are assigned in graduate school, the student is given a great deal of *independence* in the matter of how to complete those assignments. If their jobs in industry reduce freedom severely, they are dissatisfied. Another aspect of self-image is *worth*. We have already commented on the M.B.A.'s requirement of a high salary. This aspect of treatment and other aspects, such as size and characteristics of work area, and access to educational programs, must not be different from a level reflective of what they have been told in the popular literature about their worth. A final area of the M.B.A.'s feelings about themselves is their *competence*. They have each invested over $40,000[18] in the building of personal competence. If they feel that competence is not being utilized, personal satisfaction is likely to be low.

Second, the work of an M.B.A. should result in feedback regarding the effect of the work and its value to the company, if job satisfaction is to be maintained. The M.B.A. knows that the action of managers and their staff is what controls the company. An indication of a random or low effect resulting from the M.B.A.'s work makes the desirability of quitting and going elsewhere higher. An M.B.A. who produces a report wants to know what it has accomplished.

Finally, the compatibility of the M.B.A.'s organizational role with other roles is a determinant of job satisfaction. The norms and values of noncorporate associates, his or her family, and the wider world all will be compared with the requirements of life in the business organization. Time and energy requirements must also be rationed to various roles. There is now a strong folklore against selling life short in order to make it in big business. This is a new problem of uncertain dimensions. These three factors—conformance to self-image, feedback of results, and compatibility of job with other roles—all contribute to level of job satisfaction, which in turn is directly tied to desirability of quitting. When we add *availability of more satisfying jobs in the company,* we have the total story on desirability of quitting. If a new job to which the M.B.A. can look forward is seen to exist in the company, then quitting is definitely less desirable.

Ease of quitting What M.B.A.'s do when they are not satisfied with their present jobs and when they see no possibility of transferring to another job within the same organization is a function of what they believe are their alternatives. These alternatives are dependent on the state of the economy, their personal characteristics, and the visibility of other companies and organizations where they could go if they quit their present positions. The state of the economy tells them the general probability of their getting another job and what it would pay. It would also tell them the probable availability of venture capital in case they wanted to have a business of their own.

Their personal characteristics include their needs, attitudes, and values, as well as their technical and interpersonal skills. How hard will they search for a new job? In which industries will they consider a new position? For what positions are they qualified? The answers are by and large a function of the person's characteristics. The M.B.A. may very well have established personal rules of thumb about job changing, such as: No more than once every two years and only when there is a salary improvement of 20 percent.

The visibility of other organizations influences the ease with which they can identify another specific position that they expect would satisfy them more than the present one. This visibility depends largely on the effort expended by other organizations to attract experienced M.B.A.'s. Advertisements, favorable media publicity, and word-of-mouth information receive the attention of M.B.A.'s who are ready to switch. They are easily in touch with their school's placement office, which is actively helpful, or with their fellow business school alumni, who know the quality of the opportunities where they work.

The M.B.A.'s desire to quit is to some extent under the control of his or her employer, who determines rewards, punishments, and the nature of the work. On the other hand, the ease of quitting is generally *not* influenced by the employer. In the current economic downturn the employer of M.B.A.'s may be lucky on the second factor, as it is not now so easy for M.B.A.'s to quit their present jobs in favor of others. But the desirability of quitting exists quiescently in the unsatisfied M.B.A., ready to be acted upon when opportunity again appears in other firms.

SUMMARY

Hard work is required to realize the potential benefits available from M.B.A.'s educated in research-based management techniques. Hiring them represents an investment at a significant risk level, and data on the firm's historical experience with M.B.A. investments should be maintained and evaluated.[19] The characteristics of the M.B.A. which count toward performance should be discovered. This chapter has suggested several: maturity measures, quantitative orientation, educational specialty, and attitudes toward work. A strategy for each type of M.B.A. is vital if this source of talent is to be utilized effectively. Future Firm performance will rely on M.B.A.'s as a prime source for new managers.

In the early stages of their careers, many M.B.A.'s are specialized in a particular function of business, such as finance or marketing. The management of M.B.A.'s is a particular case of the management of specialization, which is the subject of the next chapter.

NOTES AND REFERENCES

1. "The Job Market Starts a B-School Stampede," June 2, 1975, p. 50.
2. Ibid.
3. Gruber, W. H., and J. S. Niles: "The Care and Feeding of MBA's," *Management of Personnel Quarterly,* Fall 1971, p. 15.
4. This group includes Harvard, Stanford, University of Chicago, University of Pennsylvania, Carnegie-Mellon, and Massachusetts Institute of Technology. The last two of these schools award an M.S. degree rather than an M.B.A.
5. *MBA Recruitment,* New York: M.B.A. Enterprises, 1968, pp. 18–19.
6. "The MBA Itch Is Mostly Myth," *Business Week,* Sept. 26, 1970, p. 30.
7. *MBA Recruitment,* pp. 218–219.
8. Ibid.: pp. 220–221.
9. Wellemeyer, Marilyn: "The Class the Dollars Fell On," *Fortune,* May 1974, p. 226.
10. Ibid.: pp. 224ff.
11. Albrook, Robert C.: "Why It's Harder to Keep Good Executives," *Fortune,* November 1968, p. 137.
12. Ibid.
13. Ibid.
14. Schein, Edgar H.: "Organizational Socialization and the Profession of Management," *Industrial Management Review,* Winter 1968, p. 2.
15. Ibid.: p. 10.
16. Ibid.: p. 12.
17. This section is an application of the employee participation model described in J. G. March and H. A. Simon, *Organizations,* New York: Wiley, 1958, pp. 93–106.
18. Say, two years at $5,000-per-year tuition and supplies and over $15,000 per year of forgone income.
19. What is the rate of return on an M.B.A.? As a clearly identified and expensive workforce category, the M.B.A. group is the perfect place to begin adding human resources to the accounting system. See James S. Hekimian and Curtis H. Jones, "Put People on Your Balance Sheet," *Harvard Business Review,* January–February 1967, pp. 105–113; also see Raymond E. Miles, "Human Relations or Human Resources?" *Harvard Business Review,* July–August 1965, pp. 148–160.

SEVEN

Specialization and Integration in the New Management

When the early advocates of decentralization cited the need to have decisions made at the level in the organization closest to the problem, they were recognizing the need for managers to focus their attention on a segment of the market. Decision making had to become more specialized. In Chapter 1 we traced the evolution of the practice of management and noted that decentralization was pioneered by Sears and Du Pont in the 1920s. Building on these innovations, the practice of decentralization as we know it today grew out of further progress made in the 1950s. General Electric is recognized as one of the important contributors to the post-World War II development of decentralization. The decentralization at General Electric has been organized according to several kinds of specialization—by product line primarily, but also by geography and functional types of work. The president of General Electric, Ralph Cordiner, described in 1956 the General Electric decentralization program, which had its beginning in studies started in 1943 and went into the actual application phase in February 1951:

> As you can imagine, the entire process involves a tremendous amount of self-analysis and education throughout the organization. Not only new ideas, but new attitudes need to be developed and accepted. Many former positions and organizations need to be discontinued, and many new and responsible positions and components are created. Persons may feel, under such changing

circumstances, that their careers and livelihoods are threatened, so that they may be inclined to be suspicious, or at least over-cautious, until the new philosophy has been thoroughly assimilated, refined, and established.[1]

Decentralization, then, was a major upheaval inside General Electric, but it was a necessary response to complexity and to the change which was beginning to appear in the General Electric environment. In a business and technological environment that is stable, it is possible for a line executive or staff professional to maintain and build a breadth of knowledge and experience and still be effective. In the "age of discontinuity" that is the environment for management in the 1970s, specialization by product, by function, by region in the world, by area of professional knowledge—in short, all kinds of specialization—are required in order to maintain a management capability that has the in-depth understanding of the current status of work and knowledge. Specialization is the only solution for keeping current in a world that is changing at a wild pace, and decentralization allows specialization.

As the president of General Electric observed,

> Unless we could put the responsibility and authority for decision making closer in each case to the scene of the problem, where complete understanding and prompt action are possible, the company would not be able to compete with the hundreds of nimble competitors who were, as they say, able to turn on a dime.[2]

Cordiner emphasized in his book that decentralization did not mean breaking up the company into smaller, more nimble pieces. To give people with specialized knowledge the authority and responsibility for making decisions does not require transforming a large company into several smaller ones, if the means to achieve a coordination of parts can be found. The fostering of specialization through decentralization and other actions requires compensatory efforts by management to *integrate* the specialized pieces into an entity which responds to the opportunities in a world of rapidly changing large markets. This fusing together of smaller pieces of an organization into a large whole has come to be called *integration*.

A strategy for the utilization of specialization will be disastrous without a complementary strategy for integration. Note in the Webster definition how integration is the act of bringing together specialized pieces into one entity.

> **integrate 1:** to make complete ... **2:** to form into a more complete, harmonious or coordinated entity often by the addition or arrangement of parts or elements[3]

Most managers will readily agree that much of their work involves this action of integration. Our experience in working with companies has led us to conclude that there are many useful techniques of integration which are underutilized. What is more serious, we find that there are very few companies in which a planned effort exists to implement strategies for increasing performance through a program to manage the specialization and integration tasks of management.

The realization of the potential in research-based management requires a planned strategy for the encouragement of specialization while maintaining a focus on corporate objectives through the effective utilization of integrating techniques. This planned strategy should include the following:

1. *An inventory of the kinds of specialization to be encouraged.* This inventory will be much longer than might be expected. For example, there is a need for specialists who provide a bridging capability between a functional area such as personnel and data processing (see example of the usefulness of this kind of specialist in Chapter 8). There is a need in many companies for a specialist whose assignment is to reduce the fees paid by the company to a CPA firm for its independent audit. In companies with a large R&D program, specialists who link R&D with marketing and manufacturing are needed.

2. *A program for the development of personnel with needed specialized skills.* Many of the needed specialists discovered in the inventory will not be available. For example, many companies appear willing to spend $5 million to $10 million a year in data processing without qualified professionals knowledgeable in such critical fields as data base management and the control of hardware failures. Other companies are willing to spend $50 million to $100 million and more for R&D without specialists who provide a bridge between R&D and marketing and manufacturing. Then there is the need for specialists who develop the personnel system to assure compliance with Equal Employment Opportunity Commission regulations. Accounting needs specialists who are current with new AICPA, SEC, and FTC disclosure regulations. To maintain someone in a company with sufficient knowledge in each of the areas of specialization in the inventory requires a development program for the assignment, education, and reward of specialists.

3. *Formal information systems and organization procedures.* These are required for monitoring progress in specialized areas and for integrating specialized tasks. How well is a company EEOC compliance program working? How should senior management review the progress on an important R&D project?

Each company and operating division must develop its own planned strategy to encourage specialization while fostering the integration required to bring together specialized activities. Problems and resources for this planned strategy will vary from company to company and from division to division within a company. As we will describe in this chapter and in Chapter 8, the historical neglect for the management of the specialization and integration tasks of management is increasingly a costly error.

If specialization and integration are so important in the practice of management, why is inadequate attention given to these tasks? We are unaware of a company in which there is a vice president of specialization or a vice president of integration. Nor do many companies even have an active program to manage these functions. In day-to-day operation the management of specialization and integration do not usually occur as clearly visible tasks of management separate from the usual responsibility for economic performance. However, in a large-scale management or organization change, specialization and integration should be managed as part of a single strategy or plan. General Electric did have a well-conceived plan for fostering specialization, while at the same time providing for the reporting procedures and organization relationships which were necessary to integrate the decentralized pieces.

To foster specialization and at the same time to integrate specialized organizational units are basic actions for any corporate management. Forces beyond the control of management have created a need for even greater efforts to specialize and integrate than were needed in the 1950s. Research on company performance indicates that judicious specialization and integration result in dramatic increases in the effectiveness of management. Many of the serious problems experienced in a large number of companies appear to have resulted in part from a failure to cope with the management tasks of specialization and integration.

Since the 1950s, there has been an increase in the rate of change in the introduction of new-management techniques. The leaders in utilizing decentralization can build on past programs. General Electric now has a much larger and more sophisticated staff of planners and systems professionals. The General Electric computer-based financial and reporting systems which are now in use provide a much stronger capability for the restructuring of activity than was available during the pioneering efforts in the early 1950s.

In this chapter we will describe the factoring of work into areas of specialization, and the integration of the pieces into an effective organization effort. We will analyze the problems and opportunities created by the ever greater need for specialists whose potential usefulness has been increasing as a result of the tremendous burst of new knowledge which has been discovered in the post-World War II period. It is hoped that the reader will improve in self-management and in the management of other specialists as a result of understanding the analysis presented in this chapter.

KINDS OF SPECIALISTS

In the development of a strategy for the utilization of specialists, it is useful to recognize that there are different kinds of specialists. We have found the following classification of specialists to be useful in our efforts to assist clients to improve their management practices related to the employment of specialists:

Experience-based Line Executives	*Research-based Traditional Specialized Professionals*	*New Research-based Specialized Professionals*
Division management	Law	Management science
Functional management	Accounting	Data processing
Marketing		Strategic planning
Manufacturing		Organization development
R&D		

Effective, research-based work on a business problem today will usually involve bringing together several specialists selected from the above categories. There will be differences in perspective among the kinds of specialist within each of these major categories and even greater differences between the different major categories. Experience-based marketing and manufacturing line executives will have similar patterns of management style, although their perspectives on problems will vary as a result of their work experiences. CPAs and lawyers have their own patterns of problem-solving behavior which are significantly different from those of other kinds of specialists, such as management scientists. This is because the work of management scientists is not as structured as the work of CPAs and lawyers. There are not the generally accepted accounting principles and other such formal guidelines in management science.

These observations about the specialized orientation of different kinds of specialists can be used to rethink the meaning of an M.B.A. degree. As our analysis in Chapter 6 demonstrated, M.B.A.'s from Harvard, M.I.T., Stanford, and Chicago have very different kinds of knowledge and conditioning. The upgrading of executives in a company is increasingly determined by the process of selection of M.B.A.'s and the strategy of broadening the experience of employees with specialized training. It is therefore critical for management to have an understanding of the differences among M.B.A.'s in education and conditioning.

Specialized Line Executives

It is often assumed that senior corporate executives are "generalists." Nothing could be farther from the truth, as we observed in Chapter 5. Everyone is a specialist. Experience-based line executives who have spent all their working lives in one company are very much specialized, indeed.

For example, the new leadership positions at General Motors were presented in *The Wall Street Journal* in an article with the headline "Top GM Jobs Likely to Go to Accountant, Engineer and Generalist."[4] The three new top General Motors officers were Thomas A. Murphy, an accountant; E. M. Estes, an engineer; and Richard L. Terrell, a generalist. Murphy, the new president, was to be assisted by Estes and Terrell, executive vice presidents in a three-man group of senior officers. Specialization is a way of thinking as well as a field of specialized knowledge or experience. A newly minted generalist such as Mr. Murphy, who "has spent all but the last four years of his nearly 37 years at GM on the all-powerful finance staff,"[5] is a very specialized generalist, despite his new responsibilities.

Companies in which there is a tradition of promoting specialists in marketing or engineering to company presidents will have different kinds of generalists on top than a company in which accountants tend to become presidents. What matters is that the *working style and attitudes of a company president, or anyone else, will reflect specialized knowledge and experience.* An effective generalist will recognize the legacy of such specialized knowledge and experiences and will seek associates who provide breadth and balance to a management team.

The Traditional Professionals

Human specialization, having been initiated as a result of entirely natural forces, tends to take on a life of its own, irrespective of the problems which need to be solved. The traditional specialized professionals, such as attorneys and accountants, can cause serious damage to innocent clients. For example, only rarely does a lawyer in an antitrust case have an adequate understanding of the economic theory which is the rationale for antitrust actions, as was noted by *Business Week* in a commentary on the IBM antitrust suit:

> The issues in major cases are so massive, complex and important to the survival of the economy that placing the responsibility for recasting entire industries on the head of a single man—a judge trained in legal procedures rather than in the science, technology, and enterprise that makes the economic system work—is too risky.[6]

Executives who do not know how to manage their lawyers or CPAs are likely to receive an unsatisfactory level of performance. Despite the history of the business–legal relationship on problems that have long existed, business executives often use their lawyers poorly, and lawyers usually do not know how to give their clients the assistance that is needed. A poor performance may never be recognized by the client (that is, a user of specialists' services). What is a good surgical operation? The proper psychiatric assistance? A good engine tune-up? It is probable that different medicine will be prescribed by different doctors, and different legal remedies or protection will be suggested by different lawyers. Various studies have shown that if the same income-tax information is given to several tax services, different income-tax–due calculations will result. In the management of specialists, when the stakes are high, several specialists should be asked the same question.

Given that the manager cannot evaluate the performance of specialists even in professional–client relationships where there have been years of experience such as those with lawyers and CPAs, one comprehends the problems created when new-management professionals in management science, data processing and other fields were added to the corporate staffs in ever greater numbers during the 1960s.

PRACTICE ON THE SPECIALIST PROBLEM

The consistent neglect of the specialist problem by personnel at all levels in the corporate hierarchy and by specialists as well as nonspecialists indicates that it is difficult to achieve a *working awareness* of the specialist problem. By working awareness, we mean an understanding of the specialist problem sufficient to cause one to operate more effectively as a user of specialists and/or as a specialist.

Skill in almost every field of activity is improved through practice and experience. The greater sensitivity to the problem of specialization that we are attempting to foster can be further improved through practice exercises. Several that we have used come to mind:

Self-evaluation

Peter Drucker proposed, in his book *The Effective Executive*,[7] that time logs be maintained in order to develop an awareness of how time is actually utilized. A similar kind of data collection is useful in the management of specialization.

First, list the kinds of specialized knowledge needed for effective performance on your current job.

Second, add to the first list the sources of this specialized knowledge.

Finally, reflect on the following questions as they relate to the list that you have prepared:

1. In what areas of knowledge are you your own source of specialized information?
2. How are you keeping current in these areas of specialization?
3. In what areas of needed specialization are your associates weak or strong?
4. How effectively is your specialized knowledge used?
5. How do the problems of specialization affect your performance as a user and as a provider of specialized knowledge?

Once you accept the fact that everyone is a specialist, the inherent difficulty of the specialist problem becomes clear.

Consider, for example, the perspective of a specialist in a working relationship. A user, who is another kind of specialist, seeks the assistance of a specialist. The user is frequently at the mercy of the specialist. What is worse, the user may be unable to explain his or her need for assistance in such a way that the specialist fully understands. The specialist may not understand the limits to his or her own knowledge or the limits to the user's ability to comprehend the specialized knowledge which is offered. How seriously does the specialist consider the question of what the user really needs to know (in contrast to the information requested by the user)? Does the specialist tell the user about the quality of the answer given in response to a request for assistance (such as, "I don't know very much about that facet of the field; . . . however, as a rough first guess . . .")? In short, is there a real dialogue between the user and the specialist?

The user–specialist problem is experienced in many unexpected ways. For example, John Hammond of Harvard Business School has observed in his research on corporate insurance decisions that a company's risk manager feels safer when he recommends more insurance than can be cost-justified. Risk management is a very specialized activity. How can experience-based executives guide the decisions of risk managers to reflect corporate needs? An understanding of the user–specialist problem is useful when attempting to answer this question. This is why a self-evaluation of user–specialist roles is very useful for increasing the contribution of specialists to corporate performance.

The development of this self-awareness is an important first stage in the progress from one level of management competence to a higher level.

Probing the Work of Others

Another kind of practice strategy which is useful for increasing one's awareness of the problems of specialization is to initiate conversations on the subject. We go out of our way to do so. Plane trips can be a source of these practice efforts. A report of one such conversation is presented below.

Consultants and lawyers tend to travel back and forth from their offices to Washington, D.C. On one such trip, we commented to an attorney sitting in a seat next to us that a number of our clients had experienced difficulties in their use of lawyers. This comment is a marvelous conversational ploy and quickly stirs the interest of most lawyers. "I don't see why this should happen," responded our victim, who was a partner in one of Boston's most prestigious law firms.

"Let's think about the problem of using a lawyer," we asked our lawyer. "Would you have any difficulty in selecting a lawyer to handle a new securities issue or an EEOC compliance problem?" After a short pause, the lawyer responded that he would have little difficulty in selecting a lawyer for even one of a long list of legal problems that we raised.

Then we asked, "Suppose you had a serious back ailment? How would you select an orthopedic specialist?" Now our lawyer was stuck. He had to admit that he had no idea about how to select a physician.

"Why was it so easy to pick a good lawyer and so difficult to select a good doctor?" we asked. "What about some of our friends who have had one physician recommend total rest for a bad back and another physician recommend exercise?" We asked if he had heard of examples of dramatically opposite treatments recommended to the same patient by different physicians. Many middle-aged lawyers have bad backs or have friends who have bad backs, and our lawyer had heard of different advice received by one person from different doctors. By the end of our conversation, our lawyer was able to describe the reasons why clients have so much difficulty in their use of lawyers.

The strategy utilized in this conversation with a partner in a large Boston law firm can be used in conversations with accountants, data processing professionals, marketing managers, and auto mechanics. The more probing conversations with specialists that are conducted, the greater will be the awareness of the specialization problem.

INTEGRATION OF SPECIALISTS

As we assist clients in increasing the effectiveness with which lawyers, accountants, data processing professionals, management scientists, economists, and other specialized research-based professionals are utilized, we emphasize that the same strategy is useful for working with all these specialized professionals. The first element of the strategy is to determine the extent of the knowledge disparity between the specialist and nonspecialist. In addition to this knowledge gap, there are frequently differences in time horizons, motivation, and method of approach to a given problem.

A second basic element of the strategy is to have a plan for the integration of the specialized pieces into a functional entity.

Once a company such as General Electric has been divided into the organizational structure presented in Chapter 2 and described earlier in this chapter, it then becomes possible to consider the enormous cost of the integrating devices used to manage the company. Note that integration is required at each level in the General Electric hierarchical structure. There is a need to integrate at the product, product-line, department, division, and group levels. At each level there is specialization by function (for example, marketing, manufacturing, finance), by geographical area, and by field of knowledge (for example, data processing, market research, R&D). Despite the complexity, General Electric usually increases its annual revenues and profits. Standards of performance are set, and actual-budget variances are monitored. Higher levels in management are informed about the performance of the operating units. Capital expenditures and new product development efforts are authorized. Task forces are set up in order to respond to new government regulations from such legislation as the Equal Employment Opportunity Act and the Pure Water Act (among dozens of other such laws).

Once we recognize integration as the result of management activities which involve such basic tasks as the reporting of financial performance on an actual and budget basis from a lower to a higher level in the organization, then it can be seen that a large percentage of all "management" activity involves the implementation of integrating devices.

How Much Integration Is Enough?

In Chapter 2, we raised the question of how much management was enough. We recommended in that chapter that the question of how much is enough should be answered by reference to the problems and opportunities that required an investment in management, with the decision on any increase in the strength of management determined by the expected improvements in corporate performances compared with the expenditures for increasing the effectiveness of management. Integration is a class of management activity, and this should be evaluated on a probable return-on-investment basis as should all other investments in management.

As a general rule, the level of resources allocated for integration increases:
1. The larger the corporation size
2. The more complex the organization
3. The faster the rate of change in the economy, in technology, in product markets, in government regulation, and in company, divisional, and operating units
4. The higher the performance standards

In order to understand this list of factors which should determine the resources allocated for integration, it is useful to compare the average company in 1955 and 1975 and discuss what has happened during the last twenty years to the importance of these factors which determine the need for investment in integration. In 1953, the *smallest* firm on the *Fortune* 500 list was Copperweld Steel, with sales of $49,694,000. On the 1973 *Fortune* second 500 list, number 501 was Allied Products with $242,109,000 in sales. How times have changed! A firm with $49 million in sales would be almost $50 million short of making the *Fortune* largest 1,000 list in 1975. The difference between Copperweld's sales of $49 million in 1953 and Allied Products' sales in 1973 can be accounted for by two factors: an inflation effect of about 50 percent and a growth in real size effect of about 50 percent. In addition to inflation and growth, the other forces which increase the need to allocate additional resources for integration include the increase in government regulation of business and the trend toward multinational and conglomerate businesses. Dramatic growth in specialization is also caused by the forces which affect the need for integration.

Integration is made possible by such research-based management techniques as strategic planning, management information systems, management science, and organizational development. Dr. Laubach, president of Pfizer, Inc., expressed his reasons for encouraging the utilization of research-based techniques by referring to the increased difficulties in the business environment: "When non-planners did as well as planners, then there was little incentive to plan. Those days are gone forever."[8] The Laubach response to a more difficult business environment was to increase the utilization of planning which was supported by a strong management information systems capability. These are two of the most important integration techniques. Dr. Laubach emphasized both the greater difficulties in the management of a pharmaceuticals company and improvement in cost effectiveness of new computer-based management information systems in his decision to authorize an increase in the corporate effort to develop research-based management techniques. These two factors which appear to be major determinants in the coming of the New Management can be seen again and again in company stories of progress that has been achieved.

Progress in the development of improved management capabilities, the move toward Future Firm, will occur because of the combination of greater difficulties in management and the improved capabilities which are becoming available to increase the effectiveness of management. When there is a sharp increase in the cost of not planning, in the cost of poor management, the ROI calculations lead to increases in the investment in good management. When improved research-based techniques cost less to purchase, an increase in the utilization of these techniques becomes cost-effective.

In a survey of utilization of management information systems, Kennedy reported that firms experiencing a high rate of technology change in the machines and professional scientific instrumentation industries had three times the MIS staffs of firms of comparable size in the primary metals industry.[9] This is one out of many studies which support the idea expressed by Dr. Laubach that management practices will vary from industry to industry and will change over time in response to new business conditions. One of the earliest teams of researchers in this field, Harvard Business School Professors Paul Lawrence and Jay Lorsch,[10] did case studies of the utilization of integrators. The Lawrence and Lorsch data were analyzed by Galbraith[11] in a study that related the importance of new products as a percentage of sales to the utilization of integrators. Galbraith discovered that the more rapid the change in the products, the greater the utilization of integrating devices; the need for integration increases when there is a rapid change in technology.

INVENTORY OF INTEGRATION TECHNIQUES

Specialization creates the need for integration, and management can respond to this need with a wide range of techniques. A specific integration technique will reflect the objectives of integration, the resources available for the integration effort, and the unique characteristics of the integration problem. The integration techniques utilized to manage within an R&D laboratory will differ from the techniques used to integrate the operations of a conglomerate multinational corporation, which, in turn, will differ from those used to integrate the specialized units in a large hospital. Integration techniques can be grouped under the following major headings:[12]

Formal Management Systems and Procedures

In large organizations, budgeting, reports comparing actual expenditures to budgeted, planning documents, and other outputs from formal systems are commonly utilized integration techniques. The coordination of the activities of specialized units in an organization is facilitated by the availability of the basic numbers produced in formal management information systems. The development of a long-range plan on the specification for a project provides the structure within which inputs from different sources can be integrated. The long-range plan provides the procedures for integrating the perceptions of the future held by finance, marketing, manufacturing, and R&D. Note the interaction effects in the development of a long-range plan. The sales forecast, insofar as it shows growth beyond the current plant output, motivates and guides the development of a plan to increase the capacity of manufacturing.

Auditing procedures can be a powerful and necessary integrating technique to ensure that a specialized unit of the firm is not going its own separate way in response to pressures on a specialized unit which are divergent from companywide goals. As one example of what can happen when auditing is neglected, consider the *Newsweek* story about the large foreign-exchange losses by Chase Manhattan Bank:

> Chase Manhattan Bank, the nation's—and, in fact, the world's—third-largest bank, announced it had discovered that its bond-trading department had been making false reports. What chairman David Rockefeller called "extremely serious errors of judgment" had resulted in a $34 million overstatement of the value of the bank's $800 million bond-trading account. . . . What evidently happened is that Chase bond traders made fictitious entries in the monthly reports they have to make to senior bank officers. According to Wall Street sources, the false reports were apparently filed to cover up losses in the bank's bond trading. The losses came as a result of Chase's mistaken belief early this year that interest rates would fall—a belief shared by many banks. Such a decline would have pushed bond prices up. Anticipating this, Chase bought bonds for its trading account, hoping to show a nice profit as their value increased. Unfortunately, interest rates dipped only slightly and then soared to record levels. That depressed bond prices, and the bank wound up losing money.
>
> Industry insiders speculated that the false reports were probably the result of heavy pressure to maximize earnings—something that's not unique to Chase. Indeed, some banking experts claimed that portfolio overvaluation is not uncommon throughout the industry.[13]

This story illustrates forces that lead to an increased need for integration, all of which were present to an extraordinary degree at the Chase:

1. Chase is a very large organization.
2. Chase is a complex organization.
3. The business environment of banking has been changing rapidly.
4. Chase management apparently applied "heavy pressure to maximize earnings."

The pressure to falsify bond-trading performance can be seen from the procedures for keeping score of performance under generally accepted accounting principles. A decline in the market value of bonds below the cost to Chase of those bonds becomes a loss on the earnings statement, whether or not the loss is actually realized through the sale of the bonds. There is an incentive to report a higher market price to cost calculation of bonds still held in the bank's portfolio in the hope that the market value of the bonds will increase by the time that the bonds are actually sold. It is much easier to falsify a market-value calculation for bonds that remain in the bank's portfolio than for bonds that have been sold and a cash (in contrast to a paper) loss realized.

Given these conditions, it is customary for senior bank management to have auditors *outside* the bond-trading department check the market to cost calculation. According to *The Wall Street Journal,* however, these "checks were carried out by the *trading department itself.* Periodic audits were also made by outsiders, but relatively infrequently, as indicated by the nine-month wait since the last previous one."[14]

The pressures of daily activity tend to cause a lack of integration among specialized activities and functions. Formal management systems and procedures are frequently a more effective device for integration than exhortations about the need to work together. Integration in large organizations is especially well facilitated by a formal system to achieve needed interactions. A *formal system* should have specifications on (1) key people involved, (2) timing of reports and meetings, (3) uses of the system, and (4) feedback on the utilization of the system. Formal management systems have the advantage that needed interactions among specialized units can be scheduled and thus made more certain to occur. Integration should not be an unprogrammed management responsibility.

Organization Techniques

Integration can be achieved through the creation of a task force (see Chapter 12 for a description of the usefulness of this technique), project teams (see Chapters 10 and 11 for more on these techniques), and other techniques for creating an organizational group which is responsible for a given activity that involves inputs from different units of specialists. It is useful to recall that specialization is a factor which affects everyone in a corporation—line executives and staff professionals; people in marketing, manufacturing, and finance. Specialized myopia is not a problem experienced only by someone in finance or data processing. Line managers in marketing see a world and have objectives which are very different from those of managers and staff professionals in manufacturing, R&D, and finance. As a general rule, people in one specialized group will give preference to their own limited objectives and will be reluctant to work toward corporate objectives that are not in almost total accord with perceived group objectives. In order to cope with this tendency to favor specialized objectives over the needs of an activity which involves a number of specialized inputs, it becomes useful to create an organizational unit which brings together specialized units in an integrated mission-based activity.

For example, in the situation depicted in Figure 7.1, product manager

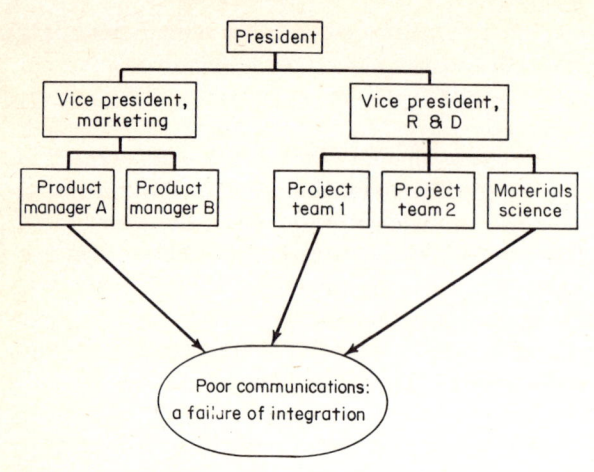

FIG. 7.1 *Illustration of an integration problem created by the organization structure.*

A is experiencing difficulties because competitors offer a more durable product. There is a need to integrate the special knowledge of the market, the R&D skills available in project team 1, and the knowledge of materials in the materials science group. How does product manager A communicate perceived needs to R&D? Can R&D project leader 1 obtain the cooperation of a materials scientist? In the example presented in Figure 7.1, the product manager wanted what he thought was a relatively minor improvement, the upgrading of a part which was wearing too quickly. The manager of project team 1 was redesigning the total product, and the materials science group was pushing for a "major breakthrough" and did not have the interest in assisting a product manager with a short-run competitive problem. The line of communication was vertical, through the vice presidents of marketing and R&D rather than horizontal through a committee or other group that included representatives from the product A profit-center, project 1 unit, and materials science. An appropriate integration device in this case would be a task force to solve the problem at hand as quickly as possible. The task force would be a temporary organizational unit with the function of letting product management influence the work of R&D to achieve a cost-effective product change.

Management Actions

Good managers recognize that the integration of specialized activities is one of their primary responsibilities. Managers, by their actions, can be a powerful force for integration. In Figure 7.2 we have diagrammed the impregnable barriers to communications and cooperation which are created by the functional organization structure which is standard practice in most corporations. Figure 7.2 is, of course, a simplified picture of the walls which prevent coping effectively with problems that cross the narrowly defined vision of functional specialists. A more complex picture would include the functional pyramids of finance, data processing, personnel, legal, and public affairs. Further complexity would include the walls created by product-focused groups and geographic-focused groups.

Given this great complexity in the relationships among the many specialized groups within a corporation and the powerful walls created by specialized interests, easy answers on a management technique which solves all problems are just not available. The first management action that leads to a reduction in the inefficiency created by the pyramidal walls diagramed in Figure 7.2 is the recognition of the problem. Once the problem has been recognized, the next management action is the decision to reduce the negative impact on organizational effectiveness that the pyramidal walls have been causing. We have observed a large number of managers who recognize the pyramidal wall problem but who have not taken effective action to correct ineffective conditions. There are a number of management actions that reduce the pyramidal wall problem. Among these techniques are (1) encouragement of informal working relationships among people in different functional areas; (2) reducing the need to cycle communications up one pyramidal ladder and then across and down the ladder in another pyramid as diagramed in communications line *C* in Figure 7.2; (3) developing management reporting systems which score performance in solving problems that involve several functional areas; (4) creating formal organizational units (see Chapters 10 to 12) which have the mission to improve conditions which involve several specialized areas; and (5) assigning responsibility for interpyramidal activity (for example, a marketing–manufacturing relationship) to integrators.

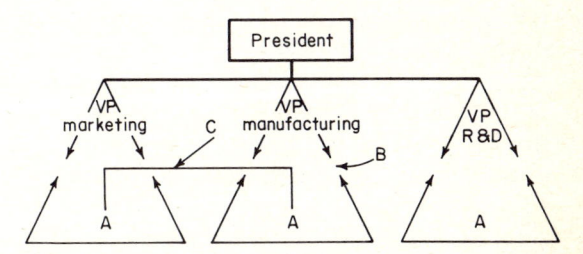

FIG. 7.2 *Corporate functional pyramids as impregnable barriers to communications and cooperation. A: Managers or staff professionals who should be working together on a problem. B: Doors in the impregnable walls of the functional pyramids. C: A line of communication between groups in two functional pyramids.*

THE JOB OF THE INTEGRATOR

A position found more and more often in corporations under various titles, but always requiring a well-rounded manager to fill it, is that of the *integrator*. This person's specific job is to take the actions that are required to integrate two or more departments of an organization. The characteristics of a successful integrator are very similar to those of a successful general manager in any broad management role, as we can see from research findings. Combining a study of six firms (described in the next chapter) with the work of other behavioral scientists, Lawrence and Lorsch isolate six determinants of an effective integrator.[15]

(1) Orientation of the integrators lies between the orientations which differentiate the departments being integrated. In other words, if sales is interested in fast responses, and research is interested in big breakthroughs that take a long time to invent, then the integrators of sales and research should be oriented equally toward short and longer run inventive efforts.

(2) Influence of the integrators stems from professional competence rather than hierarchical position. The work of integrators should be respected by both contributors to the total effort. This is most easily possible when the integrators are knowledgeable in all the facets of the work under way. Influence based strictly on authority of position will be viewed as interfering. A good integrator will frequently have worked in both of the functional units which are to be integrated. Job rotation is an important strategy for the development of integrators.

(3) Rewards to the integrators are based on joint performance of the integrative activities. The ability of all three concerned parties to focus on the same goal enhances the possibility of a team effort.

(4) The integrated departments and the integrators both feel that they have a great deal of influence in the organization of which they are a part. A feeling of meaningful involvement on the part of the organizational participants is thought by sociologists to spring from the ability to influence events. Decisions which affect a group should be made, when possible, with the involvement of that group's management. It is just too easy for a specialized group to ignore or bootstrap around decisions made without their involvement and consent. Specialization provides a cover, and failures of integration give the confidence to disregard the decision of managers who are not part of a specialized group.

(5) Within the units being integrated, knowledge about conditions is accompanied by enough influence to bring the knowledge to bear on the decision-making process. We noted above the desirability of influence of the integrators based on knowledge. The knowledge of those to be integrated should *also* enter the resolution of conflict and the accomplishment of multidepartmental work.

(6) The mode of conflict resolution is by problem-solving or confrontation. Issues are faced head on. Individual opinions are not forced on others, nor are touchy points merely smoothed over without resolution.

THE MICHELIN STRATEGY

The effective management of specialization and integration is difficult. General Electric is clearly a company that developed in one plan a strategy fostering specialization and the integration of specialized pieces into effective entities. Another example of an effective response to the problems of specialization and integration can be seen in the performance of Michelin.

Senior management "generalists" in the major U.S. auto and tire manufacturers have allowed their foreign competitors to beat them with almost every important innovation of the last twenty years. These foreign competitors have had but a fraction of the resources of the giant manufacturers in the United States, but the auto and tire industry in the United States has had a specialized focus which leads to a rejection of new ideas.

The tires produced by the traditional American tire manufacturers, Goodyear and Firestone, were first developed over sixty years ago. The decline in the market share of the standard tire is a direct result of Michelin, the French company which innovated the steel-belted radial tire. Thanks to an innovative management strategy for coping with the problems of specialization, Michelin's sales increased by four times in the last decade—"twice the growth rate of the Big Five U.S. tiremakers."[16] Michelin is now invading the United States market with an investment of $300 million in production facilities, and tire manufacturers in the United States, after neglecting the radial market for many years, are now rushing to catch up.

The huge investment by a foreign company in a manufacturing capability in the United States to produce products which are technologically superior to the products of United States manufacturers is an unusual event. Historically, it has been United States–based multinationals that invested in foreign countries.[17] Given the unusual reverse flow of management competence and technological capabilities that the Michelin invasion represents, it is useful to examine the management style at Michelin:

> The management style is so informal and flexible that Michelin is sometimes said to have no management titles or table of organization. Obviously there is a chain of command, but, as in the Chinese People's Liberation Army, only insiders know at a glance who ranks whom. Business cards used by Michelin executives in France merely identify the individual as belonging to the com-

pany—executives who travel abroad have to have extra sets of cards with titles corresponding to the custom of the countries they visit.

Michelin organizes itself pretty much as any other tire company, but the organization table is deliberately blurred by the custom of designating departments by code letters rather than functional names. Thus the letter "L" stands for marketing and "J" signifies the purchasing department, as American suppliers may have discovered by now.

In the eyes of Michelin top management, these peculiarities are not mere crotchets, but important factors in creating an atmosphere of personal initiative and flexibility. Executives who are not entrenched behind formal titles can be shifted more easily from one job to another; departments without functional designations are less apt to acquire rigid habits of territoriality.

Such a free-form system obviously requires a high degree of personal involvement by top management. To help him keep his finger on the company's pulse, François Michelin has a small staff of three or four top aides—characteristically without titles. He immerses himself successively in the affairs of the various departments, and in his relations with subordinates, the absolute monarch sometimes asks what they would do if they were in his shoes. He regards selection of those subordinates as his key responsibility. The Michelin philosophy is that decisions should be taken at the level where the problem arises, and that the *gerant* (president) should have to deal only with the well-nigh insoluble problems—what the French call "five-legged sheep."[18]

The reader is invited to think about the last time that he or she was given a business card on which the precise position and status of the person offering the card was not described. How often do magazine articles describe a company's strategy for coping with the problems of specialization? In our consulting and research experiences we have seen very little evidence that management is aware of the problems created by specialization. Companies tend not to have a strategy for the management of specialization and integration. Because of this neglect that we have observed, it is encouraging for us, if not for Goodyear and Firestone, to discover the Michelin strategy for coping with some of the problems created by a specialized focus on the world.

CONCLUSION

The practice of management increasingly involves the utilization of ever more specialized skills. The evidence indicates that management in most companies now encourages specialization by product, by geographical area, by function area. The greater the need for specialization, the larger the resources which must be allocated to efforts to integrate specialized activities in order to create an effective organization.

The performance of specialized functions such as data processing as well as performance at the corporate level are determined by the ability of management to achieve two apparently opposite effects. Management must encourage specialization while at the same time implementing the techniques which provide the integration that leads to high performance.

A concern for integration should exist at every level in the organization structure. Each manager and specialist can develop his or her own integration techniques. A company can be seen as a large number of specialized units which are integrated in a net of interrelationships. It is the responsibility of senior management to set the overall guidelines for the quality of integration which is to be maintained, although lower-level managers and specialists have the freedom to achieve a better level of integration than usually exists in most companies. As we will report in Chapter 8, there is overwhelming evidence that the effective management of specialization and integration is a major factor in the achievement of high company and division performance.

NOTES AND REFERENCES

1. Cordiner, Ralph J.: *New Frontiers for Professional Managers,* New York: McGraw-Hill, 1956, pp. 53–54.
2. Ibid.: pp. 45–46.
3. *Webster's Third International Dictionary,* Springfield, Mass.: Merriam, 1963, p. 1174.
4. Camp, Charles B.: "Top GM Jobs Likely to Go to Accountant, Engineer, Generalist," *The Wall Street Journal,* Sept. 30, 1974, p. 1. Terrell, who never went to college, was called a generalist in this *Wall Street Journal* article, defining a generalist as a nonspecialist.
5. Ibid.
6. "Telex vs. IBM: The Lesson of Second Thoughts," *Business Week,* Oct. 13, 1973, p. 26. When District Judge A. Sherman Christensen issued his Sept. 17, 1973, finding that Telex suffered $117 million damages (a possible loss to IBM of $352 million because of the triple-damages provision of the Sherman Act), IBM stock fell from $298 a share on September 14 to a low of $245 on October 4, a drop of over $7 billion in market value. Judge Christensen has subsequently admitted error in his calculation of $117 million in damages. What training qualified a judge to determine the amount of losses experienced by a plaintiff company in an antitrust suit? This IBM trial, the AT&T suit, and other large and complex antitrust suits are examples of an entirely inappropriate process. Legally trained judges are asked to rule on arguments prepared primarily by lawyers on both sides of a suit. The issues are frequently beyond the educational background of the judge and contending lawyers.
7. Drucker, Peter F.: *The Effective Executive,* New York: Harper & Row, 1967.
8. Personal communication with Dr. Gruber.
9. Kennedy, D. W.: "What a President Needs to Know about MIS," *Financial Executive,* December 1970, pp. 52ff.
10. Lawrence, Paul R., and Jay W. Lorsch: *Organization and Environment,* Homewood, Ill.: Irwin, 1969.
11. Galbraith, J. R.: "Organization Design: An Information Processing View," *Interfaces,* May 1974, p. 35.
12. These ideas were adapted from the work of J. W. Lorsch and S. A. Allen, III, *Managing Diversity and Interdependence,* Boston: Harvard Business School Division of Sponsored Research, 1973; Lawrence and Lorsch, op cit., and Galbraith, op. cit.

13. "The Chase Case," *Newsweek,* Oct. 14, 1974, p. 98.
14. "Chase Says '74 Profit Gains Wiped Out by Discovery of Overvalued Securities," *The Wall Street Journal,* Oct. 3, 1974, p. 3. Emphasis added.
15. Lawrence and Lorsch: op. cit.
16. Ball, Robert: "The Michelin Man Rolls into Akron's Back Yard," *Fortune,* October 1974, p. 139.
17. See, for example, J.-J. Servan-Schreiber, *The American Challenge,* New York: Atheneum, 1968, p. 3.
18. Ball: op. cit., pp. 142–143.

EIGHT

Specialization, Integration, and Performance

Line management and staff professionals frequently need heavy doses of encouragement before they are willing to commit themselves to an organized program to increase their effectiveness in the specialization and integration tasks of management. Interface problems between specialized functions are particularly easy to rationalize and ignore for several reasons. First, they appear exceptionally difficult to manage because several organizational units are involved in the problem. Second, blame for an interface problem and the person responsible for solving the problem are not easy to identify.

Rare indeed are champions for the funding of the integration function in management. Marketing wants a larger marketing budget and R&D wants a larger R&D budget. Who wants a larger budget to integrate marketing and R&D? Would such funds be an increase in the budgets and staffing of marketing or of R&D? In short, management must be convinced of the cost effectiveness of funds allocated for the integration function. Fortunately, the quality of integration of specialized units within a company can be shown to be a critical factor in determining the level of performance. There are now a number of studies which have discovered a strong correlation between the effectiveness of the integration of specialized functions and the level of performance.

The four case studies which we will present in this chapter are dramatic proof of the superior organizational performance which will result from improved integration between specialized groups. These studies provide strong evidence that problems at the interface between organizational units can be solved.

INTEGRATION IN SIX PLASTICS FIRMS

In a group of plastics firms studied by Harvard Business School Professors Lawrence and Lorsch,[1] they discovered that differentiation as well as integration are the hallmarks of a successful firm. The idea of differentiation as utilized by Lawrence and Lorsch is similar to our use of specialization in Chapter 7. Each organization in a corporation has unique conditions which differentiate it from other organizations. For example, sales has a very short time horizon, and in some companies daily sales reports are issued and treated very seriously. In contrast to this very short time horizon of sales management, R&D frequently thinks in terms of months or even years. Accounting insists upon total accuracy while most other functions want only reasonably correct numbers right away—usually much sooner than accounting is willing to give up the information.

Possible aspects of differentiation include:

1. Degree of formalized organization structure and procedures
2. The orientation of departmental members toward objects of work, whether oriented toward the accomplishment of tasks or toward interaction with coworkers and customers
3. Time orientation, including rate of change of conditions, certainty of information, and frequency of feedback on performance
4. Goal orientation, the clarity with which objectives are perceived

These factors can be measured with questionnaires and other methods of observation. Note that specialization of people could bear on any of these four factors.

Integration and differentiation in organizations tend to be antagonistic. Consider the marketing and production departments of a corporation. These two areas *have* to work together. The state of integration between these two functions would be made difficult to the degree that the conditions they face are differentiated. Differences between two departments in any of the above four areas could lead to conflicts. For example, a production department capable of changing its product setups every ten days would cause serious problems for a marketing department which required three-day response to orders to satisfy customers. Or, to illustrate another difference, a production engineer seeking to find the responsible person in a very diffuse and loosely organized research operation would tend to be frustrated.

We see many problems created by the differentiation between groups within a company. Marketing tends to have a very short time horizon. R&D requires much more time than any other unit in the company. Marketing, production, and finance are always pushing R&D for time deadlines. Finance talks a language that is frequently not understood by other parts of the company. The manufacturing cost standards and overhead allocations set by accounting are often accepted by senior management even though these standards and overhead allocations are incorrect and lead to serious errors when decisions are made. Data processing tends to produce elegant systems when users want a simple information capability.

In their study of six plastics firms, Professors Lawrence and Lorsch surveyed sales, production, applied research, and fundamental research departments in each of the six firms. Differentiation between departments was measured by differences in the four factors previously mentioned: formal organizational structure, personnel orientation toward work, time orientation, and goal orientation. Integration was measured by evaluation of the state of interdepartmental relations. In Figure 8.1, the relationship between levels of differentiation and integration and performance is diagramed. Performance ratings of the six firms are based on growth in profits, sales, and new product developments over five years. The two leaders—the top performer and the high performer—show the highest differentiation and integration, while four lesser performers are showing either relatively less integration or less differentiation, or both. However, it is very clear from these findings that integration achieved is a better indicator of success than differentiation, since the three top performing firms (indicated by an asterisk in Figure 8.1) all had high integration.

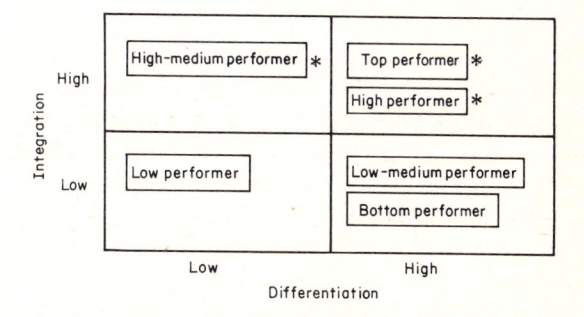

	Low Differentiation	High Differentiation
High Integration	High-medium performer *	Top performer * High performer *
Low Integration	Low performer	Low-medium performer Bottom performer

FIG. 8.1 *Integration and differentiation in six plastics firms.*
*Indicates one of the highest performers in changes in profits, sales value, and new product performance over previous five-year period.
SOURCE: Paul R. Lawrence and Jay W. Lorsch, *Organization and Environment,* Homewood, Ill.: Irwin, 1969, pp. 40, 80.

INTEGRATING EDP IN BANKS

We have been working with bank executives for several years in an effort to develop a practical checklist for the evaluation of the utilization of computers in banks. The checklist was eventually formalized as a 500-item questionnaire. This report is a summary of the findings from an analysis of the questionnaires completed by senior EDP officers in over 200 banks.[2] This large response, representing over 35 percent of all banks with deposits of $500 million and over, indicates that bank EDP executives are concerned about the problems considered in our questionnaire. This questionnaire was in the form of a worksheet for taking an inventory of management policies, procedures, and practices related to computer utilization.

In order to measure computer division performance in banks, the questionnaire listed forty-six of the most important banking computer applications. The returned questionnaires were first grouped by size of bank.[3] Then the number of computer applications utilized in each bank, weighted by the level of user satisfaction and the level of satisfaction of senior bank executives, was used to rank order computer performance within each bank size class. This measure of computer utilization, which includes both the number of computer applications and the level of user and senior management satisfaction, was defined as the "total performance index."

Banks were sorted into high- and low-performance groups on the basis of their position in the rank order of the total performance index. We then analyzed the responses to the questionnaires for each bank size and level of performance category.

In Table 8.1 we present a summary of the answers to a number of questions on the management policies, procedures, and practices which affect the integration of EDP with the needs of non-EDP executives and the users of computer division services.

For large banks, all the integration procedures and policies are generally found to a greater extent in high-performance banks than in low. Specifically, the procedures for integration (first four rows in Table 8.1),

- Use of planning in bank and EDP management
- Preparation of written EDP long-range plan
- EDP courses for management
- Review of EDP budgets by users

all occur more frequently in large, high-performance banks than in large, low-performance banks, or in the medium and small banks of either performance level. This bears out the fact that managers must work harder at integration in large organizations, and especially hard in large, high-performing organizations. In medium and small banks, the procedures for integration also showed up to a greater extent in high perform-

TABLE 8.1 Integration of Data Processing Correlated with the Performance of Bank Computer Divisions: A Comparison of High- and Low-Performing Commercial Banks in the United States, 1973

	Large banks by performance		Medium-size banks by performance		Small banks by performance	
	High	Low	High	Low	High	Low
Procedures for integration:						
Index of use of planning in bank and data processing management (based on answers to 19 questions)	163.2	123.1	143.2	118.0	125.8	73.1
Percentage of banks with a documented EDP long-range (3- to 5-year) plan	66.7	38.9	44.4	36.0	38.5	12.5
Percentage of banks with management-oriented data processing courses for senior executives	22.2	5.5	8.4	9.1	8.5	0.0
Percentage of banks in which EDP development, maintenance, and operating budgets are prepared in advance and given to user bank departments for their review and budgeting purposes	66.7	55.5	48.0	24.0	34.6	28.1
Effectiveness of integration:						
Index of communications between data processing and all levels of bank management (based on answers to 4 questions)	31.0	27.5	37.5	20.5	40.0	10.5
Index of general level of knowledge of data processing by non-EDP management (based on answers to 3 questions)	53.0	37.0	39.0	26.0	34.0	12.0
Percentage of banks with strong involvement of senior non-EDP executives in computer applications and hardware decisions	73.2	44.4	56.0	80.0	57.7	59.3

SOURCE: Study performed by Dr. Gruber for SofTech, Inc., and reprinted here with permission.

ers than in low performers, with the exception of EDP courses in medium-sized banks.

Furthermore, factors which affect the quality of integration (last three rows in Table 8.1),

- Communication between EDP and management
- Level of EDP knowledge in bank management
- Involvement of senior bank management in EDP decisions

score generally higher for high-performing banks than for low performers. This is true across the board for large banks, but there is a significant exception in medium and small banks. The one important integration indicator which does not move in the direction that we expected from our previous studies is the level of involvement of senior management in important data processing decisions. Answers to other questions suggest a possible explanation to this unexpected finding. What we may be seeing in these findings is a greater attention to the computer division by senior bank executives *in recent years* as a result of poor computer division performance. These are 1973 survey results. In our 1971 survey, there was greater consistency in the differences between the high- and low-performance banks.

The active involvement in computer division decisions by a badly informed bank president may not result in an improvement in computer division performance. Just recently one of the authors wrote a client report in which he recommended a change in the organizational structure which would result in less involvement in data processing for the company president. A commitment to better computer division performance by senior executives requires more than the elevation of the top data processing officer to a higher level in the hierarchy. *Senior management must become informed about the management factors in an effective computer division operation.* Involvement means more than making decisions. It should mean management-oriented computer courses, careful planning, and adequate staff assistance.

COMPUTER UTILIZATION IN ONE BANK

One of the techniques that has been very useful in our efforts to assist clients to increase the effectiveness of their utilization of computers is an inventory of the satisfaction of the users of a company data processing division. In Table 8.2 we report on the scores from our survey of user satisfaction. One of the critical variables which determines the satisfaction of a user division with the performance of the data processing division is whether or not the management in a user division has employed its own systems analysts to improve communications with the staff professionals and management in the data processing division. Table 8.2 shows the significantly high level of satisfaction with data processing performance in the user divisions in which there is an in-division capability to work with data processing. Placing systems analysts in user divisions is a very effective tactic for integration of EDP users and EDP specialists.

TABLE 8.2 Satisfaction by Users as Perceived by Data Processing Users in Divisions of a Large Commercial Bank with and without an In-Division Systems Capability

| | Average satisfaction scores from users in divisions ||
Question	With an in-division systems capability	Without an in-division systems capability
1. Overall evaluation	4.3*	2.4
2. Accuracy	3.6	3.5
3. Timeliness	3.9	3.2
4. Ease of use	4.1	3.1
5. Responsiveness to requests for change in functions, outputs, etc.	3.9	2.0
6. Support by data processing—answers to questions, user assistance	3.1	3.4
7. Integration with other applications	3.1	2.2
8. Average all questions for each application	3.7	2.8
Number of responses	7	18

*There were 8 user divisions with a systems capability and 12 user divisions without a systems capability. The findings are based on a calculation of the average scores in the two categories of user divisions. A score of 5 is very satisfied, 4 is satisfied, 3 is neither satisfied nor dissatisfied, 2 is dissatisfied, and 1 is very dissatisfied.

SOURCE: A report to the senior management committee of one of the largest commercial banks in the United States.

In Figure 8.2 we diagram the gap between EDP and EDP users. In some companies we have seen Condition I: No attempt to bridge the gap. No one in the user department is familiar with data processing capabilities, and there are no assigned staff responsibilities in data processing for working with specific users.

The frustration and ineffectiveness created by Condition I can lead the executives in a user department to add a systems analyst to their staff. This is a step toward integration and creates a Condition II company. Data processing management can also respond to a Condition I experience by assigning systems analysts to become knowledgeable about the needs in a specific user division. This is another step toward integration and is diagramed as Condition III.

The most effective solution occurs in a Condition IV company in which users not only have their own systems specialist, but also are represented by their own user specialists in the computer division. The great disparity

124 / The New Management

User knowledge of computers   Data processing knowledge of user needs

I. No attempt made to bridge gap

O⟶   ⟵O

II. Data processing organizes to serve users

O⟶   ⟵————————————O

III. User attempts to understand data processing

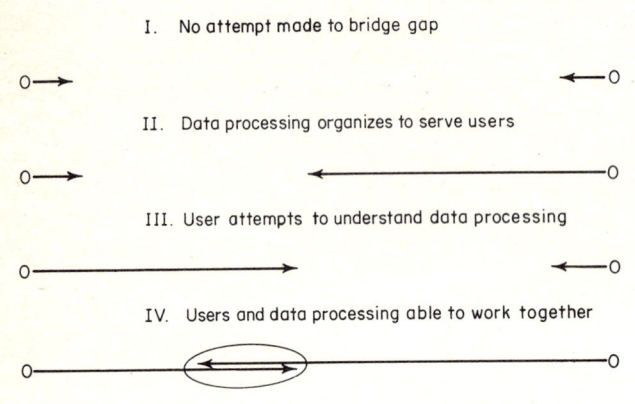

O————————————⟶   ⟵O

IV. Users and data processing able to work together

O————————⟨⟵——⟶⟩————————————————O

FIG. 8.2 *Four possible conditions in the user–computer knowledge gap.*

between the effectiveness in computer utilization in Condition I and Condition IV companies results from problems created by the need for both specialization and integration. The speed of change in computer technology requires a staff of dedicated specialists. It is necessary to work full time at being a specialist in a limited area of computer knowledge if one is to avoid obsolescence. It is the rare computer specialist who has an understanding of user problems. Discontinuities in the business of most companies require users to concentrate on problems in marketing, finance, or some other functional area. It is the rare user who has the time to learn how computers can be of assistance.

This explains the Condition IV strategy. The user staff adds a systems specialist who knows more about user problems than anyone on the data processing division staff. The EDP staff has a user specialist who knows more about data processing than the systems specialist in the user division. But when these two individuals meet, they can effectively bridge the gap caused by specialization. They are a pair of integrators. One or the other would be better than none, but two meeting halfway is the best answer to a difficult situation.

High priority should be given to the integration of the EDP systems division with its users. Given the importance of the user-systems relationship and the relatively small resources required to improve this relationship (the two integrators could have many other duties), a high return can be earned from the costs incurred to improve this problem.

INTEGRATION OF THE R&D FUNCTION

A comprehensive survey of over 270 research and development executives conducted by one of the authors found that integration of the research and development department with other corporate functions was a major determinant of R&D success.[4]

An index of total R&D performance was calculated from answers to questions which measured R&D fulfillment of company goals. The index of total R&D performance was used to rank the R&D executives in that half of the companies with research laboratories which had high-level R&D performance. The bottom half of the rank order identified the R&D executives with low-level R&D performance. Answers to questions from respondents in companies with high-level R&D performance companies are compared with answers to questions from respondents in the low-level–performance companies. This identification of respondents by level of R&D performance then provides the basis for evaluating procedures and policies associated with high and low R&D performance.

The survey results show that significant differences can exist in the quality of communications between R&D and the various functional groups in any given company. The indices for quality of communication with marketing, manufacturing, finance, and engineering are each dramatically higher for companies with successful R&D efforts. High-performing firms have worked harder at integrating R&D with other corporate functions, by involving these groups in formal reviews of R&D projects, and by putting greater emphasis on planning and the integration of goals among the functional groups.

The questionnaire checklist provides a large number of procedural items, such as groups present at R&D project reviews, the use of technological forecasting, and job rotation. The integration of R&D into the corporation does not just happen spontaneously, and it is not just a matter of feelings. Integration follows from a large number of procedures which affect the quality of communications, information utilized, and planning. In Table 8.3, for example, the index of groups present at reviews of R&D projects is made up from answers to five questions, one for each of the major corporate groups, concerning their presence at periodic formal reviews of R&D projects. High-performance firms are shown to be superior on this measure, scoring 72 percent as compared with 59 percent for low-performance firms. This measure of corporate procedures with respect to R&D involves not a subjective evaluation by the respondent but a factual presence or absence of an important procedure.

TABLE 8.3 The Quality of Planning and Communication as Reported by Respondents with High and Low Levels of R&D Performance

	Percentage of respondents reporting high scores	
	High-performance group	Low-performance group
Index of quality of R&D communications with:		
Top management	71	39
Marketing	63	34
Manufacturing	50	21
Finance	20	6
Engineering	71	49
Index of groups present at reviews of R&D projects	72	59
Planning and goals index	38	16
Index of emphasis on long-run contribution of R&D to company goals	63	35

SOURCE: W. H. Gruber, O. H. Poensgen, and F. Prakke, "The Isolation of R&D from Corporate Management," *Research Management*, November 1973, pp. 27–32.

Planning and goals is an index that reflects the pervasiveness of planning and goal orientation in the R&D system. It consists of eleven items such as: How clearly and explicitly has top management defined long-range goals and objectives for your company? To what degree are top-level people in R&D aware of long-range company goals? And to what extent has long-range planning been significant in the identification of technological areas for investigation? In Table 8.3 the high-performance firms in our survey are shown to be clearly superior to the low-performance firms on this measure of organizational integration by a score of 38 to 16.

They are similarly superior on the index of emphasis on long-range contribution of R&D which consists of three items, measuring respectively the degree to which long-range company goals actually influence the total size of the R&D budget, the degree to which contributions toward these long-range goals are considered by top management in evaluating R&D, and the degree to which performance on major R&D projects is considered by top management in evaluating R&D. Those firms which have solved the conflict over time horizon by shifting toward a greater emphasis on long-range goals have the most successful R&D.

INNOVATION BASED ON RESEARCH

These four studies of the relationship between effectiveness in the specialization and integration tasks of management, and organizational performance, have, for some clients, increased the motivation to innovate in management. These studies illustrate an important technique of research-based management: the compiling of an inventory of management practices within and between company units, and associating those practices with performance.

Practices of management can be measured and relative performance scores can be analyzed, as we have demonstrated in this chapter. In every large company there are many activities which can be compared in order to determine the effectiveness of management. A comparison of the divisions within a company for the effectiveness of integration between such interrelated functional activities as R&D and marketing or marketing and production provides an important measure of management performance. Other useful comparisons that a research-based staff can make of management performance related to integration are the effectiveness of planning and the effectiveness with which computers are utilized to produce management information.

An inventory of management interface practices integrating R&D and marketing, or data processing and marketing, or other specialized units provides a very useful checklist for discovering problems which are caused by poor integration. Inventories of interface relationships reveal problems which are frequently very easy to correct. Marketing may have information that will be useful for R&D. Data processing may be able to develop management information systems which will integrate sales forecasts and production scheduling. R&D may be able to redesign a product to ease the quality-control problems experienced in manufacturing.

The task for management is the pursuit of integration in the face of the requirement for and continual trend toward differentiation (which in turn is partly caused by specialization). Management attempts through integration to maintain the goal-seeking and work-accomplishing organization that satisfies human needs, both from employees' and managers' association with a profitable organization and from consumer utilization of the organization's successful product. An organization that is highly integrated is healthy and successful; one not integrated cannot be.

One of the most important requirements of organizational integration is the development of overall measures of performance and the creation of systems to report that performance. Developing feedback on management performance is an important part of any effort to increase the effectiveness of management. Such management information becomes the motivation for the implementation of innovations in management practice.

NOTES AND REFERENCES

1. This example is based on one of the earliest and most useful studies on the management of integration and differentiation, Paul R. Lawrence and Jay W. Lorsch, *Organization and Environment,* Homewood, Ill.: Irwin, 1969 (first published in 1967 by the Division of Research, Graduate School of Business Administration, Harvard University).
2. SofTech, Inc., a large software engineering company located in Waltham, Mass., funded the survey of computer utilization in commercial banks, and the findings presented here are published with permission.
3. For purposes of questionnaire analysis, bank size ranges were set as follows: large, greater than $500 million in deposits; medium, between $100 million and $500 million; small, less than $100 million. The total sample size for each of the three bank size categories was 52 for large, 77 for medium, and 83 for small.
4. Gruber, W. H., O. H. Poensgen, and F. Prakke: "Research on the Interface Factor in the Development and Utilization of New Technology," *R&D Management,* Summer 1974, pp. 157–163; and "The Isolation of R&D from Corporate Management," *Research Management,* November 1973, pp. 27–32. These two articles by Gruber, Poensgen, and Prakke are the first two reports on a survey of R&D performed in the United States, Europe, and Japan in which over 400 R&D laboratories are participating.

NINE

Information Is Powerful

Business executives receive more data than they know what to do with. Reports, letters, memos, telephone calls, summaries of meetings, journals, and books flood in. It is usually instructive for managers to calculate or estimate how many hours worth of reading material they receive each week. Their worst suspicions will be confirmed.

THE CRISIS IN CORPORATE INFORMATION

In many organizations, managers are faced with data overload. More data are available—indeed thrust upon them—than they can handle. Their papers are piling higher and higher; they are taking reading material home at night. The attention of management is the scarce resource, not the data themselves.[1]

When this data overload condition persists, mistakes are made in the handling of relevant data, which means a failure to process them correctly or a failure to process them at all. The manager deliberately resorts to steps such as stacking up reports to be read later or just throwing away some data. Various methods of skimming data for needed information are sometimes attempted. One can also just run away from the basic problem and turn to more pleasant activities than figuring out what to read next.[2]

To illustrate the condition of data overload, consider the reported comment of Mark Cresap, a former Westinghouse president, when the computer staff offered him daily sales and profit data: "I couldn't stand that much bad news that often. Once a month is enough!"[3]

The causes for the incoming flood of data lie both inside and outside the firm. In general, the problem is the steadily growing production of data, coupled with a fantastic ability to reproduce and transmit them. The capabilities of information technology have surpassed the human ability to use data effectively and efficiently. And new sources of data production are springing up, also. For example, the ethic of participation and involvement will increasingly reach inside the business firm, as it has already reached the universities and many communities. Information sharing, consensus seeking, questioning of authority, meetings, ad hoc research programs, and grass roots efforts to cause change inevitably bring an increased volume of data with which the manager must cope. Data, in the form of more publications and reports on new problems, have increased proportionally to new problems. If the amount of data generated in a business is a good index of the complexity of the task of management, then the increasing number of accounting reports presented in Figure 9.1 provides an awesome picture of the problems of management in the complex business environment of the 1970s. The rate of increase in government regulation that has been experienced in the last decade will continue for the next decade. The forces which have caused the sharp increase in the number of accounting reports appear to be accelerating in magnitude. Executives experiencing an information overload have little to be optimistic about as they contemplate future flows of paper across their desks.

Jay Galbraith has correctly observed "that the greater the uncertainty of the task, the greater the amount of information that has to be processed between decision makers during the execution of this task."[4] Greater uncertainty, increased government regulation, and greater complexity and scale of business operations are all forces which have increased the information requirements of management.

Office copiers, telephones, printing technology, telecommunications, and microfilm disseminate data as fast as computers, concerned individuals, and research organizations can produce them. Technology has made possible the development of equipment for the production and reproduction of the reams of data that reach the manager's desk. Can we decide if, in all this flood of data that managers receive, there is the information they require to do their jobs?

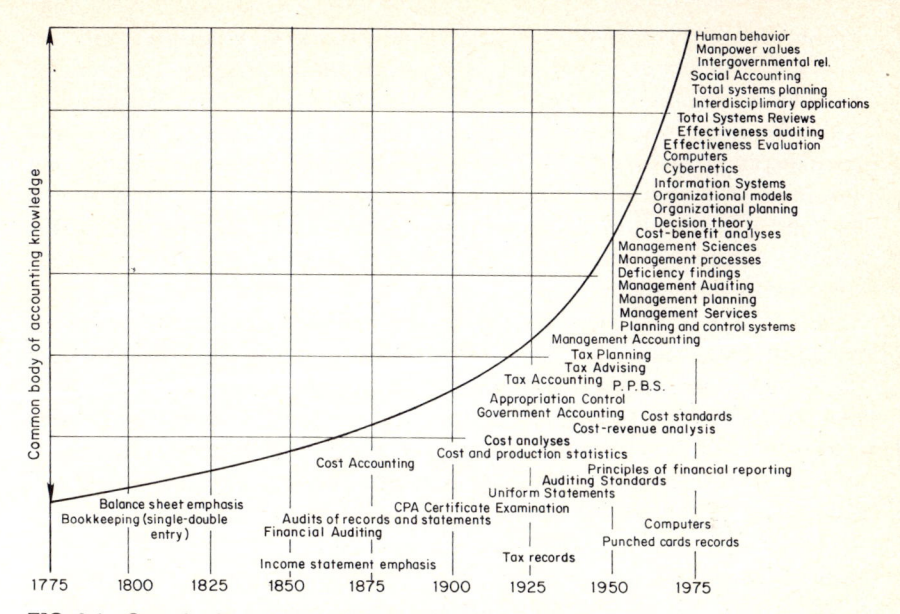

FIG. 9.1 *Growth of accounting knowledge, 1775–1975.*
SOURCE: W. N. Conrady, "Accounting Education: For What Purpose?" *The Journal of Contemporary Business*, University of Washington, Winter 1972.

As business faces environmental pressures, more rapid change, and a better-educated and more articulate labor force, information requirements for business decision making have indeed increased. Whether managers are getting the information they need is a question they must ask themselves. There is really a *series* of questions, none of which can ever be answered precisely. What is the job? What phenomena involved in the job would we like to know more about? How can we generate just enough information so that we will be able to ask the right questions of subordinates? The information needed must be brought out of the data morass.

It is difficult to find a coordinating force responsible for the management information system in many companies. As one goes from firm to firm searching for a central link that coordinates the system, all one finds are frustrated managers. These managers appear to recognize that there is critical information not easily available to them, but they do not understand how to find it or even how to find the time to look for it. Management requires making decisions with inadequate information; the world of complete information will never exist for managers. But that does not mean they should have to manage without basic, easily provided information.

For example, the controller in a division of a billion-dollar corporation with computer resources so plentiful that it rents out computer time had so much difficulty getting financial reports from the computer center that he asked for a little IBM 360/20 of his own. When told that all computers had to be part of the computer system, he fought for and received a NCR bookkeeping machine. In his haste to get the machine, he neglected to get a trained NCR operator. His personnel wanted to continue doing reports by hand (because they could not get the financial summaries from the computer center). The accounting of this division of a sophisticated company is a shambles.

As another illustration, an executive in one of our client companies reported to us that the accounting division in his company was not providing adequate information for management decisions. We noticed that some of the financial reports were in a computer printout. If the data were stored in the computer, we suggested, then the accounting department could just program for management reports as well as the financial statements. Then we discovered that the computer printouts were a mirage. After the financial statements were prepared by hand, the data were punched line by line onto computer cards, and a program was used to prepare the financial statements. All the program did was perform the calculations for comparing a month's operating statement with the results from the previous year and the budgeted figures. A large multimillion-dollar computer system was used to do a few worker-hours of arithmetic in order to provide comparisons with last year and to calculate the variance from budget.

In some cases, information systems are underdesigned with respect to computer capabilities. For example, the manufacturing manager in a plant of a large company complained that he had to forecast production and shipments for the fourth week of every month so that the accounting department would have time to produce a monthly income statement four days after closing. Forecasts did not equal actual results for that fourth week, and the monthly statement was usually wrong. It was difficult to control costs or motivate his managers because of the uncertain nature of the performance measures. When we informed him that the custom of making a forecast for the last week of the month was a precomputer habit that should be no longer necessary, he grinned and said that he could not wait until the plant accountants asked for the next month's forecast.

In other cases, the information system is engineered beyond the abilities of managers to use it. An executive vice president described to us his company's decision *not* to put a management control room in its new world headquarters building. The computer consulting firm which recommended the investment in an information control center brought the top management of this company to visit a large bank which *had* invested in such a control center. The bank executives at first talked enthusiastically about time-share capability with CRT visual display terminals; however, when pressed for an explanation of how these electronics devices were used to make decisions and to manage more effectively, they admitted that all this computer equipment was not really used.

It would be possible to continue page after page on the present inadequacy of information for management. Management information needs and computer capabilities are not matched up. In a given company, the design of an integrated information system is enormously complicated. At the close of the 1960s, it was taking companies from two to five years longer than they had planned to develop such systems.[5] And furthermore, the level of success may not yet be increasing. Tom Alexander, in the *Fortune* article "Computers Can't Solve Everything," quoted many findings such as:

> As more and more business operations become more mechanized or computer-based, fewer companies actually use the computer for a cost-effective tool.

and

> Computers are oversold and underemployed . . . and the gap between the capabilities of computers and their actual applications is wide and widening.[6]

Unfortunately, computers have made it possible for the naïve research types to overwhelm experienced management with mountains of paper containing data, rather than information. The task of management is to insist upon the screening and analysis of data at staff level until the information needed to make good decisions is available. The better the information received (and understood) by the experienced executives responsible for making decisions, the better will be the decisions made.

The Financial Executives Institute survey found that 95 percent of the respondents agreed with the following definition of MIS:

> . . . a system designed to provide selected decision oriented information needed by management to plan, control and evaluate the activities of the corporation. It is designed within a framework that emphasizes profit planning, performance planning, and control at all levels. It contemplates the ultimate integration of required business information subsystems, both financial and non-financial, within the company. To be effective, it requires interrelated coding, processing, storage, and reporting. It involves a systematic approach toward providing information that is timely, meaningful, and readily accessible. The subsystems will satisfy both the routine and special reporting needs of management efficiently and effectively to plan and control the acquisition, use, and disposition of corporate resources.
>
> A successful management information system must consider the current and future management information needs of the administrative, financial,

marketing, production, operating, and research functions. It will have the capacity to provide environmental (competitive, regulatory) information required for evaluating corporate objectives, long-range planning (strategy) and short-range planning (tactics).[7]

This definition of the corporate MIS specifies a management accounting capability far superior to present standards, even in companies with progressive managements.

The quality of management information systems appears to vary widely among firms and industries. Firms in the backward (in MIS) industries will be forced to compete for investor evaluations with firms which have higher-quality management information systems. Where there is interindustry competition, such as chemicals versus steel, advantages in MIS capability may affect the outcome of the battle.

DATA AND INFORMATION

To comprehend the underutilization of computers in many firms, it is useful to distinguish between data and three kinds of information.

Data are represented by the gross body of written and oral words and numbers that can be obtained by the manager. When managers receive a report, a budget, a copy of *Business Week,* or a telephone call, they get data. They may not care about most of the data which come their way. The total flow of data across a manager's desk is inside circle A in Figure 9.2.

The total flow of data received does not include information needed, but not received (indicated by D in Figure 9.2).

Optimal information ($B + C + D$ in Figure 9.2) is the data a manager *should* be using on the job. It is not a precise concept, because information needs change over time, and there is uncertainty both in a manager's job and in what information he or she should have to do the work. To be as precise as possible, optimal information for a manager is defined by the answers to the following questions about information needs as they relate to the decisions made:

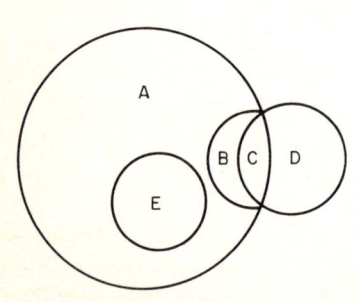

FIG. 9.2 *Data and information in the practice of management. A = total data flow to a manager; B + C + D = optimal information required for effective management; C = optimal information received and utilized; B = optimal information received and not utilized; D = optimal information not received because not part of the data flow to a manager; E = data utilized that are not optimal information.*

1. What must be done?
2. How do I decide what to do?
3. What information is needed to decide?

4. How accurate should the information be?
5. How often do I need the information?
6. What is the source of the information?
7. What is the best way to obtain the information and receive it on my desk?[8]

Utilized information ($C + E$ in Figure 9.2) includes optimal information (C) which was needed and relatively useless data (E) which was utilized.

Unutilized optimal information ($B + D$ in Figure 9.2) is information which is received but not utilized (B) and information which was never received (D).

Figure 9.2 reflects our observation that executives receive much more data than optimal information. A significant percentage of the information that should be utilized for effective management (D) is never even considered by executives in their decision making.

Professor Ackoff explains optimal information this way in his article "Management Misinformation Systems."

> For a manager to know what information he needs he must be aware of each type of decision he should make (as well as does) and he must have an adequate model of each. These conditions are seldom satisfied. Most managers have some conception of at least some of the types of decisions they must make. Their conceptions, however, are likely to be deficient in a very critical way, a way that follows from an important principle of scientific economy: the less we understand a phenomenon, the more variables we require to explain it. Hence, the manager who does not understand the phenomenon he controls plays it "safe" and, with respect to information, wants "everything." The MIS designer, who has even less understanding of the relevant phenomenon than the manager, tries to provide even more than everything. He therefore increases what is already an overload of irrelevant information.
>
> For example, market researchers in a major oil company once asked their marketing managers what variables they thought were relevant in estimating the sales volume of future service stations. Almost seventy variables were identified. The market researchers then added about half again this many variables and performed a large multiple linear regression analysis of sales of existing stations against these variables and found about thirty-five to be statistically significant. A forecasting equation was based on this analysis. An OR team subsequently constructed a model based on only one of these variables, traffic flow, which predicted sales better than the thirty-five-variable regression equation. The team went on to *explain* sales at service stations in terms of the customer's perception of the amount of time lost by stopping for service. The relevance of all but a few of the variables used by the market researchers could be explained by their effect on such perception.[9]

The experience in this oil company cited by Ackoff is consistent with what we have observed in our efforts to assist executives in client companies. The selection of the critical variables on which to focus a model for decision making is the most important stage of a model-building effort. Computers have made it possible to process very complex models. The low cost of processing data is an insufficient reason to put a busy executive into an information overload condition.

It has been our experience in working with clients that executives rarely have sufficient time to think about the optimal information $(B + C + D)$ that they need to make good decisions. As a result of this failure to specify their information requirements, executives are dependent on the many sources of data inputs (A). The uncontrolled flow of data inputs results in an information overload condition. This overload leads to:

- The failure to specify needed information
- The utilization of useless data
- The failure to utilize important information which is received

Given that managers are in fact not receiving the information needed to do their jobs effectively, there is an information gap despite the overload of data. Corporate information efforts so far have spent too much time on data flow and not enough time on control of information content for management performance.

Because of advances in computer technology, the cost of producing data has dropped precipitously, perhaps by a factor of 100 in the last thirty years.[10] The cost of producing information is also going down, but less rapidly. At the same time, the size and complexity of corporations have been increasing. To manage them requires more information. Though a person's ability to perceive information through eyes and ears has not increased dramatically over the years, information aggregation has put more usefulness into fewer pages. This means that the value of utilized information is increasing, even when it is not optimal. Because the cost of information is decreasing, its profitability is rising dramatically, as seen in Figure 9.3.

The timing and quality of financial reports have improved significantly in the last fifty years. The *adequacy* of a management information system is not based on an absolute level of sophistication. Adequacy is a relative concept. Management information systems must be judged against the needs of management and the possible systems that can now be developed as a result of computers and the recent advances in quantitative methods. By these two standards the average management information system is seriously inadequate.

FROM INFORMATION TO MODELS

How do the models produced by management scientists relate to the management information system? Models are the fruits of an understand-

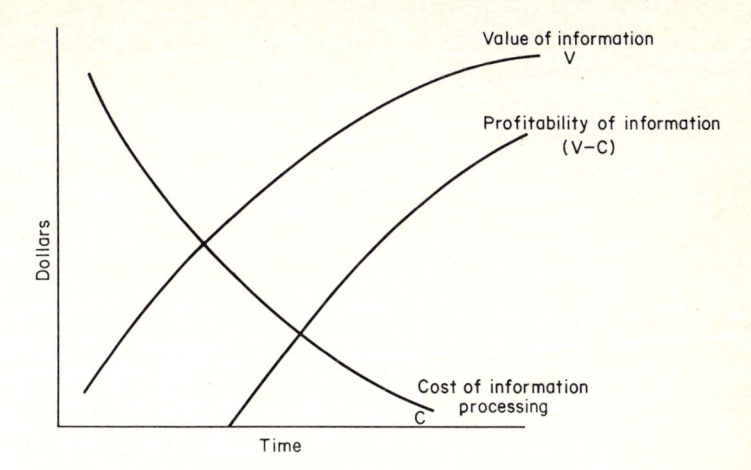

FIG. 9.3 *The increasing profitability of information.*

ing that comes from working with management information. To see this, we have to describe the evolution of management.

If we view management as a process in which managers continuously learn how to achieve better organizational performance, then we can make a parallel between management and the development of other human activity. Agriculture, weather forecasting, and bridge building have come to depend more and more on the work of people who develop knowledge about these activities and their settings. Similarly, we see in management a continuing evolution away from totally intuitive judgmental behavior toward activity that is increasingly broad in scope and includes the work of scientists and engineers. The development of a knowledge base underlying the practice of management is the result of a research and development process occurring in many companies, although not recognized as such. There is a close analogy between the growth of management knowledge and the growth of scientific knowledge. The first step in learning about a phenomenon through a scientific approach is to collect data, and management in most firms is in the stage of data collection. These data are accounting figures for the most part, although some companies are achieving a broader focus on management information which goes beyond mere financial reporting of past results into personnel, logistics, and environmental data. Forecasts, market shares, and probability data will make larger inroads on management's attention over the next few years.

The next step of scientists after data collection is data analysis. Managers have always analyzed at least some of the information they received, and the tools are becoming increasingly sophisticated. Analysis of data is the work of staff specialists. Regression analysis, variance analysis, and cross classification tables are made easy with computers. These analyses structure data into a format that gives the reader information. Even the juxtaposition of present results and last year's results is an analytic step, albeit an easy one.

Eventually, in the activity of science, there can be theorizing and model building. Through theories and models of the total business environment, managers can understand "what is" and predict "what will be." Furthermore, they can ask "what if" questions. This stage of work inside business is arriving through the model-building, theorizing activity of quantitative and behavioral specialists.

Tremendous growth lies ahead, with increasing emphasis on models for integrating data and producing decision rules. Yet management needs information that fits the *present* mode of decision making before it needs sophisticated quantitative models. To suggest that the solution to information problems is quantitative models is reminiscent of Marie Antoinette saying of the starving people in France, "Let them eat cake!" Information for management is so weak that model building does force the collection and restructuring of data. However, the understanding of critical relationships results from thinking about the relevant data rather than running complex models through the computer. As Rayford L. Roark, director of the Ford Motor computer systems office, noted, "The process of building a model is usually more instructive than putting it through the computer after it is done."[11]

The coming of the New Management has been made possible by the availability of computers. Many of the new-management models eventually involve the processing of such large quantities of information or the calculation of such difficult equations that computers must be used if the implementation of the new techniques is to be cost-effective. But in the initial stages of progress, rather than spend corporate resources on models, management would do well to commit its energy to directing improvements in the information it judges necessary to decision making by present procedures.

There is a crying need in large companies for a centralized management information staff group that can accurately determine just what the utilized information is in the current decision-making process. The vast majority of the utilized information in companies today is nondocumented, verbal, current, and unorganized, but managers use it anyway and even prefer it to computer reports that do not tell them what they want and need to know. Understanding what managers actually do and taking the first halting steps toward organizing the information they currently use is the only way to build relevancy into a formal management information system. The biggest mistake in much of the current information system design work is that it does not proceed from where managers are now but, instead, builds information output products that serve some assumed decision-making process which real managers do not carry out.[12]

The personnel who will serve on such a staff group will probably include accountants, but it is certain that accountants alone cannot do the job, as we will see next.

THE FAILURE OF ACCOUNTANTS

Management progress since World War II has been largely a direct result of improvements in the management information capability. During about the first fifteen years of the period, from 1945 to 1960, industrial accountants were in charge of information. These professionals were a major force in the development of new-management concepts and techniques. Consider these achievements which have been developed by accountants in many of the better-managed companies of the country:

1. Cost accounting, including standard costs and variance by cause
2. Budgets and rolling target estimates
3. Monthly reports five days after end of month
4. Contribution margin
5. Profit and cost-centers
6. Return-on-investment calculation
7. Discounted cash flow technique
8. Decentralization by transfer prices

The leading-edge position once enjoyed by the accounting profession has now been lost. Accountants are oriented to providing only financial information—not logistics, personnel, marketing, or strategic information. Information required by management is presently formed and processed by new and old staff groups in accounting, systems, market research, personnel, long-range planning, and EDP. The resulting balkanization of information control has been dysfunctional. There are duplicative sources. Some management needs are not met. The information system is out of balance.

The trend in the control of corporation information has been away from traditionally trained accountants and toward professionals trained in the new-management fields of EDP and management information systems. Note the Chapter 3 analysis that the value of computers in use rose from about $130 million in 1955 to almost $24 billion in 1970, an increase of about 200 times. This growth in computer power has been primarily for accounting data processing. In the next decade, the ratio of management to accounting data processing will increase rapidly, as diagramed in Figure 9.4. A new corporate management information systems capability will emerge, and the corporate accounting function will become a specialized activity with responsibilities far more limited than at present.

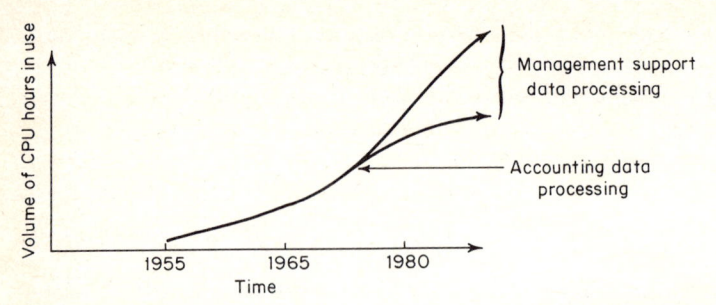

FIG. 9.4 *Trends in the utilization of accounting and management-support data processing.*

Many accountants are aware of the forces leading in the direction suggested in this forecast. A 1968 survey, *Corporate Organization Structures*, by the National Industrial Conference Board, found a trend toward the establishment of information system units. In many firms the *processing of accounting information has been taken away from the control of the accounting-finance division and given to an independent department.* The failure of accountants to understand the opportunities possible with the computer has fostered this reduction of the responsibilities of the accounting function. As Stieglitz and Wilkerson noted in reporting the results of the National Industrial Conference Board Survey:

> Electronic data processing—the computer—offers management a range of possibilities as a management tool. Its impact on the management process, company experience attests, depends largely on the uses to which the computer is put. To some companies, it is the biggest, best, and fastest adding machine so far invented. And it is used that way. To other companies, the computer is looked at as a kind of Rorschach test: its possible application is limited only by the imagination (and the ability to develop the accompanying software). In some companies, it has brought about a whole new concept of planning and control and made possible a technique increasingly referred to as systems management. . . .
>
> The first home of EDP equipment in most companies was within the finance department—in accounting. There has been a move to get it out of accounting or out of the controller's domain. In more and more companies the stress on EDP and management information has given rise to a new staff function—management information systems. A unit of this kind shows up more often at the corporation level. Its function is to widen and exploit the possible uses of EDP so that it is not just a bigger and better adding machine.[13]

Even more recent information has been reported by the Committee on Management Information Systems of the Financial Executives Institute. The Financial Executives Institute survey discovered that 46 percent of MIS managers reported to "someone outside of the financial area. Since just a few years ago, the MIS reported almost exclusively to someone in the financial area, responses to the questionnaire would seem to indicate that MIS is moving away from the responsibility of the financial executive."[14]

There is reason to expect that this increase from near zero to 46 percent of MIS groups reporting outside of the financial function represents a trend that will continue. Probably this organizational group which has recently been created in many corporations will be given additional responsibilities.

The MIS capability will not be a passive force relative to accounting-finance activities. Traditional information supplied by accounting-finance will be reorganized and related to new information such as comparisons with performance by competitors. What role will accounting-finance professionals have as information they controlled is used in new ways? Even more serious is the problem of the speed with which the MIS competence is developed within a corporation, now that it is widely recognized that the information traditionally supplied by the accounting-finance function is inadequate (and often misleading for management decisions).[15]

The trends toward MIS, new-management techniques, and the growth in the importance of management services challenge the CPA profession. An adequate background in quantitative management is becoming more important for professional accountants. Are undergraduate accounting departments responding to this need? Has the CPA qualification examination been altered to encourage education in these new-management skills? Our findings indicate that:[16]

- Undergraduate accounting majors are reluctant to take quantitative courses in the new-management topics of computers, statistics, and operations research.
- The uniform CPA examination emphasizes traditional accounting problems; it can still be passed with absolutely no knowledge of the new tools used in accounting, such as computers.
- Partners in the Big Eight CPA firms were not satisfied with the breadth of training received by students with undergraduate accounting majors.

At Northeastern University there are only three required new-management courses in the undergraduate accounting curriculum. Although more than twenty-five courses in the new-management area are offered as electives, only 8 percent of a recent graduating class of accounting majors elected courses in this vital area, and those courses represented less than 2 percent of the total elective courses taken. The findings from an analysis of the Northeastern University accounting majors graduating in June 1969 are given in Table 9.1. There are reasons to believe that the North-

TABLE 9.1 Willingness of Accounting Majors to Take Courses in Quantitative Management*
(June 1969 Graduates at Northeastern University)

	No.	Percent
Total elective courses possible in sample†	392	
Electives taken in quantitative management	5	1.3
Quantitative electives taken by honor students	4	
Total students in sample	49	
Total students taking quantitative electives	4	8.2
Honor students in sample	7	
Honor students taking quantitative electives	3	42.9
Nonhonor students in sample	42	
Nonhonor students taking quantitative electives	1	2.4

*Quantitative management defined as including mathematics, computers, statistics, and systems analysis.

†A sample of the first 49 names in the graduating list.

SOURCE: W. H. Gruber and L. L. Logan, "The Education of Professional Accountants," *The Journal of Accountancy*, May 1971, p. 87; unpublished data.

eastern University experience is similar to what was happening at other colleges of business administration. However, there is relatively little published information on activity in other universities with which to compare the Northeastern experience.

In an attempt to understand why 92 percent of the accounting students avoided this important area of study, the uniform CPA examinations for the years 1960, 1965, and 1969 were analyzed, on the theory that accounting majors prepare for these examinations. Each of the problems and questions on the practice and theory portions of the examinations was analyzed to determine if new-management knowledge would have been helpful in understanding the question and developing a good solution to the problem. As indicated in Table 9.2, each of the six examinations could have been passed with no knowledge of new-management techniques.

In a recent publication by Price, Waterhouse & Company entitled "A Self-Study Program for CPA Preparation," the authors present a classification of all the questions and problems in the CPA examinations for the ten-year period from May 1957 through November 1966. This study reveals heavy emphasis on such traditional areas as cost accounting, taxation, governmental accounting, inventory evaluation, and application of funds and cash flow. During this same period, there were only two questions on computers and their applications. Prior to 1967, problems relating to mathematical programming, matrix algebra, and other quantitative techniques were never used. Since the serious student interested in a career in public accounting will take elective courses that will help him or

TABLE 9.2 New-Management* Knowledge Tested on CPA Examinations, 1960–1969†

	Percent of total required and alternative points for which New Management useful			
Year	None	Some	Great deal	Total
1960	100	0	0	100
1965	98	2	0	100
1969	92	4	4‡	100

*New Management defined as management science, mathematics, systems analysis, and computer applications.
†Review of Problems in the Accounting Practice, Parts I and II, and Theory of Accounts sections in the examination.
‡On an alternative (i.e., not required) question.
SOURCE: CPA examinations.

her pass the CPA examination, the lack of interest in new-management courses may have resulted from the failure of the AICPA examination to reward students who have taken difficult new-management courses.

Greater breadth of competence in information management is now required. If corporate accountants define their responsibilities narrowly in terms of traditional accounting reports, a smaller slice of the management information pie will be left under their control. However, if they accept the challenge for advances in the use of information for new-management requirements, then once again the leading edge in management improvement can be identified with the accounting function.

The fragmentation of information control has been dysfunctional. Consolidation in the control of management information can be expected. Once again there will be a shuffling around of responsibilities for control. The information content of management will continue to increase in importance. Whether industrial accountants can rise in response to new opportunities, as they did in the postwar period from 1945 to about 1960, or whether the erosion in the level of responsibility for management information held by accountants is to continue in the 1970s will be determined by the vision of corporate accountants.

CORPORATE INFORMATION STRATEGY

The corporate information strategy should reflect the findings presented in this chapter:
- Critical information not utilized
- Data overload pressing on management

- Extraordinary improvement in the technology for processing and distributing data and information
- Research-based professionals working on models rather than information
- Accountants poorly trained to work with new information technologies
- Dysfunctional balkanization in the control and processing of information

Now is the time to formulate a corporate information strategy which reflects the opportunities and problems specified in this summary listing. The corporate information strategy should reflect the new resources for management described in Chapter 3. Recall that Withington dates the utilization of computers as information custodians as starting in 1974. Withington's opinion that information management with computers is a very recent ability is supported by Nolan's article, "Computer Data Bases: The Future Is Now."[17]

Staff resources, the computer technology, and the management know-how are all available for the corporate executive who has the vision to initiate the development of a corporate information strategy. A small number of companies have made some important progress in the development of a corporate information strategy. Successful development of a corporate information strategy requires an experience-based line executive working together with research-based staff professionals from several areas of specialization.

The urgent need to gain control over corporate information is a result of thin management. An increase in the effectiveness of management and improvements in corporate performance can be achieved with a modest investment in the development of a corporate information capability. In only a small number of companies is there an adequate level of resources and senior management time committed to the development of a corporate information capability, because thin management provides resources only for crisis fighting. Efforts to meet this week's budget consume the attention of management. Hundreds of millions of dollars are spent in uncontrolled ways in some companies. Compare this willingness to spend money so freely in traditional ways (such as advertising, plant, equipment, R&D for new products) with the reluctance to allocate funds for the development of a corporate information capability. If the executives in corporations made this comparison, greater willingness to invest in the control of corporate information would result.

NOTES AND REFERENCES

1. Simon, Herbert A.: "Applying Information Technology to Organization Design," *Public Administration Review*, May–June 1973, p. 270.

2. Katz, D.; and R. Kahn: *Social Psychology of Organizations,* New York: Wiley, 1966, pp. 231–233.
3. Alexander, Tom: "Computers Can't Solve Everything," *Fortune,* October 1969, p. 129.
4. Galbraith, Jay: "Organization Design: An Information Processing View," *Interfaces,* May 1974, p. 28.
5. "Data Processing Industry Assessed by Consultant," *Communications of the ACM,* vol. 13, no. 11, November 1970, p. 704.
6. Alexander: op. cit., p. 126.
7. Kennedy, D. W.: "What a President Needs to Know about MIS," *Financial Executive,* December 1970, pp. 52–53.
8. Adapted from H. Justin Davidson and Robert M. Trueblood, "Accounting for Decision-Making," in Alfred Rappaport (ed.), *Information for Decision Making,* Englewood Cliffs, N.J.: Prentice-Hall, 1970, p. 23.
9. Ackoff, Russell L.: "Management Misinformation Systems," *Management Science,* vol. 14, no. 4, December 1967, pp. 149–150.
10. IBM estimates that the cost of 100,000 multiplications has fallen from $1.26 in 1952 to 1 cent in 1974.
11. Alexander: op. cit., p. 129.
12. Mintzberg, H.: "The Myth of MIS," *California Management Review,* Fall 1972, pp. 92–97.
13. Stieglitz, H., and C. D. Wilkerson: *Corporate Organization Structure,* Studies in Personnel Policy, No. 210, New York: National Industrial Conference Board, 1963, p. 4.
14. Kennedy: op. cit., p. 54.
15. See note 10 to Chapter 1.
16. This section is based on William H. Gruber and Louis L. Logan, "The Education of Professional Accountants," *The Journal of Accountancy,* May 1971, pp. 85–88.
17. Nolan, Richard L.: "Computer Data Bases: The Future Is Now," *Harvard Business Review,* September–October 1973, pp. 98–114.

TEN

How to Innovate in Management

The rate of improvement in the practice of management varies among companies. In some companies (those of an almost-to-Future Firm category), there is a high level of commitment and a well-conceived effort to increase the effectiveness of management. At the other extreme, there are companies (of Prior Firm classification) in which senior management appears to be totally unaware of the opportunities for increasing the effectiveness of management.

In all companies there is an opportunity for innovation in management at every level in the organizational structure. It has been our experience that managers are rarely so tightly controlled that there is not the freedom to improve the practices with which they fulfill their responsibilities. In fact, *most managers are given more freedom than they use.* Rarely can a lack of innovation be blamed on stupid and myopic superiors. Rather, management innovation is not achieved because managers do not know how to innovate.

We will report on our experience in assisting the executives in client companies to innovate in management. The strategy for an innovation effort is similar whether the company is a multinational conglomerate, a large commercial bank, a relatively small manufacturer, a book publisher, or almost any other kind of organization. Departments in state and city governments, nonprofit hospitals, and even universities can all benefit from the application of this strategy for management innovation.

FACTORS IN A SUCCESSFUL INNOVATION EFFORT

The factors which determine the success of an effort to innovate in management are:
1. Time availability of line management
2. Commitment by line management to the innovation effort
3. Involvement of line executives
4. Competence of staff support for the innovation effort
5. Relationship between line executives and research-based staffs
6. Strategy for the management-innovation effort

These six factors in the improvement of management effectiveness will be analyzed in this chapter. All six factors must be working if the full potential of a program of innovation in the practice of management is to be achieved.

Line-Executive Time

The creation of a research-based management improvement capability involves experience-based line executives and research-based staff professionals working together. The failure of line executives to gain control of their time is a major reason why corporate problems continue for years after they have been recognized. Line executives are so busy fighting yesterday's crises that there is just not the time or the interest to work on efforts to improve the effectiveness of management. We have here a vicious circle. Because there are yesterday's crises to solve, there is not the time to develop the management effectiveness which is required to reduce the time spent on solving crises.

If we accept the idea that attention is a measurable resource in the form of executive person-hours, we can pose a key question. How do managers decide to allocate their attention among the large number of tasks they carry out in fulfilling their responsibilities? To a large extent, their attention is allocated by others: telephone calls, meetings, required reports, required procedures.[1] But attention is the most precious resource managers have in their control, and they should reserve as much of it as they can to utilize at their own discretion. This is fundamental.

How often our clients tell us that they will get on a recommendation just as soon as possible—but there is "too much to do now!" The president of one large corporation asked us to develop a plan for turning around a division which had been losing its market share to competition. For several years, this division with sales of $25 million a year had been performing poorly, and yet corporate management had not the available management attention to move in and take control.

In another situation, there was a job shop operation with very high fixed setup costs. This made the length of production run, inventory decisions, and the marketing effort highly interrelated. Someone had to decide how much inventory buildup to risk in order to achieve a lower unit production cost. Sales of this operation were over $100 million a year. For several years, we have been talking with top management about what could be done to integrate manufacturing and marketing in order to control the uncertainty in the length-of-production-run decision. The top management of this company has not had the time to decide what should be done about what appears to be one of its most serious problems.

These two corporate situations are examples of a very common ailment: there tends to be no line-executive time available within corporations for the management of innovation. Even after a problem is recognized, it often takes several years before any action can be taken!

The initial step in innovative management therefore is finding discretionary time so that attention can be directed to the process of improvement. Peter F. Drucker has spelled out three steps for making such time:

1. Executives must ensure that the uses of their time are systematically recorded for later study. The manager cannot really seek to improve his or her productivity in the work day until one has an objective record of how time is being used currently on an hour-by-hour basis. One can record this personally or have a secretary do it.

2. When a personal time log is available for examination, the manager will be able to start improving beyond the present situation. He or she does this by examining the log for useless meetings, trips and other activities; inefficient scheduling; areas for delegation and opportunities to implement better practices.

3. From a consideration of what the time log shows, the manager can proceed to the goal of creating one hour or longer chunks of discretionary time, time blocks one can use for thinking through, planning and otherwise initiating innovative management activity.[2]

There are available today books and short executive-development courses on the efficient and effective use of time. Taking advantage of such knowledge is an important first step in breaking out of the tyranny of programmed activity and reaction to crisis. Setting goals and obtaining feedback on progress toward goals is the method prescribed by behavioral scientists for changing individual behavior.[3] If managers have the will power to decide they are going to improve their use of time, study the present situation objectively, and take positive steps toward achieving blocks of discretionary time, they have shown they can be innovation-minded managers; such a goal-setting, situation-measuring, improvement sequence is the prototype for all management improvement efforts.

Commitment of Resources to Innovation in Management

Line executives have the budgets. Line executives make the decisions. If a line executive is not investing his or her resources in planning, in the management information available for the evaluation of performance and for making decisions, or in anything other than meeting today's sales budget, then little will be accomplished in an effort to improve the effectiveness of management.

Typical of the responses that we hear from line executives who are not committing their resources to improving the effectiveness of management are:

- Just not time. There is this or that threat or problem. No time to think about . . .
- We are winning! Sales above budget. Profit margin improving. We don't have to think about . . .
- My boss wants me to meet today's sales budget. He doesn't care about . . .

All these statements occurred in discussions with line executives in client companies. All the line executives who made these statements had good performance records in meeting this year's budget. They were good managers. They were providing some verbal support for the effort to improve the practice of management. They were at a Present Firm level of management competence and expressed some interest in moving toward a Future Firm management capability. But until they are willing to provide a larger budget for a research-based staff, their rate of progress in increasing the effectiveness of management will be unnecessarily slow.

Managers are always balancing the allocation of their resources between the short-term and the long-term future. The dilemma becomes especially apparent in a recession when just surviving the next six months can be of paramount concern. Is investment in research-based management improvement justified in a recession? This question should be answered affirmatively. Research-based staffs can be just as effective in a period of retrenchment as in a period of growth, if line management will stay involved in defining their mission and keeping it relevant to current needs. In fact, major decisions occur because of depressed profits and sales. Serious errors are often made during recessions, and research-based staffs can be particularly helpful in preventing the bad decisions which occur so frequently during periods of instability.

Involvement of Line Executives

The commitment of line executives should not be measured only by the *funds* allocated for an effort to improve the practice of management.

Commitment should be measured by the time given by line executives in the effort to improve the practice of management. Much can be accomplished on a small budget if a line executive devotes sufficient attention and time to interaction with the research-based staff which is working on his or her problems. While research-based staffs in such areas as planning, management information systems, and organization development provide specialized knowledge for solving problems, line executives provide a knowledge of the business. Furthermore, line executives must understand the solutions which are proposed in a management-innovation project. To understand a solution, they must have helped to develop it. Then they will be willing to implement the recommendations of a project team. Implementation may mean the use of a new management information system or a decision-support model, or it may mean action on a strategic plan.

The most effective involvement occurs when a line manager serves on a project team. At the first National Bank of Boston, for example, the project director on a new systems development effort is frequently a bank officer in the user division for which the new computer application is being developed. It is critical that the relevant line manager be on a management-innovation team right from the start of a project. The most important decisions in a management-innovation project are made early in the effort. Consequently, inputs from line management are particularly important in the early stages of an innovation project.

The horror stories of useless efforts to improve the practice of management are often the results of line executives sufficiently committed to a management-innovation project to provide the funds, but not their attention or involvement. This puts the awesome responsibility for improving the practice of management on the frequently frail shoulders of young, inexperienced, myopic staff professionals trained in some specialized area such as computer systems or organizational development. Note that in many graduate schools it is possible to obtain an M.S. or Ph.D. in organizational development or operations research without learning how to read an income statement.

Assignment of the Professional Staff

Since the time and involvement of even a line executive who is very committed to a management-innovation effort is limited—to say nothing of the executive's lack of specialization in needed management technology—assistance from staff resources is usually required. The determinants for the success of a management-innovation effort are seen as more complex when the quality of professional staffs is added as a factor. The types of people who can be said to make up the new-management staffs are, to say the least, very diverse. They can be more or less specialized in their professional competence. They can know much or very little about the environment of business. They can be very good or very bad at interacting with line managers and solving their problems. We concentrated on the diversity of just one group of new-management professionals, the M.B.A.'s in Chapter 6, although much of what we said there is true of specialists generally. When a manager is deciding if he or she wants to hire (either from outside the firm or from an internal staff unit) a particular research-based professional, we would advise that the manager focus on the ability of the specialized individual to make his or her approach to problem solving clearly understandable.

The problem of finding a suitable person within a professional category is one issue. Another problem for a manager using research-based people is finding the proper mix of professionals needed to carry out a particular project. We believe, for example, that the development of a new management information system for the evaluation of divisional performance should involve, in addition to line executives, (1) the MIS staff, (2) the data processing staff, (3) the organization development staff, and (4) the finance staff.

The above list of the kinds of people resources to be utilized in the development of a new management information system must frequently be expanded to include other kinds of specialists. In the effort to adapt its commercial loan application to a change in a state law, for example, one large bank included the corporate lawyer, several members of senior management, a staff professional from corporate communications, and one from branch management in order to respond effectively to the change in rules for lending money in that state. This example illustrates the large number of line and staff interrelationships which now occur very frequently when a change in the practice of management is attempted.

For a particular management-innovation project, the staff should include those knowledgeable in the functional area concerned (for example, marketing, manufacturing, or finance), representatives of the technology involved (for example, data processing, accounting, or industrial engineering), specialists in changing people (for example, organizational development personnel), specialists in the larger environment (for example, from the legal or public affairs departments), and of course the line managers who have the responsibility for the performance which will be affected by the implementation of the management innovation.

Relationship between Line Executive and Research-based Staffs

How should line management and staff professionals work together in an effort to improve the effectiveness of management? This question can be answered in several ways. It is critical that both line and staff recognize that they have an interrelationship problem that goes beyond their immediate responsibilities. One writer summarizes the successful manager–staff advisory relationship as follows:

- The manager turns to the specialist-advisory group with his problems, largely on his own initiative, with the feeling that he can discuss his problems freely with a sympathetic listener who will not hurt his position. . . .
- The line executive understands what skills and knowledge are embodied in the advisory group—how far they can go—and in turn the advisory group comes to understand the needs and objectives of the line groups.
- The manager is aided in understanding the full dimensions of his problem and is helped to develop skills in evaluating alternative solutions.
- The manager increases, over time, his ability to cope with these problems in his own area; perhaps he has to call on an advisor less often. At least he regards such problems as a means of developing new abilities and insights.
- The advisory group develops greater acceptance for its ideas and points of view, not by putting pressure on the line but by developing confidence in its helping role and by proving in practice that it can contribute to the manager's effectiveness.
- The line manager gets credit for any improvements that result.
- The advisor is evaluated, not in terms of the number of his plans and projects, but in terms of his ability to solve problems that the line manager sees as problems.[4]

We will examine the relationship between line and staff in several other sections of this and the following chapter. The importance of specialized staffs and the sheer number of areas of specialization have increased so rapidly in the last decade that it is now necessary to focus on the line-staff relationship as a critical determinant in the effectiveness of efforts to improve the practice of management.

Strategy for the Management-Innovation Effort

In our consulting and research, we have observed wide disparities in corporate capabilities to innovate in management. The process of management innovation should be governed by a strategy formulated after a serious effort has been made to think through the objectives for the management-innovation effort. The basics for an effective strategy for management innovation are presented in the next section.

STRATEGY FOR THE MANAGEMENT-INNOVATION EFFORT

The funding of an innovation in management effort is similar to the funding of an R & D project to create a new product. Success in both of these kinds of innovation should be measured by the effect on the bottom line. A new product which turns out to be a technological achievement that does not sell is not a success. An innovation in a management project which does not contribute to a significant improvement in the performance of management is a failure. There is no shortage of examples to cite for both kinds of failures. Innovation efforts for new products and for increasing the effectiveness of management require a well-organized strategy.

There is a paradox here that should be explained. It has been our experience in working with clients that improvements in the effectiveness of management are easy to achieve. Yet many efforts to innovate in management end in failure. We estimate that about four out of every five efforts to improve the practice of management are either total or partial failures. One reason that the success-to-failure ratio in efforts to improve the effectiveness of management is so unsatisfactory in most companies is that management has not been organized to manage the process of innovation in management. A second reason, related to the first, is that the management in most companies has been so buried in the daily details of work that there has been little experience in efforts to innovate in management. Put more bluntly, *management frequently does not know how to increase the effectiveness of management.*

In the remainder of this chapter and in Chapters 11 through 14, we will provide instructions for the development of an effective management-innovation program. These instructions will involve lists of concepts and lists of stages in the management-innovation project cycle. One unfortunate experience that we observe all too frequently in client companies is the tendency for management to give inadequate attention to all the critical stages in the management-innovation project cycle. A failure to take positive action on even one of the concepts and stages that are fundamental to a management-innovation program can cause a serious reduction in the effectiveness of the effort.

Beginning a Management-Innovation Program

A description of a typical beginning of a management-innovation program in flowchart form provides a useful summary of the stages of effort. We have diagramed these stages in Figure 10.1. Note that the first stage involves the decision to improve performance. Most managers believe that they are always attempting to improve the effectiveness of management. What we are considering, however, is a *planned program* of management improvement similar to a program of R&D for new products. A program of management innovation is not a random, half-hearted effort to "do better."

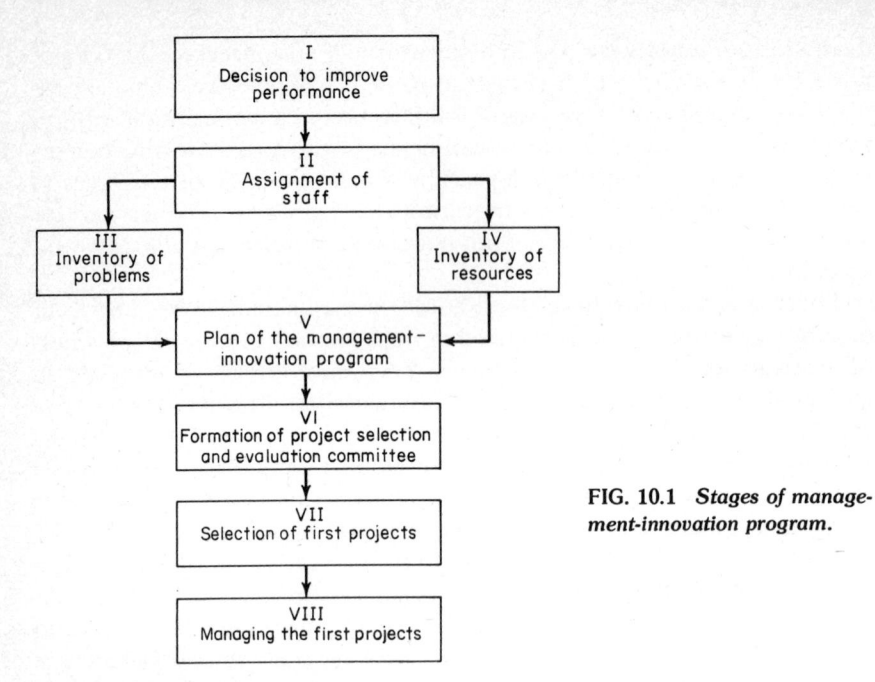

154 / *The New Management*

```
        ┌─────────────────────┐
        │         I           │
        │  Decision to improve│
        │     performance     │
        └──────────┬──────────┘
                   │
        ┌──────────▼──────────┐
   ┌────┤         II          ├────┐
   │    │    Assignment of    │    │
   │    │        staff        │    │
   │    └─────────────────────┘    │
┌──▼──────────┐              ┌─────▼───────┐
│     III     │              │     IV      │
│Inventory of │              │Inventory of │
│  problems   │              │  resources  │
└──────┬──────┘              └──────┬──────┘
       │      ┌───────────────┐     │
       └─────►│       V       │◄────┘
              │Plan of the management-│
              │innovation program │
              └───────┬───────┘
                      ▼
           ┌─────────────────────┐
           │         VI          │
           │Formation of project selection│
           │and evaluation committee│
           └──────────┬──────────┘
                      ▼
           ┌─────────────────────┐
           │        VII          │
           │Selection of first projects│
           └──────────┬──────────┘
                      ▼
           ┌─────────────────────┐
           │        VIII         │
           │Managing the first projects│
           └─────────────────────┘
```

FIG. 10.1 *Stages of management-innovation program.*

The decision to improve the performance of management with a set of formal procedures and responsibilities (stage I) leads to preliminary assignments of line management and staff professionals for the management-innovation program (stage II). These assignments need not be a full-time commitment of people to the management-innovation effort. An assignment means that a working group (which may mean one person) has responsibility for developing a plan for a management-innovation program. In order to develop the plan (which is diagramed as stage V in Figure 10.1), it is first useful to take an inventory of problems (stage III) and an inventory of resources which are available for the management-innovation program (stage IV).

The preliminary assignments represent a rescheduling of the time of people who are required to develop the plan for a management-improvement program. This plan (stage V) should include the procedures for proper selection and evaluation of innovation projects and procedures for the evaluation of performance in the operating unit for which the management-improvement plan has been developed. This operating unit can be an entire company, an operating division of a company, or a functional area such as marketing or R&D. In these days of rapid discontinuities in business, we recommend the creation of a senior-management-level committee for the continuous monitoring of plans and performance (stage VI). Actual improvement in management performance begins when the first projects are selected (stage VII) and carried out (stage VIII).

This summary of the stages in a management-innovation program will be expanded after a brief analysis of the problems experienced by managers who believe that they have no resources for a management-innovation program.

For Managers without Resources

During the 1974–1975 recession we were frequently told by managers that they have had to cut into bone and muscle on orders from above. Their reaction to an organized program of innovation in management such as the one that we are describing in this chapter will frequently be one of apathy. When a manager is so tightly controlled for funds that doing the minimal work required to avert a crisis is a major accomplishment, it is difficult to think about improvements in the practice of management other than ones which will solve today's crisis. Tomorrow may never come, and next month is an eternity away.

It has been our experience that a small number of days of effort on a bootstrap, bare bones management-improvement program can pay a very high rate of return—thereby creating more resources for further efforts to improve management performance. The reader whose operations are under severe financial pressure should think about ways to use the suggested actions presented in this chapter. Some will require a very low level of resources and will produce a rapid payback. We know from experience with clients that low-cost, fast-payback management innovations are possible and even relatively easy to achieve.

STAGES IN A MANAGEMENT-INNOVATION PROGRAM

The strategy for a management-innovation effort should include the following basic concepts:

Stage I: The Decision to Improve Performance

All executives are for improved performance. The question is whether executives *will commit the resources* required to achieve an increase in the effectiveness of management. This commitment can be made at almost any level in the hierarchy. The management of a department in a division of a company can make the decision to improve performance by the allocation of some resources for the effort to innovate in management. For example, the supervisor of accounts payable, a unit in the accounting function in the controller division in a product-line department of a large company, was experiencing difficulty in managing the flow of work through her unit. On her own time, she analyzed the paper inputs that were processed and discovered several tasks which could be made more efficient. She was able to reduce the pressure on her limited staff resources and increase the overall effectiveness of her unit without any assistance or approval. Another example: The sales manager for a small product line in the division of a large company asked his systems group for an analysis of how often his sales representatives should see each customer. The analysis resulted in a major reallocation of sales efforts which almost doubled sales and resulted in a more than doubling of profits. The sales force manager was able to achieve this analysis and reallocation of effort without anyone's approval! There is no question that almost every manager has far more power to innovate than is utilized.

Stage II: Assignment of Staff

After the decision to improve performance is made, one or more people, starting with a respected, experience-based manager, should be assigned to the program for the purpose of doing front-end planning work. Again, in a small unit, the staff to do this work might be only the one person who made the decision to improve performance.

Since the entire strategy of management innovation we propose is based on demand pull (see Chapter 3), rather than supply push, the staffing emphasis here should be on problem finders,[5] not on people who have techniques to apply but no particular understanding of what is going on in terms of business performance. After projects are selected in a later stage is the time to think about who has the right research-based techniques to solve a particular problem.

Stage III: Taking an Inventory of Problems

In the initiation of a management-innovation program, it is not necessary to commit specified amounts of funds. The first stage of an innovation effort is to create an inventory of problems. Only a small amount of time is required to prepare a list of serious management problems. Our experience has been that we can prepare a list of serious management problems just by spending a small number of days in interviews with managers and staff professionals.

Aha! the reader may exclaim. You are experienced in finding problems. What about me? The answer to this question is that many of the problems experienced in management are widely recognized. A company president, an outside or inside consultant, the manager in a division—almost anyone in management or staff—can be assigned the responsibility for preparing a list of management problems.

Who is interviewed and how the interviews are structured (top down or bottom up) will vary from one company to another. Some effort to think about the development of a list of management problems is useful.

If there is any doubt about the ease of preparing a list of serious management problems, the reader is urged to prepare a list for his or her own organization. A management problem is defined as a condition which, if corrected, can result in a higher level of performance. Typical of the management problems on which we have worked are:

- R&D division of a company not linked to marketing and production
- Quotas set for a sales force without reference to potential in a market area
- High turnover rate of sales representatives with loss of knowledge about buyers
- Excessive inventories
- Market research poorly done and performed manually at great expense
- Financial records of a company out of control
- Poor track record of acquisitions

Note that the list of management problems is just a list of briefly described problems. At this stage of the management-innovation effort, it is not necessary to do an extensive analysis of a problem. Most of the problems will be so visible (and recognized by management—frequently for several years), that a brief description of the problem will be sufficient to communicate why the problem was put on the list.

In this portfolio-building stage of the search effort, the manager should not be concerned with evaluating these areas for net value of improvement or even feasibility. The idea in brainstorming is to come up with as large a list as possible. To spur creativity, those responsible for the preparing of the inventory of problems should view the operations from as many perspectives as possible. How do things look from the marketing angle, from the financial side, from the viewpoint of production or research? What is top management saying? What are the employees saying?

We have found it useful to bring together several people involved in a given problem area. For example, we find that when the users of a given data processing system meet with the data processing professional responsible for the system, the exchange of opinions is very useful in the effort to define the problem. The users may be causing many of the problems that they, the users, are experiencing. When production and sales personnel are brought together, stock-outs, quality-control, and delivery-time problems are perceived in a very different way than appears when one interviews the production and sales personnel separately.

A focus on irrationalities and inconsistencies in management is one way to find problems. Questions bring out the areas needing innovative problem solving. For what intended use are the long reports filled out by the sales force? When sales quotas are set, how are they determined? How are standard costs calculated, and what is their effect on pricing? Activity needing change becomes evident when an effort is made to understand the way managerial work is done. Automatic acceptance of what has gone on before is no way to manage; this attitude of complacency and custom must be eliminated. An inventory of serious management problems is simple to compile once complacency as a major force shaping management activity is rejected.

Stage IV: Compiling an Inventory of Resources

Simultaneously with taking an inventory of problems for the management-improvement program, an inventory of personnel and other resources to solve problems should be compiled. The inventory of problems and the inventory of resources should each suggest additions to the other. For example, in one large manufacturing company, the users of data processing in finance, marketing, and production reported that data processing required weeks and months to make even the most trivial (in the eyes of the users) modifications to computer programs. We examined this problem when taking an inventory of management-innovation resources and discovered that the data processing division was using patched programs (that is, programs that had been changed again and again over a number of years) and, in addition, had not developed a good data base management system. It became clear to us that solutions to the problems experienced by data processing users would require a big investment in time and money. In another company in which users were dissatisfied with data processing, there was much greater technical strength in DP and a rapid rate of progress was possible because the problem was one of user/DP interface—and such problems are often easier and less expensive to correct than are technical problems.

Stage V: Planning the Improvement Program

The staff assigned in stage II can now begin work on a work plan for the management innovation program to follow. The inventories of problems and resources are an appendix to the plan, and of course shape the overall nature of the work to be achieved, depending on the nature of the problems and the resources.

The plan should also reflect how performance is to be measured in the operating unit where performance is to be improved. The plan should include priorities, the procedures for selecting management innovation projects, and the procedures for monitoring progress and implementing the innovations.

Stage VI: Forming the Project Selection and Evaluation Committee

There will always be more management problems than resources for improving unsatisfactory conditions. The project selection and evaluation committee has the important task of rationing scarce resources. This committee is responsible for overseeing performance on the management-innovation projects. The transfer into practice of the recommendations of a management-innovation project team can be made easier if the project selection and evaluation committee has access to senior management (of the company, division, or department in which innovations are to be implemented). This access to senior management can best be achieved through actual membership of one or more senior executives on the committee.

We recommend that a number of project selection and evaluation committees be created in a company in order to involve management in the operating divisions with the process of innovation. When there are centralized resources (such as data processing or organizational development staffs) which must be allocated across a number of operating divisions it then becomes useful to have a corporate-level committee to assign resources to the divisions. As a general rule, membership on the project selection and evaluation committee should include senior management in the operating divisions to be affected by innovations plus functional management if the research-based staffs are involved in the innovation effort (for example, data processing, accounting).

Stage VII: Selecting the First Projects

After the project selection and evaluation committee has been formed, it is ready to begin the work of the program by selecting the first situation to be improved by the initiation of a management-innovation project.

The list of problems and opportunities to improve the effectiveness of management will usually result in more high-return management-innovation projects than there are resources available for project staffing. For this reason we like to think of a management-innovation project as a matching of both a problem (or opportunity for improvement) and the resources necessary to confront the problem and solve it. This matching process is diagramed in Figure 10.2. Keep in mind that once resources are committed to one project, they are unavailable for use on another.

More or less staff time can be applied to creating a portfolio of management-innovation projects, depending on the amount of committee staff

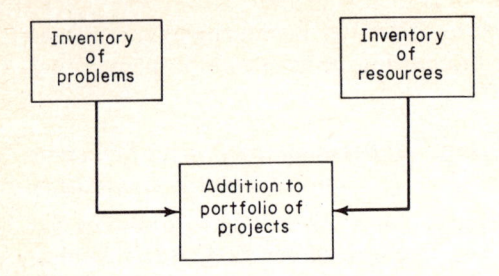

FIG. 10.2 *A management-innovation project combines a problem and the resources to solve it.*

time available. Each project proposal in the portfolio need be defined no further than a few pages of written description, because the problem-solving team assigned to the project should have the task of specifying the project in more detail. After a portfolio of proposals has been assembled, the project selection and evaluation committee should select from it a first management-innovation project. The choice of the first project is crucially important to later progress. It should be a fast-payback, low-risk venture, so that success is as close to certain as possible. If possible, the project should be one with which the selected problem-solving team is familiar, but which for some reason management has just not gotten around to. These types of projects were selected in the innovation effort described in "Step-by-Step Management Innovation,"[6] an article in which one of the authors described the increases in management effectiveness achieved in a client company. From that company the projects selected by the director of systems and planning had the following characteristics:

- Low risks
- Low technical complexity
- Tight funding
- Fast payback
- Acceptance by line executives

The selection of the first project is not a simple task for several reasons. First, there is the sheer size of the list from which the first project is to be selected. Second, there are the different measures to be used in the selection process. There is a temptation to select the most important project even if this project involves greater costs, risks, and time than a project with a smaller payback.

Bear in mind that projects with the goal of increasing the effectiveness of management can themselves get out of control. It is not wise to start too many projects at the same time during the first year of a management-innovation program. We recommend a concentration on projects which have clear, visible returns and which would be relatively easy to complete once the resources were applied. Every project is a matching of resources and returns, along with an associated risk. In the first year of a management innovation program, it is reasonable and correct to select projects that require only limited resources. In other words, the risk in this first set of possible management investments should be low.

Stage VIII: Managing the First Projects

Consider the management involvement that went into the introduction of the Vega by the Chevrolet Division of General Motors. A week of overrun, or a 2 percent cost difference, and management would have moved in fast on the situation. When a new product is being made ready for production and marketing, there is a mission, there is a set of expectations as to quantity and quality of work, and there is evaluation of performance against expectations. In contrast, consider how passive management has been in utilization of research-based professionals toward the goal of improved management.

At the very least, there should be an effort by responsible executives to estimate costs and benefits of management innovation ahead of time. If corporate officers feel that it is necessary to calculate return on investment from new plant and equipment, is it not reasonable to ask for similar analysis before initiating management innovation? This follows from the old principle of knowing objectives before proceeding. If a comparison of costs and benefits from an investment is not calculated, it is much less probable that a correct decision on a potential investment will be made. Skilled people—the major resource in management innovation—are an investment, and their utilization deserves a high level of sophisticated management. The goals and accomplishments of a problem-solving team must be expressed in quantitative terms wherever possible—in particular, in contributions to the quantitative performance of the division.

Although a team of research-based staff personnel should be managed with deadlines and a budget, the division manager cannot stay at arm's length if he or she expects the effort to succeed. We have stressed involvement of the manager, who must take a personal interest in the team efforts. The manager and the team leader must ensure that the team's resources are not being spread too thinly over excessively ambitious efforts.

It is also important to let project visibility stem from successful results, rather than from fanfare which precedes substantive work. Management innovation as a philosophy can eventually prevail throughout a division, but first a process that works must be observed.

What we are talking about in this chapter is the strategic process of managing management innovation—a different process from the actual tactical steps of research-based staff personnel in changing the work of line managers. Let us summarize what we have learned about managing management innovation.

The strategy requires:

1. Making time for innovation
2. Finding commitment to change among line managers
3. Involving line managers in the management of innovation
4. Developing a pool of competent staff
5. Requiring staff of different disciplines to work together
6. Building inventories of problems and resources
7. Knowing which projects to pick first
8. Monitoring performance in various projects

A strategy for managing management innovation is often overlooked. A strategy for innovation contrasts sharply with randomly hiring various types of management scientists and turning them loose on problems of their own choosing. The strategic process of managing management innovation recognizes that the integration of specialized staff resources is required if management is to achieve a return on the investment in maintaining such a staff.

Although this chapter was written to be read from the corporate division manager's point of view, the steps of systematic management innovation can be initiated by anyone in a position of responsibility in line or staff. Every executive or professional has problems in his or her area of responsibility, and a businesslike approach—that is, marshaling resources to meet problems and opportunities—is like motherhood and apple pie to the boss. If economic results are posed as the initial objective of innovation, rather than advancement of knowledge, or professional development, or utilization of the latest ideas, then resistance to change from those who are responsible for performance will be made less serious.

The next chapter will describe in greater detail the management of management-innovation projects.

NOTES AND REFERENCES

1. Mintzberg, Henry: *The Nature of Managerial Work,* New York: Harper & Row, 1973.
2. Adapted from Peter F. Drucker, *The Effective Executive,* New York: Harper & Row, 1967.
3. Kolb, D. A., S. K. Winter, and D. E. Berlew: "Self-directed Change: Two Studies," *Applied Behavioral Science,* vol. 4., no. 4., 1958, pp. 453–471.
4. Sayles, Leonard: *Managerial Behavior: Administration in Complex Organization,* New York: McGraw-Hill, 1964, pp. 91–92.
5. Pounds, W. F.: "The Process of Problem Finding," *Industrial Management Review,* Fall 1969, pp. 1–19.
6. Gruber, W. H.: "Step-by-Step Management Innovation," *Management Adviser,* March-April 1972, pp. 21–27.

ELEVEN

Management of a Management-Innovation Project

We are now ready to move from the development of the strategy for an effort to improve performance through a management-innovation *program* to the actual implementation of a management-innovation *project*. Some important progress toward increasing performance has been achieved when a manager has moved along the innovation cycle to the stage of thinking about the management of a management-innovation project. In order to understand the significance of this progress, we urge the reader to think about other efforts to increase the performance of management. What is the reader's opinion of these other efforts to improve the effectiveness of management? Most readers will report that they have seen relatively few, if any, formal, well-organized efforts to increase the effectiveness of management—with the exception of the introduction of new management information systems.

The basic concept is that a management-innovation project can be managed in the same way that an R&D-for-a-new-product project is managed. In Chapter 10, we described the stages in the management-innovation cycle and noted that the initiation of a management-innovation program is similar to the funding of a program in R&D for new products. We are now ready to consider stage VIII (see Figure 10.1) in a management-innovation program, the management of projects.

The very high historical failure rate of efforts to innovate in management practice has been caused by poor management of improvement activity. For this reason, we will describe in some detail the effective management of a management-innovation project.

There should be milestones, cost estimates, and a management reporting system to monitor results. If well-managed, a given management-innovation project will usually involve the following stages:[1]

1. Problem discovery (addition of problem to the portfolio)
2. Project selection
3. Project specification and justification
4. Diagnosis and solution specification
5. Implementation of new-management practices
6. Project documentation
7. Evaluation of project
8. Termination of project and monitoring of new activity

A management-innovation project can fail or be only partially successful because of poor management of *even one* of the above stages. This may explain why it is that there is such a high failure rate for management-innovation efforts.

The degree of formality in the management of a management-innovation project will vary according to the level in the organization, the size of the organization, and the magnitude of the problem to be improved through the implementation of a management innovation. Our description of the management of a management-innovation project can be adapted to a particular organizational level, size of organization, and seriousness of problem.

FLOWCHART OF A PROJECT CYCLE

In Figure 11.1 we have diagramed the stages of a project cycle from problem discovery to project implementation and the monitoring of a management innovation.

As an example of how the management-innovation cycle can be factored into these stages of effort, with the work in each stage based on the progress made in the previous stages, consider the interrelated problem set of unit manufacturing cost, production run size, and inventory carrying costs experienced in one company. This set of decisions has become a very serious problem because of shortages in raw materials, the high cost of interest, and the fall in corporate liquidity. As a result of these pressures in this company, senior corporate management recognized the inadequacies of old ways of making the decisions which affect unit costs, production run size, and inventory levels.

Management of a Management-Innovation Project / 165

FIG. 11.1 *The management-innovation-project cycle.*

```
Actual practice  ──►  1. Problem discovery:
Preferred condition ─►    addition of problem
                          to the inventory
                              │
                              ▼
                       2. Project selection
                              │
                              ▼
                       3. Project specification
                          and justification
                              │
                              ▼
                       4. Diagnosis and
                          solution specification
                              │
                              ▼
                       5. Implementation
                          of solution
                              │
                              ▼
                       6. Documentation of
                          project
                              │
                              ▼
                       7. Evaluation
                              │
                              ▼
                       8. Project termination and
                          monitoring of results
```

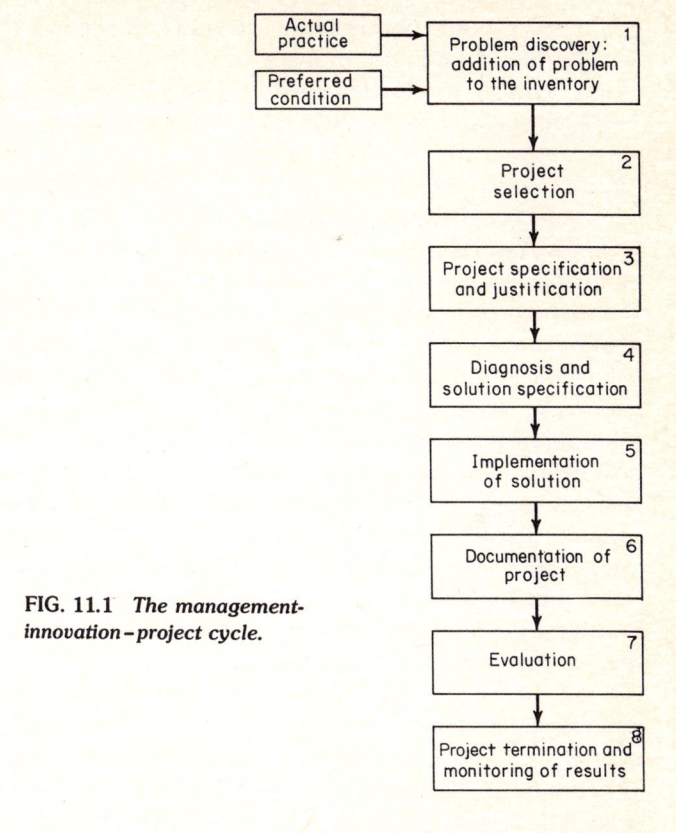

Stage 1: Problem Discovery

This stage occurs when management questions the current procedures for making these decisions and learns that previous experience as a basis for the making of these decisions is no longer a viable option. An addition is made to the list of proposals to be evaluated in the management-innovation project-selection stage.

When we say a problem is discovered at this stage, we want to emphasize that the "problem" is by no means necessarily clearly understood. Rather, the addition of an unsatisfactory condition to the inventory of problems indicates that further attention of management appears to be warranted. A given "problem" will frequently be factored into many management-innovation projects. For example, the problem of unit manufacturing cost, production run size, and inventory carrying costs involved the following management-innovation projects:

1. Sales-forecasting system
2. Production-scheduling system linked to sales-forecasting system

3. Sales force bonus system to move goods in excessive inventory
4. Reduction in the number of styles
5. Longer production runs on jobs with high setup costs
6. Improved cost standards and cost controls

Stage 2: Project Selection

This stage occurs when the problem of unit cost, production run size, and inventory level is accepted as a project and staff resources and responsibility for project management are determined. There may be several stages within the project-selection stage. Management may request further information about a given problem area, and a miniproject may be started to determine the scope of the problem and the cost/benefits from several alternative ways of solving the problem. There are different levels of solution. In the set of decisions involving unit cost and inventory level, it is possible to go in and get some quick and dirty answers in order to solve a crisis. A more complete solution might involve such tasks as a study of variable manufacturing costs and the development of a management information system for the integration of sales forecasts and production scheduling and for monitoring the unit-cost and inventory-cost interrelationships as the production run and the cost of carrying inventories fluctuate from month to month.

Stage 3: Project Specification and Justification

This can be a separate stage in the management-innovation cycle or it can be included in the project-selection stage, as noted above. By this stage in the cycle, the first member(s) of the project team are assigned, and the process of establishing working relationships between line and staff can begin. In the development of a financial planning system, the corporate controller and a senior systems professional served as the start of the project team. In a project to reduce manufacturing costs, the vice president of manufacturing and an outside consultant began the project. The project team was joined by a plant accountant, a systems analyst, an R&D manager, and several product-line managers. From the diversity of people on a management-innovation–project team, it follows that an effort should be made to ensure that line management and the research-based staff professionals have a similar understanding of the nature of the problem, the objectives of the project, and how the workload is to be divided. It is useful during a project specification and justification meeting to review the items on the following checklist of issues to be understood by the line management and research-based professionals on the project team.

1. Goals of the project; the expected financial return
2. Problem definition
3. Relationship of the problem to the overall divisional activity
4. Resources available from the line manager
5. Resources available from the research-based staff professionals
6. Broad approach to the problem and major milestones
7. Nature of the relationship between higher line management and the problem-solving team
8. Benefits for the line managers
9. Benefits for the staff
10. Ability of new-management staff to influence line management and vice versa.

On the example of the size of the production run, it may be necessary to make some major decisions either during this stage or even at the project-selection stage of the cycle. For example, how good are the cost data on which to calculate the relationship between production run size and unit cost? What will be the carrying cost of inventory? Do we have the specialized staff required to work on a problem of this complexity? Should we work on this project for a small number of products in order to determine the probable benefits from a full-scale study of all manufacturing?

This checklist of questions, which should be answered at an *early stage* of a management-innovation project, is of critical importance. It is so easy for line executives and research-based staff professionals to get close to the end of a project without a shared understanding of the major objectives of the project. The bringing together of line and staff on new projects can be an unproductive effort unless communications about the major questions listed above have been programed into the management of the project.

A few of the many failures we have seen in management-innovation projects are:

- A data-processing problem was bigger than line management wanted to solve, but the research-based systems staff began work on a project of very large scope. As soon as the total costs of the systems effort became known, the project was canceled.

- In a problem involving bad debts and excessive accounts receivable, the sales department would not cooperate on the project because of a fear that changes would affect the volume of sales. The company president was needed to bring together the vice presidents of sales and finance, but he was unavailable. Improvement of this problem situation was not achieved, despite the fact that the financial viability of the company was jeopardized by the seriousness of debts and by overdue and excessive receivables.

- The price of a new product was set too high because of some serious errors made by the management scientists who prepared the market model on which the pricing decision was made. In this case, a young, inexperienced management scientist was asked to solve a problem with inadequate direction from the marketing staff.

Stage 4: Diagnosis and Solution Specification

This is the stage in which solutions are recommended, selected, and scheduled for action. In the production-run problem, this is the stage in which the unit costs, inventory costs, sales forecasting, and production scheduling are interrelated into a set of new procedures. The management information system required to control production scheduling, inventory, and sales fulfillment would be specified in this stage of the project.

The New Management, with its advocates of sophisticated management technology who are sometimes in the position of looking for an application of what they know rather than a solution to a management problem, has led to confusion about the basics of diagnosis and solution development. Management consultant Leo Moore grasped the basics many years ago when he wrote: "The central theme of the improvement procedure is a methodology which is a systematic, common-sense and direct approach to action in the true management sense."[2] He identified five major steps that will exist in the improvement process whether computers or behavioral sciences are involved:

1. Understanding the situation
2. Specifying the problem
3. Accumulating possible solutions
4. Selecting the best solution
5. Devising a plan of action

Steps 1 and 2 are what we mean by diagnosis and steps 3 to 5 constitute solution specification.

Understanding the situation is a step where descriptive facts and data are gathered in a way that does not prejudice managerial thinking on the limits of the problem. As Moore points out, "It is typical for managers to think in terms of the problems that they have, as contrasted to the whole situation that they manage. It is important to the improvement procedure that we orient ourselves toward the situation in order to avoid making a flash decision as to what the problem is. Such flash decisions will push us into finding answers to problems which are not the key to the situation."[3] This is obviously true, but in the heat of a business crisis in a tumbling economy, management problem-solving teams are under severe pressure to move out fast on the problem at hand, even before the situation is understood. One reason that problems are often so clear to a particular manager is that he or she may have a *solution* in mind. In other words, there is a tendency for one to work backward from top-of-the-head, impressionistic solutions to problems. In a new-management professional with a full bag of analytical techniques, this working backward is particularly dangerous.

Adequately specifying the problems in a situation goes a long way toward solving the problem and making the situation better. For example, a consumer products manager with a failing product line may look at the marketing strength of Procter & Gamble and decide what he or she needs is more advertising, more promotion, and a more effective sales force. Yet it is apparent that Procter & Gamble took a hard look at the entire consumer products situation a long time ago, and decided that developing demonstrably superior products was the first problem to solve. In reporting on P&G's secret ingredient, *Fortune* notes:

> Before Chairman Edward Harness will allow a new product to be put on the market, he insists that its superiority (meaning consumer preference for it) be demonstrated by actual tests. "Some people suggest that product differences in our field are minimal or infinitesimal," he says. "I can't agree. When you find a significant body of women who believe the characteristics of what they want are found in a product—this is the essence of consumerism, giving them what they want."[4]

The facts relating to a problem are a subset of the facts describing the situation, but they are a manageable subset, and the *correct* subset to the extent possible. Problems should, of course, be laid out for solution in an order determined by priorities.

The possible solutions are now ready to emerge in a creative, brainstorming process of managers and staff professionals putting their minds to work. As many solutions as possible should be allowed to come out on the table. Evaluation and choosing of solutions is inappropriate here if the full range of possibilities is to emerge. The tough management decision here is how much time to allocate to the generation of alternatives. Some solutions may crosscut other possibilites, especially when varied specialists are contributing to the list of possibilities. The input of line managers and other specialists in the synthesis of management technology is of value here; solutions can be clustered into packages of "real" alternatives, wherein are contained similar or compatible solutions that can be worked into a plan of action later.

Selecting the best solution is the decision-making step to be made by the person with the responsibility for solving the problem. As Drucker has pointed out often, most recently in the November 1974 *Fortune*, a decision maker—from the President of the United States on down—should not insist on consensus of staff advisers, of the varied professionals who make up the management team: "The chief executive who insists on 'consensus' deprives himself of understanding. He becomes a poll taker and conciliator rather than a decision-maker. In effect, he abdicates."[5]

Finally, a plan of action needs to be devised to implement the chosen solution. Once again, the situation where the problem arose needs to be brought sharply into focus. The management team should once again be brought together to lay out a schedule of concrete tasks to be done with a specified amount of personnel and financial resources by a scheduled milestone date. These aspects define the scope of the management-improvement project.

It is frequently possible to implement some facets of the management innovation before the total project is completed, and partial implementation should be encouraged. It may take a number of months to develop the computer-based management information systems for controlling the interrelationships of production run size, inventory, and sales. It may be possible to implement some decision rules and achieve savings in unit costs and/or inventory savings within a short time of completing the diagnosis that resulted in the decision rules.

And complexity must be faced. Changes in the size of production runs will have many effects. New standards for manufacturing costs will have to be determined. Workers on piece rate will be affected. Warehouse space requirements are likely to either increase or decrease. It is critical to evaluate the effects of all the possible consequences of the changes recommended in this project.

Stage 5: Implementation

The best strategy for change as developed in the plan is then implemented. If the phases completed before the action phase have been properly carried out, actions should proceed according to plan without significant hitches. As Kolb and Frohman have explained:

> The failure of most plans lies in the *unanticipated consequences* of the change effort. In industry these failures often take the form of technical changes (e.g., a new information system) which fail to anticipate and plan for the social changes which they cause (e.g., increases and decreases in power at various levels of the organization). The result is that managers and administrators become annoyed at the stupidity of those subordinates who resent the very "logical" improvement. Yet, the subordinates often are not resisting the logic of the improvement (hence logical arguments do not help) but are resisting the social changes which management has not recognized or anticipated. When it occurs, this resistance is often treated as an irrational, negative force to be overcome by whatever means are available. In some cases, however, resistance to change can be functional for the survival of the system by

insuring that plans for change and their ultimate consequences are thought through carefully.[6]

In other words, a plan, to be effective and implementable, must take into account all pertinent factors. When the implementation of a management innovation is not going well, brute-force orders by higher-level authority are not the answer. Resistance to change, which is *not* a unified, fixed characteristic of people, must be factored down to its specific causes in the particular situation at hand, and each cause faced squarely as a separate issue to be written into the plan for behavior change. This is the critical stage in which the practice of management is improved. A "solution" which is not implemented is really not a solution. A solution may not be implemented for several reasons. The procedures required to implement may be too difficult. Users may be unwilling to cooperate. The solution may prove to be not cost-effective when all the information is in.

One peculiar reason for the failure of a management-innovation effort is the apparent unwillingness of management to commit the resources required to complete the last stages of a project. In one systems development group, this failure of management caused a serious morale problem. The systems staff would bring a project to the point where the first computer output was provided for users. This was sufficient evidence for management that the systems development project was completed. In fact, a new computer system is far from complete when reports are first produced—a difficult reality for line management to accept. In our client report for this company, we called this a "Catch-22" problem. The systems group faced the dilemma of either revealing no progress or else revealing so much that they had to start new projects and leave old ones incomplete.

What happens at the implementation stage determines the return on the investment in this management-innovation effort. Better decisions which save millions of dollars each year in production costs and inventory costs can be achieved. In other management-innovation efforts, quality control can be improved with an important saving in warranty and return costs, turnover of personnel can be reduced, market share can be increased, new products more attuned to the needs of users can be developed, and the data processing ratio of output to costs can be improved. These examples of what can be achieved in the implementation stage of a management-innovation project all have one basic element in common: the contribution to corporate performance depends on the effectiveness of the implementation effort. A grade A solution implemented with a grade C effort is likely to produce less than a project with a grade C solution and a grade A implementation. There is a tendency to focus on the solution and forget the implementation stage of a management-innovation project.

Stage 6: Documentation

A management-innovation project represents an investment to improve the effectiveness of management. When the project was funded, expectations were established: a serious management problem was to be made less serious as a result of the progress achieved in a management-innovation project. Documentation of the total cycle of management innovation should be standard practice for the following reasons:

1. Traces are left of the decisions made. A follow-on effort will be facilitated by the record of what was accomplished. Questions about the changes created can be answered by reference to the documentation, which can be especially important when key personnel leave the company.

2. There is a visibility for what has been accomplished. An important by-product of a successful management-innovation project is a greater willingness of management to be creative about the solution of problems. We have seen companies in which serious problems continued for years. This acceptance of bad conditions is fostered by an attitude of resignation; yet bad conditions are not inevitable. A successful management-innovation project can make a big improvement in a very short time. The results of this project will lead to a more determined effort to solve other problems. Documentation in the form of a report distributed to management or a seminar by the project leader increases the visibility of what was accomplished.

Stage 7: Evaluation

The line manager responsible for the problem area should evaluate the effect of the problem-solving team's work; this implies that the team should help the manager develop the data and procedures for evaluation. As this phase proceeds, the team and the manager can decide whether further innovative work in the area is warranted. A management-innovation project should be evaluated with a formal set of procedures. How useful were the project specifications? How effective was the solution? Was the potential in the solution realized in the implementation stage? How much resistance was experienced in the implementation effort? Are follow-on and educational efforts necessary?

We encourage our clients to maintain a management-innovation–project notebook. This management technique is one of several that we have adapted from procedures which are commonly used in R&D management. The project notebook has sections on the project objectives, budget, and actual performance against objectives. The performance evaluation of a management-innovation project is based on the following factors:

1. What was expected (i.e., the objectives set for the project compared with what was accomplished)

2. Actual versus budgeted costs in time and money
3. Performance by stage in the management-innovation cycle
4. Satisfaction of management and other employees who are affected by the management innovation

The actual evaluation format will vary by class of project. Management-innovation projects which involve data processing should be evaluated somewhat differently than an effort to increase the efficiency of the sales force. That a formal evaluation procedure is an accepted stage of a management-innovation project is the important idea to be considered.

Stage 8: Termination of Project and Monitoring of New Activity

The relationship between the new-management staffers and the line manager responsible for the problem area is temporary. The length of the relationship, in fact, should be budgeted ahead of time. Once the mission of the team is complete, their relationship with the line managers should be limited to the point where the line managers can feel that the situation under their control is completely theirs once again. However, the new patterns of activity resulting from the project should be monitored to see if further work is warranted.

The effectiveness of management may continue to improve as a result of a management-innovation project long after that project has been formally completed. Some management-innovation projects lead to new projects because enhancements to a new system or procedure can continue to be made. Management is rarely stagnant, and the development of the capability to upgrade on a continuing basis the management of a given activity is to be encouraged.

As an example of the continuing nature of a management-innovation program, consider the system that was developed for allocating sales personnel to customers. A project was initiated with the objective of specifying the number of sales calls per year for each customer as determined by the evaluation of the potential for each customer. The first finding from this effort was that some low-potential customers were seen as frequently as twice a month and some high-potential customers were seen as little as five or six times a year. A large increase in sales was achieved by a reallocation of sales calls from low- to high-potential customers. A second finding from this analysis was that the sales force was relatively uninformed about the customers. This lack of information was caused by the rapid turnover in the sales force and the failure of marketing to provide the sales force with customer information. This management-innovation project will continue for a number of years. A customer information system is being developed which will provide for the storage and reporting of marketing information by customer. The effectiveness of the sales force should continue to increase over a period of years as the customer information system improves in usefulness, as sales training is linked to the customer information system, and as sales quotas and bonuses reflect more accurately the potential of each customer.

SUMMARY

There has been a very rapid increase during the last five years in the utilization of new-management professionals in such specialized activities as the development of computer-based management information systems and organizational development. Our procedures for the implementation of a program of management innovation are a synthesis of what is good practice in management systems development efforts, organizational development programs, and R&D for new products and processes.

The steps in a particular management-innovation project may be fairly summarized as follows:

Problem discovery:
- To add to the portfolio of problems

Project selection:
- To match the problem with the resources for a project

Project specification and justification to spell out:
- Goals
- Definition of the situation
- Relationship of situation to overall picture
- Resources available from line management and from research-based staff for the project team
- Broad approach to the situation, with milestones
- Relationship between line and staff
- Benefits for line and for staff
- Staff and line influence on each other

Diagnosis, whereby the project team:
- Understands the situation
- Specifies the real problem

Solution specification, whereby the project team:
- Accumulates possible solutions
- Selects best solution
- Devises a plan of action

Implementation of the plan in action
Documentation of project and results
Evaluation of project
Termination of project and monitoring of new activity

The research-based staff skills and line management with knowledge of research-based techniques now exist in many large companies. The implementation of programs of management innovation that are producing an important contribution to corporate growth in profits and sales is occurring today in a small number of companies. Companies that can manage a good R&D program or an efficient data processing operation can use this experience to build a program of management innovation which makes an important contribution to increased sales and profits. There is nothing particularly difficult to implement in the strategy for management innovation which has been described in this chapter. We have observed the successful implementation of many of these recommendations in a number of companies. The plan for implementing a management-innovation program should be tailored to fit the unique needs in each division and functional area of each company.

It is difficult to believe that just twenty years ago R&D for new products was not a serious activity in the majority of all large companies. And so it is with management-innovation efforts. Ten years from now it will be possible to reflect back on the decade ending in 1975, a decade in which the first real accomplishments in the development of management-innovation programs began to show returns in improved corporate performance.

As a test of the usefulness of our strategy for a management-innovation program, the reader is invited to evaluate the process in which effectiveness of management is improved in his or her company. The first step in this evaluation should be a list of management problems which have continued to exist over a period of several years. What inefficiencies are present which could be made less serious by a management-innovation effort? Why have these inefficiencies continued to hurt performance for months and years? Is there a formal procedure for improving these conditions? Is there adequate staff support for assisting the effort to correct management problems? Are several kinds of staff specialists coordinated in an effort to improve a management problem? For example, do you find an organization development specialist working with a systems analyst in the development of a new management information system? Is there a portfolio of problems available for evaluating the relative payback on the investments required to improve the different kinds of problem conditions which exist? Is the process of improvement in the practice of management controlled with a competence equal to that which occurs in the management of R&D for new products? We could go on with this list. Any executive able to give an affirmative answer to most of these questions is seeing incipient Future Firm management capability. Our experience has been that executives in the majority of all companies will give a negative answer to the majority of these questions. The process of improving the practice of management is well conceived and well managed today in only a few companies. How to improve the unsatisfactory status of the capability to innovate in management has been described in this chapter. Our experience indicates that the implementation of a management-improvement program provides high return on investment. It is from this experience that we forecast the coming of the New Management.

NOTES AND REFERENCES

1. Kolb, David A., and Alan L. Frohman: "An Organizational Development Approach to Consulting," *Sloan Management Review,* Fall 1970, pp. 51–65, develop a similar list of stages.
2. Moore, Leo B.: "How to Manage Improvement," *Harvard Business Review,* July–August 1958, pp. 82–83.
3. Ibid., p. 83.
4. Vanderwicken, Peter: "P&G's Secret Ingredient," *Fortune,* July 1974, p. 75.
5. Drucker, Peter F.: "How to Make the Presidency Manageable," *Fortune,* November 1974, p. 149.
6. Kolb and Frohman, op. cit., pp. 60–61.

TWELVE

Task-Force Management

How revolutionary is our proposal that management-innovation programs be funded in industry with procedures that are very similar to those utilized in the management of R&D for new products and processes? What evidence is there that the management-innovation program procedures, described in Chapters 10 and 11, actually work?

There are several ways of answering these questions. During the last twenty years when company-financed R&D for new products and processes increased from $2.2 billion to $13.0 billion, procedures similar to those that we have recommended for a management-innovation program were implemented for the management of R&D in many companies with effective R&D programs. The growth in the value of installed computer hardware increased from $150 million to $25 billion during the last twenty years, and procedures similar to those that we recommended in Chapters 10 and 11 have been adopted for the management of computer software development programs in many companies in which a high level of computer utilization has been achieved. We stress that these procedures have been adopted in companies with *effective* R&D management and computer utilization programs. There is, of course, a very wide range in the quality of management of R&D and data processing for the reasons that we have analyzed in this book. (Note the findings of differences in R&D and computer utilization performance that were described in Chapter 8.)

The speed with which new products and new computer software programs are developed and utilized is strong evidence that project-based management techniques can be effective in achieving a revolutionary rate of progress in some facets of corporate activity. It is easy to accept the speed with which new products and new computer software programs are developed without giving credit to the management techniques which have made possible this rate of progress. Management problems of trivial complexity relative to technical issues in R&D or computers remain unsolved because the same project-based techniques are not widely used.

There is another source of evidence that a management-innovation program can make an important contribution to improvements in the effectiveness of management. This evidence is company experience in the utilization of task forces. When a serious problem or an important opportunity must be managed, senior executives will frequently create a task force with responsibility for the management of this problem or opportunity. These task forces bring together research-based staff professionals and experience-based line executives in a team effort to achieve an objective. As we will illustrate with a number of examples, a well-managed task force is very effective for solving serious management problems.

Why, then, has the utilization of task forces not been developed into the kind of management-innovation program that we described in Chapters 10 and 11? We have asked several company presidents this question, and the answer appears to be that the need to develop a capability for innovation in management that is funded and managed like R&D for new products is an idea that just has not been considered. It is useful to recall that when company-financed R&D funds were only $2.2 billion in 1953, there were many large companies that did not have serious programs of R&D for new products. Before the decentralization movement in the 1950s, most companies were centralized in management. And so on. Accepted management practice evolves over time. In this chapter, we will demonstrate that there is ample evidence that management-innovation projects going by the name "task forces" are effectively improving management performance in a number of companies.

BACKGROUND FOR THIS CHAPTER

In 1974, Dr. Gruber was asked by the Presidents Association of the American Management Association to do a study of how company presidents utilize specialists.[1] The research methodology for this study was interviews with company presidents. The theme of the interviews followed some of the ideas in this book. Specialists have become more important—how do you (the company president) utilize them?

An effort was made to select presidents from different industries and different-sized companies. In manufacturing, the participants in this study were Gerald D. Laubach, president of Pfizer, Inc., Sheldon G. Gilgore, president of Pfizer Pharmaceuticals, Robert A. Charpie, president of Cabot Corporation, and John A. Fox, president of H. P. Hood. In banking and financial services, they were William H. Dougherty, Jr., president of NCNB Corporation and George B. Rockwell, president of State Street Financial Corporation. J. R. Fowler, president of Jacobson's, and C. Peterson, president of SofTech, Inc., provided information about their experiences in retailing and software systems, respectively.

Despite the breadth of experience represented by presidents who participated in this study, there was a remarkable consistency with which they reported that the establishment of task forces was the management procedure utilized after a decision had been made to solve a serious problem or to move decisively to take advantage of an important opportunity. Company presidents are, by definition, interested only in serious problems and important opportunities. Thus, a presidential task force differs from a management-innovation project as described in Chapters 10 and 11 by the importance given to the work of the task force.

Although we will be reporting on the utilization of task forces by company presidents, the same strategy and procedures can be utilized in the lower levels of an organization. The creation of a task force should imply an effort to improve a serious problem situation or to realize the potential in an important opportunity, since task-force members have jobs in the regular organization structure. Problems and opportunities of enough magnitude to justify a task force exist in many divisions and functions within a company. For example, manufacturing can set up a task force to increase the efficiency of energy utilization. Marketing can set up a task force to develop the techniques for measuring the effectiveness of different kinds of promotion. Sales can set up a task force for the development of procedures for the management of the sales force (for example, determination of potential by customer and territory, setting of quotas and bonuses, and development of a system of customer service). Data processing can set up a task force to evaluate future computer hardware requirements.

In other words, an adaptation of the basic task-force strategy which we will describe in this chapter can be utilized for line and staff activities at almost any level and function in a company.

BASIC TASK-FORCE STRATEGY

A major function of the chief executive officer is to bring together specialists and line executives to solve serious company problems or to implement action in response to important opportunities. Most task forces involve both specialists and line executives selected in an effort to bring together the diverse set of skills and authority which are required to solve a given problem.

The active role of the company president can be seen in the way that John M. Fox, president of H. P. Hood, sees his role in the utilization of task forces.

> Task forces are an important procedure that I utilize to increase the effectiveness of management. I have assigned task forces some very difficult problems, and the results have made an important contribution to company performance.
>
> My role is to write specifications for the task force assignment which include:
> (1) A detailed description of the problem as I see it.
> (2) Specifications for the solutions that I expect the task force to produce.
> (3) A time schedule for when answers are to be produced.
> (4) A reporting routine and a schedule of meetings.
> (5) Identification of the chairman and members.
> In operation, the task force provides the following:
> (1) Analysis and the hard numbers needed for a decision.
> (2) Options—what are our alternatives?
> (3) Recommended actions.
> (4) Implementation plan which the task force will live with until fulfilled.
>
> My selection of the chairman and the members of a task force is a factor that critically affects its performance. The chairman must be strong. The task-force members must include the necessary specialized staff, and line executives who have authority to take the required action.
>
> I expect a task force to continue in operation until the recommendations are implemented. This is one reason why it is necessary that task-force members be taken from the line managements in the areas affected by the recommendations of the task force. When members agree with task-force recommendations, they are also agreeing to take the necessary actions in their own areas of authority.
>
> Actions implemented are compared with the task-force recommended actions. The way to cause change is to monitor performance and keep the task force alive until performance achieved fulfills the reasons that we set up the task force.

John Fox's description of how he utilized task forces to achieve important improvements in performance in H. P. Hood was similar to what was reported by a number of the other company presidents. For example, Robert A. Charpie, president of Cabot Corporation, noted his utilization of task forces:

> The task force is the basic technique we use in this company. We say to people, now, in addition to what you are doing, we want you to work on this problem

for a while. . . . You pick the best guys you have from different parts of the company; . . . you balance the people in terms of discipline in order to get coverage.

CASE STUDIES OF TASK-FORCE MANAGEMENT

It is useful to recall that company presidents reported on their utilization of task forces *when asked questions about the usefulness and management of specialists.* As these case studies indicate, a task force provides a way of creating a team of line executives and specialists. These case studies also provide examples of the usefulness of research-based management.

Robert A. Charpie, President, Cabot Corporation

The following analysis by Dr. Charpie of how he manages specialists provides some particularly valuable insights into the specialist–user relationship. In a response to a statement that the world was changing in ways that only lawyers and accountants could understand, Dr. Charpie observed:

> I don't find the world changing in ways that only lawyers and accountants understand. What lawyers and accountants can tell me stems from their careful and precise professional interpretation of what's going on around us, but the forces which are driving us, the new circumstances that they look into and interpret are perfectly visible to all of us. We understand the background of the problems at least as well as they do, because it's often originally more of a business than a technical problem. For example, consider the complex of regulations in the occupational safety or the environmental quality areas. It seems to me that while the lawyers interpret the regulations, we deal with the circumstances in which those regulations operate. Line management and general management have a much better feel for the problem.
>
> What is the factory environment? The worker on the manufacturing floor—what's around him? What's in the air? How noisy is it? What are his performance problems? How annoyed is he? While we don't have problems with these background issues, we do have problems related to technical compliance. A very high level of technical compliance is required, in part because of the proliferation of agencies and the simultaneous attack on many different facets of the problem. Every aspect of the working environment is under scrutiny.
>
> Compliance involves more than the lawyers and accountants can tell us. It involves the development of new management information systems for analyzing our activities, for setting standards in all the operations affected by a new regulation and for monitoring actual performance in order to compare it with what we have set as our standard of acceptable practice.

> In wage and price controls, we created a task force inside the company that consisted of a lawyer, an accountant, and someone on the personnel staff connected with salary administration. Its assignment was to provide us with a reporting system so that we could tell at the end of every month how we were doing, and a forecast system that would tell us beforehand how we would look at reporting time. They created the reports in dummied up fashion before filing so that we could look at them, understand them, and develop a management understanding of the sensitivity of the reporting controls to certain actions that we might take.
>
> In the case of environmental controls, we have designated an individual whose job it is to be aware of the changes in requirements made by the states and the federal government as they affect us, and to supervise our compliance. For this purpose, we have assigned that individual an R&D group that reports to him, although the staff is part of R&D. Within that R&D group is a full-time specialist who develops measuring techniques and provides in-house consulting to all of our plants and subsidiaries. He is concerned with air quality, water quality, noise levels and all the other environmental control problems covered by local, state, and federal regulations.

Note Dr. Charpie's research-based management response to the government's new regulations. He created task-force teams that included research-based specialists. He and other line executives were very much involved in the work of the task forces. Charpie has recognized the usefulness and the limitations of specialists, and has acted accordingly. A response to new government regulations will involve a series of activities. First, there will be the task-force interpretation of the new regulations as they effect company operations. Second, there is a corporate plan for responding to the new regulations. This plan will frequently include standards for compliance and procedures for communications with the managers and staff professionals whose operations are affected by the new government regulations. Finally, in order to assure compliance, it is frequently useful to specify the management information systems which will monitor progress toward the fulfillment of standards.

Sheldon G. Gilgore, President, Pfizer Pharmaceuticals

The pharmaceuticals industry is in one of the most rapidly changing sectors of the economy. It is one of the most heavily regulated industries and an industry very dependent on new scientific discoveries. When asked about management in such an industry, Dr. Gilgore noted his utilization of task forces:

> The faster the rate of change in our business, the more task forces we set up to study a problem; thus the rapid increase in the size and quality of my

specialized staffs. I have confidence in my intuition, but I can't rely on it. When I perceive a problem and a possible solution or when I just perceive a problem, I set up a task force. Sometimes its detailed and careful analysis proves my intuition to be correct; sometimes it is not.

For example, several of our competitors had begun to adopt a new distribution strategy. I conceived of a plan in which we might also adopt this strategy. I set up a task force to study the matter. It included the chief financial officer, the director of systems, the company lawyer, top sales and marketing executives. After doing their staff work, they reported back to me. The room was filled with the members of the task force, some of their specialized staffs and senior management. When all of the hard numbers were in, it was clear that my intuition about the utilization of a new distribution system was incorrect.

Not suprisingly, I am delighted when I find my intuition proven incorrect by good staff work. I would question the quality of the quantitative evidence developed by specialized staffs if I were always correct.

You might say we make decisions by committee. When a report with recommendations for decisions is submitted by a task force, we meet and senior management asks questions which frequently haven't been considered by the task force. This means another cycle of staff work. When all of the hard data and analysis are in after several meetings, our senior management usually reaches a decision by consensus. Consensus is usually easy to achieve when the right questions have been asked. It is startling how black and white many answers are when the needed data is available to support a decision. Thus an important part of my role is to assure that there is good staff work, which will provide the information and analysis we need to make a sound decision.

Dr. Gilgore was one of several company presidents who reported the usefulness of research on problems to test his ideas. Apparently, the faster the rate of change in the economy, in technology, in business, the more useful it is to assign specialists the responsibility for testing out ideas with hard evidence. A second experience reported by Dr. Gilgore (also experienced by other company presidents) is the consensus that resulted after a thorough task-force study of a given problem area. When all the facts are in, there is less room for disagreement among the executives who meet to make a decision. *A lack of facts appears to encourage the maintenance of strong conflicting opinions.*

TASK FORCES OR A PROGRAM OF INNOVATION IN MANAGEMENT?

There is only a small number of companies with a well-organized program to improve the effectiveness of management. Task forces, such as those described in this chapter, are utilized in a large number of companies. The basic differences between a random series of task forces and a program of innovation in management are (1) the level of commitment to increasing the overall effectiveness of management, (2) the comprehensiveness of the planning that is utilized to select problem areas to be improved, and (3) the management procedures utilized in the effort to improve management performance.

There are some executives who are very skilled in the management of task forces. The company presidents who participated in the American Management Association study described in this chapter were carefully selected on the basis of strong performance records. The task-force management procedures of John Fox, Robert Charpie, and Sheldon Gilgore that were described in this chapter are not found in all companies. These are management procedures that high-performance company presidents have found to be useful. Similar procedures are not necessarily utilized by other managers in these companies. A program of innovation in management should be managed with clearly specified procedures that are similar to the list utilized by John Fox. A program of innovation in management will differ from the utilization of task forces by virtue of the standardization of good management practices in guiding the total management-improvement effort.

A senior executive can often create a task force on the day that the idea is conceived. When we encounter a serious management problem in our consulting, we frequently recommend that a task force be created with responsibility for the management of the effort to secure an improvement in the unsatisfactory condition. Most managers respond to an immediate problem. *Managers rarely want to think of all their problems at one time.*

After an executive has observed the usefulness of a task force in improving the effectiveness of management in one situation, the moment is at hand to initiate a discussion of extending the task-force procedure to create a strategy for improving the many other problem conditions which all executives live with year after year. We often suggest a task force as a prototype management-innovation project. Experience with efforts to improve management performance contributes to the success of a formal program of innovation in management. An executive who has successfully managed a series of task-force efforts will easily learn how to manage a management-innovation program.

USEFULNESS OF RESEARCH-BASED MANAGEMENT

In an earlier chapter, we described some of the problems which have been experienced in the utilization of specialists. Lawyers, accountants, R&D

scientists and engineers, management scientists, and other specialists have caused difficulties for the managements in many companies. The experiences reported in this chapter indicate that when specialists are skillfully managed, the results can be an important contribution to company performance.

We have reported on disasters and good performance. The effective management of specialized resources is clearly possible, as the performance reported in this chapter illustrates. Some of the difficulties reported in earlier chapters about the inadequate integration of specialized units into a problem-solving team can be overcome by the creation of a task force. If a more impressive title than management-innovation project is needed to bring together marketing, R&D, manufacturing, and research-based management professionals in an effort to improve management performance or respond to problems such as new government regulations, then the use of the task-force strategy as described in this chapter should be considered.

The utilization of task forces and management-innovation–project teams provides the temporary organizational unit for increasing the effectiveness of management. A task force or an innovation-project team should be initiated with the same deliberation that is given to the funding of an R&D effort to produce a new product. The higher the stakes, the more care should be taken in the definition of a task force or innovation-project team. Management will frequently find it useful to begin exploratory work on a problem or an opportunity at an innovation-project level of activity and then scale up the effort into a task force if the preliminary stages of the effort indicate that this will be an activity of major importance.

The creation of a task force is one of the techniques that has proved to be useful in the integration of experience-based executives and research-based professionals into an effective problem-solving team. The adaptation of a company or a division to a changing condition is one of the most difficult tasks of management. In this chapter we have demonstrated that the presidents in some companies have discovered how to assign research-based task forces the responsibility for the management of change. As we will observe in the next chapter, there is strong evidence that the disruptions in economic, regulatory, and technological conditions which have been experienced in this past decade can be expected to become more serious in the next decade. Therefore, the utilization of task forces and management-innovation–project teams will be of greater importance during the more difficult years that now must be anticipated. The company experiences reported in this chapter and in earlier sections of this book indicate that research-based management techniques have been an important resource in some companies for coping with the business problems of the 1970s.

NOTES AND REFERENCES

1. For a full report on this study, see William H. Gruber, *The Utilization of Specialists by Company Presidents,* Presidents Association Special Study 200.6, New York: American Management Association, 1975. Parts of this special study are reproduced here with permission from the American Management Association.

THIRTEEN

Environmental Forces in the Development of Future Firm

Executives in many well-managed companies are accelerating their efforts to increase the effectiveness of management during the decade of the 1970s. We have analyzed some of the reasons for this willingness to invest in research-based management. First, there is the greater availability of employees with research-based skills. Second, there has been the extraordinary increase in the effectiveness of research-based techniques as well as improvements in the cost effectiveness of computer hardware and software. Third, there are now available case studies of research-based techniques increasing corporate performance, as we illustrate in Chapters 12 and 14.

Yet, there are many pressures to maintain existing management procedures. Executives are programmed to survive today's crises. Very good reasons for change are frequently not sufficient to overcome forces which slow the rate of implementation of innovations. There is something very comfortable about staying with tried and tested practices. The executives in the majority of large companies will continue to lag in their investment in research-based techniques throughout this decade. We see only a small number of Future Firms by 1980.

How, then, can we predict the rapid improvement in the effectiveness of management in at least some companies by 1980? The answer lies in the more difficult economic and regulatory environment of business of the

1970s. Many of the corporate executives who have been tentatively seeking assistance from research-based management techniques are finding that there is indeed a powerful set of tools now available for coping with the devastating economic and regulatory conditions of the 1970s. Executives in a number of companies are responding to the greater difficulty experienced in managing their companies by making investments in research-based techniques which are now readily available. The 1970s has been a period in which the executives in many companies have begun to recognize the need to turn away from intuitive, experience-based management procedures that are not adequate for coping with a harsher business environment.

LIMITS TO GROWTH

The happy days of the post-World War II economy in the United States that were enjoyed until sometime in 1974 represent a discontinuity with the history of the United States economy in the twentieth century. That is, a comparison of the periods 1900–1940 and 1948–1973 leads to the conclusion that the United States has enjoyed an unusually bountiful economy in the post-World War II period; we do not expect that this superior performance will be maintained through the next decade.

A related factor is the end to the freedom of action which has been enjoyed by United States business. Government regulation and limits on growth are causing a severe decrease in the freedom of American business leaders to make decisions in their self-interest.

Economic and Business Performance

It is easier to produce good business performance when the economy is increasing rapidly in size, when prices and costs are rising slowly, and when productivity (that is, output produced per unit of labor input) is improving rapidly. On all these measures, the economic environment in the United States since 1940 has created an extraordinary stimulus for the growth of business. In Table 13.1 we present the increase in sales since 1940 of the ten companies with the largest sales in 1973. Even with inflation as a source of dollar sales growth, a reading of Table 13.1 indicates the impressive increase in the sales and financial resources of this sample of large United States companies. During this thirty-year period, the gross national product in current dollars (that is, *not* deflated for inflation) increased from $99.7 billion to $976.4 billion, or an increase of less than ten times. In contrast, GM increased in sales by 20 times, GE by 28 times, and IBM by 239 times. Price increases contributed significantly to the growth in GNP. Given that $1 in IBM sales in 1970 purchased far more computer power than $1 for IBM equipment in 1940, the IBM

TABLE 13.1 Sales of the Ten Largest United States Companies in 1973 and 1940 (in Millions of Dollars)

	1973	1940
General Motors	35,798	1,795
Exxon	25,724	934
Ford	23,215	*
Chrysler	11,774	774
General Electric	11,575	412
Texaco	11,407	343
Mobil	11,390	444
IBM	10,993	46
ITT	10,183	†
Gulf	8,417	273

*Ford was not a public company in 1940, and sales figures were not listed in *Moody's* for 1940.

†A large percentage of the growth of ITT has been through acquisitions, and thus the comparison between 1940 and 1973 sales for ITT differs significantly from the experience of the other companies on this list.

SOURCE: *Moody's Industrials,* 1973 and 1940.

growth has not been inflated and represents an extraordinary increase in the contribution of one company to the well-being of the United States.

Business rode a wave of surging economic activity which, in turn, was made possible by dynamic business leadership. Whether business performance will continue at the post-World War II level is another question. We are pessimistic about the continued rate of high macroeconomic performance. In Table 13.2 we compare the rates of growth in real GNP and output per hour worked in the United States between the periods 1900–1940 and 1948–1970. Forecasts of growth to 1985 are included in Table 13.2. The first conclusion that follows from an analysis of Table 13.2 is that the post-World War II economic growth is approximately 30 percent (3.7 ÷ 2.8) above the rate of increase that was experienced in the 1900–1940 period. Real GNP improved faster in the 1948–1970 period primarily because of the extraordinary increase in real output per hour worked in the private sector, which increased at over 3 percent per year in the 1948–1970 period and by only 1.7 percent in the 1900–1940 period.

The standard forecast is for a continuation of post-World War II performance rather than a rate of progress closer to the 1900–1940 experience. The basic question before us is whether the historical performance of the United States economy since 1948 can continue through 1985 as forecasted by the U.S. Bureau of Labor Statistics, Division of

TABLE 13.2 Comparison of Rates of Growth in GNP and Productivity in the U.S. Economy, 1900–1940 and 1948–1970, and Forecasts for 1972–1980 and 1980–1985

	Annual rate of change, %			
	1900–1940	1948–1970	1972–1980	1980–1985
Real GNP	2.8	3.7	4.6	3.2
Real GNP in the private sector per hour of work	1.7	3.1	3.2	2.8

SOURCE: U.S. Bureau of Economic Analysis, *Long Term Economic Growth*, 1860–1970, Washington, D.C., 1973, pp. 103 and 109 for the 1900–1940 and 1948–1970 time periods; and Ronald E. Kutscher, "The United States Economy in 1985," *Monthly Labor Review*, December 1973, p. 28.

Economic Growth. A factor to be considered when asking this question is the pressure that size creates in the calculation of a rate of change. In 1950, when General Electric had $2 billion a year in sales, a 10 percent increase in sales involved $200 million. Now that General Electric has $13 billion in sales, a 10 percent increase involves $1.3 billion in sales. Such an increase must be translated into the utilization of steel, energy, and other inputs. Even if the GNP should continue to increase at forecasted rates, will the large companies experience a rate of growth several times as fast as the rate of increase in GNP? Our analysis of the forces to be described in the following section has led us to conclude that the rapid rate of progress achieved by American business so far in the post-World War II period will not be experienced in the decade ahead.

A MORE DIFFICULT BUSINESS ENVIRONMENT

Our forecast of a more difficult business environment is based on the following forces which have a negative impact on the future of business in the United States:
1. Dysfunctional government-business relations
2. Government growth and inefficiency
3. A legalistic environment
4. Shortages of investment capital
5. Shortages and costs of natural resources
6. Deterioration in multinational activity

In this chapter we will analyze the impact of these negative forces on the management problems of American business. There are a number of other negative forces which should also be considered when evaluating the prospects for the growth in sales and profits of U.S. corporations during the next decade. The McGraw-Hill Economics Department noted in a forecast of the U.S. economy to 1988 that "the 3.2% annual rate of growth (between 1973 and 1988) now expected is significantly lower than the 3.9% we projected a few years ago for the 1970–85 period"[1] and cited the following changes which caused the department to lower its forecast.

    (1) Relatively rapid rate of inflation (5 percent through 1988)
    (2) Basic energy shortage
    (3) Raw materials shortages
    (4) Growth of U.S. population slowing to a zero rate
    (5) Increasing tendency for today's young people not to get married
    (6) Productivity gains not accelerating in the future
    (7) Slowdown in U.S. research and development expenditures since 1967

We think that the McGraw-Hill forecast, although lower than the standard forecasts, such as the U.S. Department of Labor forecast presented in Table 13.2, is still too optimistic about the long-term growth prospects for the United States economy. Furthermore, we expect that business in the United States is likely to experience a lower rate of growth in profits than might be expected from the performance of the United States economy.

However one selects a list, it appears that negative forces began to be a more serious problem for business during this last decade, and we expect the seriousness of these adverse conditions to increase during the next decade.

One reason for a pessimistic forecast is the interaction of these negative forces. That is, the increase in the severity of one force results in an increase in the severity of the other forces.

Dysfunctional Government-Business Relations

The government, for all its good intentions, has devastated almost every industry which has been subject to detailed regulations. Think about the deterioration of the railroads, stock market, airlines, mass transit, maritime industry, and a number of other industries.

In energy, transportation, product safety, environment, banking, pensions, equal employment, food, pharmaceuticals, health care, housing, education, and many other important activities, the government will be setting rules in the next decade which will represent a level of regulation that would not have appeared possible in the 1950s and early 1960s. Increases in government regulation are now gaining momentum. The history of government inefficiency in regulation of business does not encourage optimism about a future in which the government assumes a larger and larger role in the management of economic activity. The government appears to shoot from the hip with regulations that involve billions and billions of dollars of costs which are paid for by the American people. Some opinion leaders believe that the government should do more regulation of business, and some believe that it should do less. Where these leaders in conflicting camps agree is on the ineptness of existing government efforts to regulate economic activity. As Paul W. McCracken, former chairman of the Council of Economic Advisors has observed: "To anyone willing to look it is clear that with distressing monotony [government] regulation has produced sick and arthritic industries."[2] The history of government regulation in pollution, safety, and equal employment suggests that a terrible loss in efficiency results when the government attempts to correct some of the abuses of business.

The acceleration in the increase in government regulation of business will be caused by a number of factors. First, there is the distrust of business by the American people. Surveys by the Opinion Research Corporation indicate that there has been a very serious deterioration in public attitudes toward business. A second factor is the trend toward participation in politics. Younger and more aggressive political leaders are emerging as a result of the increase in the involvement of the people in political campaigns. The establishment politicians are facing difficulties which are similar to those experienced by business: their credibility and usefulness are increasingly questioned by populist politicians. One way for politicians to prove fidelity to national objectives is to attack the performance of business. The recent campaign-financing laws, of course, encourage politicians to use polemics which attract small givers. The "little" people apparently like to hear how their political leaders will offer protection from rapacious "big" business.

Another factor which has encouraged politicians to attack business has been the increase in the special-interest groups—women, minorities, environmentalists, and others—which are a new, rapidly increasing source of countervailing power in the United States.

There is very strong evidence that business, government, and the universities have all discriminated against minorities and women. How to correct these past abuses is another question. Hyatt notes that the Equal Employment Opportunity Commission (EEOC) has a backlog of about 100,000 unresolved charges.[3] In 1972, Congress gave the EEOC the right to sue employers directly, and by October 1974 the EEOC had 280 attorneys—which made it one of the country's largest law offices.

Business and government in the United States have an adversary relationship. The distrust and dislike which prevails on both sides of this relationship obstructs any cooperative approach to the solving of problems. *An effective national response to the energy shortage, environmental controls, rapid inflation during a recession, and other such problems requires a quality of business–government cooperation which we do not see happening.* Improvements to the problem conditions that we describe below will be very difficult to achieve without a significant improvement in business–government relations. The following forces will hamper efforts to improve business–government relations.

1. The trend during the last decade toward a worsening of feelings on both sides
2. A huge increase in government employees to control business (for example, the almost 300 EEOC lawyers)
3. The antibusiness political climate which encourages attacks on business by government leaders and regulators
4. The almost total failure of business leaders to reverse the trend toward ever more counterproductive government regulations

Antitrust may be the cutting edge of the government attacks on business. As reported in *The Wall Street Journal:*

> The antitrusters are coming.
> President Ford is leading the charge, part of the government's war against inflation, with the vow that his administration is going to "zero in on more effective enforcement" of antitrust laws. Joining the attack are Attorney General William B. Saxbe and Federal Trade Commission Chairman Lewis A. Engman.
> Mr. Saxbe's cry is that price-fixers and monopolists are as crooked as muggers and should be thrown into jail for as long as five years. Mr. Engman (FTC Chairman) says the FTC is looking for the types of trade restraints, collusion and unfair marketing practices which reduce competition and lead to higher prices for comsumers. . . .
> Meantime officials at both the Justice Department and the FTC are generally expanding their antitrust arsenals. For example:
> - Federal Bureau of Investigation agents have been instructed to help ferret out possible price-fixing and contract bid-rigging. "This will give us manpower that we've never had before," boasts a Justice Department antitruster.
> - Mr. Saxbe recently told the 93 U.S. attorneys' offices that trustbusting is as much a part of their job as cracking a local Mafia ring. To set an example, a model antitrust task force is being established at the U.S. attorney's office here.
> - The FTC is shifting emphasis from traditional consumer protection, such as policing deceptive advertising, to antitrust activities—"where we can have more impact" on prices, Chairman Engman says. More people and money are being devoted to antitrust work, and the agency's 11 regional offices are being reorganized to enforce the antitrust laws more effectively.

- Both the Justice Department and the FTC are using economists as well as lawyers to look more closely at the structure of entire industries to discover possible anti-competitive practices that may keep prices up or retard product innovation.[4]

As Edward M. Cole, president of General Motors, reflected in an interview with *Newsweek* on his planned retirement: "'The joy of trying to run a business and do an effective job is gone. If I were a young man, knowing what I know now, would I do it again? No, I wouldn't go into the auto industry.' Cole's complaint is not with General Motors per se. The basic problem is the glut of new laws that now regulate everything from exhaust emissions to the weight of new car bumpers."[5]

In response to the critics of business who are of the opinion that the government has been too soft on business, it is probably correct to say that the government failed until recent years to control the societal damage caused by business (for example, the lag between the scientific demonstration in 1950 that autos caused serious levels of air pollution and the Clean Air Act of 1965). But, however slow the government may have been to control the societal problems that are caused by business, the surge of new regulations during the last ten years has certainly gone a long way to correct the situation. Unfortunately, there has not been a cooperative effort by business and government to solve societal problems. Instead, an adversary relationship deprives the country of the knowledge which business can bring to the improvement of national problems.

A process in which government, business, and labor communicate together in order to reach a consensus on economic policies exists in other developed countries such as Japan and West Germany. As James Reston has aptly observed, confrontation rather than consensus appears to best characterize government–business relations in the United States:

> Precisely on the day when the stock market hit a twelve-year low and the unemployment total went beyond anything in the last thirteen years, the Attorney General, Mr. Saxbe, announced that the Department of Justice was looking into antitrust charges against the auto industry, Big Steel and other primary-metal industries, tobacco, coal, chemicals, beef, newsprint and other paper products, and heavy electrical equipment.
>
> Suddenly, in the middle of the energy crisis, the auto crisis, the housing crisis and the stock-market crisis, the Ford Administration brought a suit against AT&T. No warning was given. Mr. Saxbe merely called them down and said they were going to be sued, and when the President was asked about this, he merely said he had been informed, and had left it all up to the Justice Department.
>
> This is only one illustration of what is going on here now. The government, business, labor and the public are all caught up in an economic crisis, but they

are not talking together about their common problems, and there is no effective way for them to do so.[6]

Such behavior does little good for the country, the government, and business. It leads to little confidence in government–business relations during the next decade, when the need will become acute for a cooperative effort to solve serious national and business problems.

Government Growth and Inefficiency

It is widely accepted that government spending has increased as though it were out of control during this last decade. The welfare system is in chaos. The Medicare-Medicaid funding of health care has created an extraordinary inflation of medical costs.

The total of federal, state, and local government expenditures has consumed an increasing percentage of the GNP, as shown in Table 13.3. As we write this chapter (April 1975), the federal government deficit for the fiscal year beginning July 1, 1975, is forecasted at between $80 billion and $100 billion, and the deficit for the fiscal year ending June 30, 1975, is expected to be $45 billion. The government, in order to sell its debt, is forcing interest rates up for both government and private borrowing.

The public has good cause to be concerned about the increasing share of the GNP that is spent by the government because the problems which should be solved by the government appear to be getting worse. Given trends in crime, health care and welfare costs, public transportation, education, and unemployment, it appears that the government should be doing much more for the American people. Despite the increasing share of the GNP spent by government, many citizens feel that public services are woefully inadequate. Massachusetts is a case in point. As Michael

TABLE 13.3 Gross National Product, Total Government Expenditures, and Debt: 1950, 1960, and 1972

	1950*	1960	1972
Gross national product, billions of dollars	284.8	503.7	1,155.2
Total government expenditures, billions of dollars	70.3	151.3	397.4
Government expenditures as a percentage of gross national product	24.7	30.3	34.4
Total interest-bearing government debt outstanding, billions of dollars	281	358	609

*Excludes Alaska and Hawaii.
SOURCE: *Statistical Abstract of the United States,* 1974, p. 373 for GNP, p. 246 for total government expenditures, p. 234 for government debt.

Dukakis, the new governor, lamented in his inaugural address, "We, as a commonwealth, face the most serious fiscal crisis that has ever confronted an incoming administration. Many of our human services programs are not working. Our public transportation system is a public disaster."[7]

Large expenditures or a remarkable increase in the cost effectiveness of Massachusetts government will be required if basic tasks of government in this state are to be performed adequately. Given the uncontrollable costs such as pensions and interest on a large debt, the increasing unionization of public employees, the limitations on the employment and transfer of personnel as a result of civil service regulations, a very expensive union contract in the Massachusetts Bay Transit Authority and many other problems, it is unlikely that Governor Dukakis will succeed in bringing cost-effective administration to the commonwealth of Massachusetts. The political pressures to provide new services and the built-in inflation in many existing services will result in a faster growth in government expenditures than the rate of increase in the private sector. This will mean an increase in taxes and a further loss of jobs as employers leave the state.

Massachusetts is a center of management education with schools such as the M.I.T. Sloan School of Management and the Harvard Business School. The state is the home office of several of the world's most famous consulting firms, such as A. D. Little and Harbridge House. It is a center for the development of advanced computer technology and is the home office of companies such as Honeywell Information Systems and Digital Equipment Corporation. Despite this proximity to education, consultants, and computers, state and local governments are incredibly ineffective in the utilization of computers and other techniques of research-based management.

The government appears to have lagged behind the private sector in the effective utilization of the basic techniques of research-based management. It is not that government leaders do not have access to skilled research-based professionals. Rather, *there is an inadequate integration between those who have specialized knowledge and those who make decisions.* The recommendations of many research-based government task forces appear to be totally ignored by our leaders. A chairman of a number of government task forces reported to one of the authors that he frequently repeated recommendations from earlier studies in his writing of a current study. The problems become worse, but the government does not act on the collected knowledge in task-force reports. President Ford has recommended that a new commission be created to study the country's regulatory agencies which have fallen into disrepute. Why should a new commission be any more successful in improving the functioning of the regulatory agencies than the Brownlow Commission created by Roosevelt, the Hoover Commissions of Truman and Eisenhower, the Landis Commission in the Kennedy years, and the numerous commissions in the Johnson and Nixon years? Whatever happened as a result of the Ash Council Report?

The total costs to United States business and to the economy are much greater than the government expenditures would indicate, as Murray L. Weidenbaum has demonstrated in his *Government-mandated Price Increases*.[8] In Table 13.4 we present Weidenbaum's table on extension of government regulation of business from 1962 to 1973, but have added "partial list" to the title. The states and cities have added many new regulations of business during the 1962–1973 period, and there are also many new federal regulations not on this list (such as the wage-price

TABLE 13.4 Extension of Government Regulation of Business, 1962–1973 (Partial List)

Year of Enactment	Name of Law	Year of Enactment	Name of Law
1962	Food and Drug Amendments	1970	Amendment to Federal Deposit Insurance Act
1963	Equal Pay Act		
1964	Civil Rights Act	1970	Securities Investor Protection Act
1965	Cigarette Labeling and Advertising Act	1970	Poison Prevention Packaging Act
1966	Fair Packaging and Labeling Act	1970	Clean Air Act Amendments
1966	Child Protection Act		
1966	Traffic Safety Act	1970	Occupational Safety and Health Act
1967	Flammable Fabrics Act		
1967	Age Discrimination in Employment Act	1971	Lead-based Paint Elimination Act
1968	Consumer Credit Protection Act (Truth in Lending)	1971	Federal Boat Safety Act
		1972	Consumer Product Safety Act
1968	Interstate Land Sales Full Disclosure Act	1972	Federal Water Pollution Control Act
1968	Wholesome Poultry Products Act	1972	Noise Pollution and Control Act
1968	Radiation Control for Health and Safety Act	1972	Equal Employment Opportunity Act
		1973	Emergency Petroleum Allocation Act
1969	National Environmental Policy Act	1973	Vocational Rehabilitation Act
1970	Public Health Smoking Act		

SOURCE: Murray L. Weidenbaum, *Government-mandated Price Increases*, Washington, D.C.: American Enterprise Institute, 1975, pp. 4–6.

controls, phases I to IV). There are quasi-governmental regulations such as the rulings of the Financial Accounting Standards Board, and there are numerous actions which business fought in the 1962–1973 period that have become new regulations in the 1974–1975 period (such as the FTC Product Line Disclosure action and the Pension Reform Act of 1974).

The real problem before the country is not whether new standards of social performance for business are necessary. Rather, it is the terrible inefficiency of government attempts to achieve improved business performance. Weidenbaum offers hope for more reasonable government regulation:

> As these government-mandated costs begin to visibly exceed the apparent benefits, it can be hoped that public pressures will mount on governmental regulators to moderate the increasingly stringent rules and regulations that they apply. At present, for example, a mislabeled consumer product that is declared an unacceptable hazard often must be destroyed. In the future, the producer or seller perhaps will only be required to relabel it correctly, a far less costly way of achieving the same objective.[9]

However, Weidenbaum shares our pessimism about whether there will be an improvement in the cost effectiveness of government regulation and rejects his own hope, cited above, with the conclusion: "Yet, the recent trend is clear—more frequent and more costly regulation of the private sector."[10]

A Legalistic Environment

There has been an alarming increase in lawsuits for the settlement of grievances. The number of lawsuits presented in Table 13.5 is only the tip of the iceberg for the increased utilization of lawyers. As *Business Week*

TABLE 13.5 Business Lawsuits: A Comparison of Activity in 1964 and 1974

Class of suit	Lawsuits 1964	Lawsuits 1974	Percentage increase 1964 to 1974
Civil rights	709	2,453	246.0
Labor	3,187	5,400	69.4
Commerce	271	3,925	1,348.3
Marine contracts	2,399	3,195	33.2
Securities and commodities	439	2,378	441.6
Patent, trademark, and copyright	1,885	2,084	10.6
Antitrust	422	1,287	205.0
Totals	9,312	20,722	122.5

SOURCE: "How Companies Fight Soaring Legal Costs," *Business Week*, Nov. 16, 1974, p. 104.

noted in an example of the effect of the 1974 pension law, "Companies must submit every existing plan—and all new ones—to both the Treasury and Labor Departments. The legal work involved, according to one lawyer used to high fees, will be 'expensive.' A company defense against a relatively simple EEOC suit, says one New York lawyer, could easily cost $100,000, not counting potentially staggering costs if the court awards plaintiffs a lot of back-pay."[11]

These are happy days for the partners in the major law firms who frequently charge $100 or more for *each hour* that they work. Business spends millions to work with a complex, crazy system of legalistic procedures and almost nothing to improve the efficiency of government regulation. Fortunately, law school enrollment has tripled since 1953 and jumped 70 percent in just the last six years.[12] Thus there will be no shortage of lawyers even if business persists in its reliance on lawyers to solve problems. The large number of new government regulations and the decline in the public's estimation of business has created an environment in which a larger and larger share of the time of business executives will be allocated for defense against lawsuits or in response to government regulations. Because of the inefficiencies created by the excessive use of lawyers, the trends presented in Table 13.5 deserve the careful attention of business leaders.

That the use of lawyers is related to government actions can be seen from the population per lawyer of 49 in Washington, D.C., compared with a national average of 626.[13] *The regulatory problems of business have been the exclusive happy hunting ground for lawyers.* It is time business recognized that regulatory problems are also economic, managerial, behavioral, and technological issues which can best be solved by task-force teams which include (1) specialists in such research-based management skills as economics, R&D, management information systems, and organization development; (2) line managers whose work is affected by a given government regulation; and (3) a (team of) lawyer(s).

However effective the business response to government regulation, it appears that the trend toward a legalistic society will reduce the profitability and productivity of business with increasing severity in the decade ahead.

Shortages of Investment Capital

The growth of the United States economy will be severely restricted during this next decade by a shortage of the capital that is needed by business for investments in plant and equipment. The New York Stock Exchange (NYSE) has predicted a cumulative shortage of business investment capital of almost $650 billion by 1985.[14] If government deficits increase as a result of an effort to bring the country out of the 1974–1975 recession, this NYSE forecast of a capital deficit for private industry will be too low because increases in government debt are in direct competition with business efforts to raise funds.

One of the big unknowns in forecasts of the growth of the United States economy to 1985 is the availability and cost of investment funds. Gross private investment as a share of GNP, which increased in the United States at an annual average of 10 percent between 1970 and 1972, has been much lower in the United States than in other countries, such as France and West Germany with an average of 17 percent and Japan with an average of 19 percent.[15] The position of United States industry relative to foreign competition has been eroded as a result of the lag in modernization that has been experienced because of lower rates of investment in new plant and equipment.

As we look ahead to 1985, we do not see the investment funds at acceptable costs to maintain the post-World War II rate of growth in the private sector. It is unlikely that the stock market will provide the price/earnings ratios which will make new equity issues as attractive in this next decade as in the more bountiful years of the 1950s and 1960s.

Forecasts of the availability of funds for capital investment should focus on the costs and returns to invested capital. When a significant percentage of capital investment is allocated for the equipment and replacements required in compliance with Environmental Protection Agency regulations, this is a force which raises costs and lowers the rate of return on investments. This kind of investment increases the total demand for investment capital, but does not increase the capacity of American industry over precontrol conditions. As the demand for capital is increased by new regulations, so will the cost of capital funds be increased. A high cost of capital tends to reduce the rate of capital investment, and this, in turn, will result in a slower rate of real economic growth.

The economy increases in size as a result of an expanding demand for goods and services which is satisfied by an expansion in supply. Future economic growth can be sharply curtailed if increases in supply are limited by a shortage of investment capital. What capital for expansion is available can be made less productive by other negative forces. For example, the time lag between the decision to build a nuclear reactor and the time when the reactor produces new electricity has increased from about five years in 1960 to over ten years in 1975 as a result of government regulations and environmental pressure groups. This greater time lag has had a very serious impact on the cost of expanding nuclear electrical capacity which, in turn, has put pressure on the supply and costs of fossil fuels (the most common alternative to nuclear capacity). Nuclear plants are built in Europe and Japan in less than half the time required in the United States.[16] This combination of a larger share of GNP invested in new plant and equipment and greater efficiency in government regulation of industry may be providing insurmountable advantages for the foreign competitors of United States companies.

Shortages and Costs of Natural Resources

Innovations that work tend to be imitated. For example, there once was a time when planes were not subject to skyjacking. The idea did not cross anybody's mind until some clown had the inspiration. Suddenly, skyjacking appeared to be a marvelous opportunity for people with certain psychoses or political motives. The first skyjacking was an innovation which was imitated with alarming regularity until costly detection devices were installed at airports and paid for by passengers with a "security surcharge." The Oil Producing and Exporting Countries (OPEC) cartel is another example of an innovation which has proved itself to be an effective means of increasing the revenues of the oil exporters.

There appears to be little question in the minds of the experts that the United States government will assume a major role in the control of the use and supply of energy. As Harvey Brooks and Carl Kaysen note:

> ... as a nation we are faced with a long-run energy problem with which we are unlikely to deal in a desirable way by relying chiefly on the workings of the market. This is what we have done until now, with sporadic, diffuse and uncoordinated interventions by government—sometimes to assist producers, sometimes to protect consumers, sometimes to preserve the environment, sometimes in the name of national security.[17]

Two years after the oil embargo by OPEC, the United States still did not have an energy policy. This failure is widely recognized. What is not well known is the fact that the energy crisis of the 1970s was forecasted in a 1952 study prepared for President Truman.[18] The recommendations in this 1952 report were ignored and were *repeated* in the 1973 materials report prepared for the President and the Congress.[19]

It must be an unnerving experience to serve as a member of a commission which recommends actions that were recommended by earlier commissions on the same subject—and then ignored. Jerome S. Klaff, chairman of the commission which prepared *Material Needs and the Environment: Today and Tomorrow* in 1973 for the President and the Congress, expressed his dismay about the failure of the government to act as follows:

> Some recommendations of the earlier [1952] Commission, *never implemented, but still valid in 1973*, were repeated in the more comprehensive recommendations of our Commission. Such, for instance, was the repeated recommenda-

tion for a central source of data on material resources. Surely our recent energy crisis showed how wanting we are in basic data from which policy decisions are formulated. [20] [Italics added.]

The world watches in awe while once backward countries become international bankers and industrialists; the lesson is there for the leaders of other countries with basic natural resources. The developed countries in the West, such as the United States, France, and the United Kingdom, have become identified as imperialistic powers by many leaders in the Third World countries. It is the United States, not Russia or China, that bombed Asians in Vietnam. United States corporations have invested heavily in white South Africa. There is a conviction in Third World countries that rich nations (and the United States ranks number one for wealth) should share their wealth with the poor nations. As Paul Lewis, Washington correspondent for *The Financial Times of London,* observed:

> But while the O.P.E.C. action has left the industrial countries frustrated, angry and suspicious of one another, *the rest of the world has greeted the oil-price increase as an act of justice.* Even the poorest countries, for whom the new prices are an impossible burden, have pointedly refused to make common cause in public with the industrial world against the producers' cartel. Instead, they have accepted that its members have a perfect right as developing nations to extract the last penny they can from the rich in return for what remains of their mineral resources, on which the industrial world's prosperity has been built.[21] [Italics added.]

Leaders in several of the oil-rich countries in the Middle East identify with the downtrodden people of the world, and it appears that at least some of the huge flows of oil-created cash will be converted into arms and other assistance needed for the liberation and development of Third World countries. This assistance will strengthen efforts to form cartels for the control of national resources which have historically been imported by the rich countries on favorable terms. The anti-Western ideology of the oil-rich countries bodes ill for countries such as South Africa, in which United States companies have invested heavily.

Lest there be any doubt about the seriousness of the threat to supplies of raw materials, United States mineral imports as a share of United States consumption are presented in Table 13.6.

It is one thing to have the people in desperately poor countries dislike the United States and the United States multinational corporations. It is quite something else again to have very rich countries with similar feelings. Estimates of *excess funds* (those funds not needed for internal consumption) of the OPEC countries range from $250 billion to $500 billion by 1980. Felix G. Rohatyn has put these excess funds into perspective as follows:

TABLE 13.6 Mineral Imports as a Share of United States Consumption, 1972

Minerals	Percent
Asbestos	81
Bauxite and aluminum	87
Chromium	100
Cobalt	92
Copper	8
Iron ore	30
Lead	24
Manganese	95
Nickel	90
Platinum group	93
Potassium	45
Tin	100
Tungsten	44
Zinc	51

SOURCE: *International Economic Report of the President, 1974,* Washington, D.C.: Government Printing Office, 1974, p. 26.

Whether ultimately $250 billion or $500 billion is closer to the truth, the figure should be compared with a total market value of all companies listed on the New York Stock Exchange—approximately $600 billion accumulated over 100 years—and a total of approximately $120 billion invested abroad by the United States over 50 years. It should be compared with approximately $45 billion of total debt and equity financing by all United States corporations in 1974, of which approximately $5 billion was equity. Within five years a small group of countries will have excess funds available for investment ranging from 50 per cent to 100 per cent of the value of all corporations listed on the Stock Exchange.[22]

There are some who see these huge flows of funds to the OPEC countries as a marvelous source of new business for United States corporations. An opposite view is based on questions about what the OPEC countries are likely to do with these excess funds. For example, how well will the United States multinational corporations compete with OPEC-financed companies who have such a tremendous advantage in low-cost funds and low-cost energy?

Deterioration in Multinational Activity

The basic strategy of the senior executives in large United States multinational corporations has been to regard the world as a market in which profits and growth are to be increased without reference to national boundaries. Raymond Vernon, director of the Harvard University Center of International Affairs, titled the summary book from the Harvard

Multinational Enterprise Series *Sovereignty at Bay: The Multinational Spread of U.S. Enterprises*.[23] The book documents the extraordinary increase in worldwide activity of 187 companies which were selected by Professor Vernon on the basis of a specified level of involvement in multinational activity. According to Vernon,[24] United States companies in 1969 managed about $110 billion in overseas assets. Many large United States corporations received over half of their net profits after taxes from overseas operations. The stakes are of great magnitude for the United States economy and for a large number of the most profitable United States corporations.

The theme of Vernon's book is represented in its title. "Suddenly it seems, the sovereign states are feeling naked. Concepts such as national sovereignty and national economic strength appear curiously drained of meaning."[25] Thus Vernon begins his story about United States multinational corporations.

The idea that sovereign states stand naked appears less comforting today than in 1971, when Vernon published his book. United States multinational corporations have been a dominant force in expanding world markets. The factors which contributed to the United States dominance in multinational activity have been documented in a number of studies.[26] Size of firm and investments in R&D were two of the critical factors which contributed to the advantage of the United States multinationals.

In the decade ahead, it appears that foreign activity will contribute less to the performance of United States multinationals for the following reasons:

1. *Foreign competition.* The lead of United States multinational corporations after World War II has been lost in many industries.

2. *Foreign governments.* The relatively passive role of governments toward multinational activity appears to be changing. Hard bartering between governments will become more important, and the free enterprise dealings of private corporations will become less important (for example, the December 1974 deal arranged by French Prime Minister Jacques Chirac for $6 billion in capital goods, industrial plants, and agricultural equipment with Iran).

3. *Fear and dislike of the United States.* The capitalistic system associated with the United States is seen as exploitive to the leaders in many countries. As Richard L. Strout reported on his experience in the Rome World Food Conference in December 1974, "What startled me at first was the suspicion of America. . . . For 'capitalistic imperialism' read, generally, the United States. . . . Next in my education were the Chinese and Russian speeches. They were rather alike. Scarcity, hunger, famine—these were all due to capitalism, to imperialism. . . . Since this is a subjective account, I will add another discovery that I made: the widespread suspicion by poor countries of the multinational corporations."[27]

The new power of the less developed countries has cast such a cloud of uncertainty over the supply and cost of raw materials that business planning has become very difficult. For example, what will a trend toward the manufacture in the OPEC countries of petrochemicals, steel, aluminum, and other products mean for the future of United States corporations? Note the recently announced plans of several Arab nations to build aluminum plants—using flared (i.e. wasted in the process of oil drilling) natural gas for power. *The Wall Street Journal* reports that "Several Arab nations have moved to guarantee a raw material supply for the smelters. Saudi Arabia, Kuwait, Libya and Egypt recently joined the government of Guinea to exploit that African country's deposits of bauxite, the aluminum ore, and to process the ore for its alumina, or aluminum oxide."[28] In addition to the impact that new sources of supply of aluminum will have on prices received by the United States aluminum companies, foreign sources of the raw material supplies of the United States manufacturers may be diverted by less developed countries such as Guinea to other less developed countries such as the Arab nations who will be able to afford to pay more for this raw material because of power-cost and investment-capital advantages over the United States manufacturers. What will it mean if most of the raw materials now imported into the United States are exported by cartels such as the one recently formed by the iron-exporting nations?

The comfortable assumptions about the security of the earnings and assets of United States multinational corporations appear to be overly optimistic given the experiences thus far in the 1970s. United States multinationals have created intense competitive pressure on the firms in other countries. There is likely to be a significant reversal of this pressure during this next decade. In the new economic environment in which governments negotiate for a large share of total business activity, how well will the United States multinationals be able to compete? Now that there are so many large United States multinationals with a significant percentage of assets, profits and sales from overseas business, the abrupt change in the climate of world business is particularly threatening.

REDUCED ECONOMIC PERFORMANCE

The net result of the negative forces discussed above will be a slower rate of growth in the economies of the United States and other developed countries. As business allocates an increasing percentage of available senior management time to fighting regulatory battles, as governments at all levels absorb a larger share of GNP while at the same time reducing the efficiency of economic activity, as foreign markets become less profitable, and as foreign sources of raw materials become more expensive and less dependable—as these and other negative forces decrease the efficiency of economic activity—the rate of economic growth will fall below the high performance achieved since the end of World War II.

An additional consideration is that countercyclical government fiscal and monetary policies have decreased in effectiveness during the last two decades. Prior to the Keynesian revolution in economic knowledge in the 1930s, governments did not know how to fine-tune economic activity. The business cycle in the "good old days" of little government control over economic activity created a wildly fluctuating economy with booms and severe recessions and depressions. In the post-World War II period, governments in most of the developed countries of the world have been able to slow down booms in order to achieve a longer upsurge in economic activity. When economic growth begins to falter, governments have learned how to provide the stimulation which slows the rate of decline until a recovery can be initiated. This moderation of economic activity is constrained by a tradeoff between inflation and unemployment. The Full Employment Act of 1946 made it government policy to maintain full employment and a stable price level. The moderation of booms fostered a low rate of inflation; the stimulus in a recession lowered the rate of unemployment.

As reported by Geoffrey Moore, vice president of research of the National Bureau of Economic Research, this tradeoff between inflation and unemployment appears to have become a less functional force. The high unemployment rates in the last quarter of 1974 and first quarter of 1975, during a period of high inflation, are but another experience in a historical trend in which declines in economic activity are no longer causing a proportional decrease in inflationary pressure. As calculated by Dr. Moore and reported in *The Wall Street Journal:*

> Consumer price changes associated with a recession or a period of slow growth in the economy:
>
> | | |
> |---|---|
> | 1948–49 | −4 |
> | 1951–52 | −1 |
> | 1953–54 | −1 |
> | 1957–58 | 0 |
> | 1960–61 | 0 |
> | 1962–63 | 2 |
> | 1966–67 | 2 |
> | 1969–70 | 3 |
>
> The lowest rate of increase in consumer prices over a six-month span expressed in annual rates, during the five generally recognized post-war recessions plus the periods of retarded real output growth in 1951–52, 1962–63 and 1969–70.[29]

In order to understand the findings of Dr. Moore, it is useful to include in the analysis the severity of the decline in each recession. In the 1948–

1949 recession, real GNP decreased by 3.6 percent and consumer prices fell by 4 percent. In the 1957–1958 recession, real GNP decreased by 4.4 percent *without a corresponding decrease in prices*. The 1974–1975 recession is likely to be more severe in terms of a reduction in real GNP and an increase in unemployment than either the 1948–1949 or the 1957–1958 recessions, but the rate of inflation will range between 8 and 12 percent for most of this period of recession.

The freedom of the government to use strong fiscal and monetary policies to stimulate the economy in the 1970s is sharply constrained by the need to control the rate of inflation. The 1974–1975 experience of a combination of high inflation and a rapidly deteriorating economy has created an unprecedented challenge to government, business, and labor leaders in the United States. The old rules guiding public policy do not apply.

BUSINESS INEPTNESS

Experience in working with business leaders indicates that there is a fairly wide agreement with our analysis of a more difficult future. Many business executives, while recognizing the need for the protection to the public and to workers that is provided by OSHA, EEOC, EPA, the Pension Reform Act, and other such new regulatory activity, deeply resent the arbitrary, autocratic, inefficient, inequitable, and unpredictable nature of the implementation of the new regulations. Business leaders appear to recognize the threat to the efficiency and growth of economic activity that is represented in the problems analyzed thus far in this chapter.

One might expect that business would be mounting a vigorous effort to improve business–government relationships. There has been an extraordinary cost to business and to the country as a result of government regulation. The magnitude of the total costs of the new regulations is unknown, but estimates of the costs of some of the new regulations are available. The White House Council on Environmental Quality increased its estimate of industry and government pollution equipment costs during the 1977–1983 period from $152.7 billion to $194.8 billion, an increase of $42.1 billion or 28 percent from the earlier forecast.[30] The total cost of the new government regulations is very difficult to estimate for a number of reasons. For example, what was the full impact on the economy when the government set a very high standard for water pollution control on an industry when products were in short supply? Cost increases and a slower increase in supply have a direct impact on inflationary pressure.

Many of the new government regulations appear to be in response to unsatisfactory performance by business. The government has demonstrated to the country that it can force business firms to correct clearly visible business-created societal problems. What we have not seen is an effort by business to enter into a dialogue with the government about the solution to societal problems. We have seen very few studies by business of the costs which unreasonable government regulation has imposed on the American people.

A process of government–business cooperation in the regulation of economic activity has been developed in a number of other countries. There is clearly a need in the United States for the kind of mutual respect between business and government that has existed in Japan, West Germany, Sweden, and several other developed countries. The "business as usual" attitude of many business leaders just will not work for very long given the present deteriorating conditions for business.

The inadequate response to the new business environment by executives was analyzed by Carl G. Burgen, management editor of *Business Week:*

> No chief executive could be oblivious to the economic and social turmoil of the past decade and to the impact it has had on his job. If the typical CEO has been slow to respond, it is because there was next to nothing in his training or conditioning to tell him how to respond. Besides, given the incredible amounts of time required just to manage today's huge, diverse, far-flung companies, few CEOs have found time enough to formulate a suitable response.[31]

That business is willing to invest billions of dollars in R&D for new products, plant and equipment, and other expenditures gives evidence that there is a belief in the future. These are the traditional ways that business has invested in the future. Socioeconomic research to improve the communications between business and government has not yet been seen as an investment which may be of greater importance to the profits in 1980 than investments in new plant and equipment. Business has not had a long-range plan to work toward a more effective regulatory climate. Each time the government takes an adverse action, business responds with a crisis-level push to defend itself. Then business sits back and does very little to improve the government regulatory process—until the next government action creates a new crisis.

Business has placed its chips on lawyers and lobbyists rather than on economists, management scientists, and R&D professionals. This myopic response to new business problems may have delayed some onerous government regulations. It has done little to build a healthier business environment. And it has done little to help the government to develop policies for reducing the rate of inflation, restoring the rate of economic growth, creating new supplies of energy—or taking other actions to resist the negative forces in the economic environment which only the government can control. Although business should allocate resources in harmony with problems and opportunities, there has been an unwillingness to commit resources for efforts to improve the process of government regulation. Business associations in Japan, Sweden, and West Germany have a much more active role in government decisions which affect economic activity. In the United States new problems and opportunities require a rethinking of business behavior. This has been occurring in the utilization of research-based management techniques for internal decisions. The failure of business leaders to expand the scope of their concern beyond the narrow confines of their firms may be the most costly error of American management in the decade of the 1970s.

Murray Weidenbaum has concluded that a managerial revolution is now in process:

> ... a silent bureaucratic revolution—in the course of which the locus of much of the decision making in the American corporation is shifting once again. This time the shift is from the professional management selected by the corporation's board of directors to the vast cadre of government regulators that influences and often controls the key decisions of the typical business firm. The added costs flowing from this change are ultimately borne by the public, in the form of higher taxes, higher prices, and lower real standards of living.[32]

Our analysis supports Weidenbaum's conclusion, and Future Firm management capability seems the probable response of United States business to the ongoing revolution in economic and regulatory conditions.

FUTURE FIRM MANAGEMENT

Our forecast of the rapid improvement in the effectiveness of management that will be achieved in a small number of high-performance companies by 1980 (a Future Firm level of management competence) stands in marked contrast to our doom-and-gloom analysis of the problems which will be confronting the nation's political and business leaders during this next decade.

This is because the rapidly changing world will offer many new opportunities as well as problems. Huge increases in market size will appear rapidly. Consider the potential in such markets as health care, mass transit, educational systems, pollution-control equipment, and energy-related equipment. Experience provides little guidance for efforts to respond to the opportunities and problems created by the possible payments to oil-exporting countries of over $700 billion between 1975 and 1980.

Business must develop the management capabilities to anticipate extreme changes in the economic and regulatory environment. Wage-price controls, a new oil embargo, a long period of slow economic growth and high inflation are but a few of the problems that are likely to be experienced. Decisions that were sound when the rate of inflation was 1 or 2 percent a year may be a source of huge losses when the rate of inflation is 10 to 12 percent. Business must rethink its basic assumptions. What has worked for years may be doomed to failure—perhaps *this year.*

In the decade of the 1970s there will be an extraordinary improvement in air and water quality, safety conditions, pensions, equal employment, disclosure on financial statements, efficiency in energy utilization, and many other conditions related to business activity in the United States. Business has had a history of responding rapidly and effectively to new conditions, and the emergence of Future Firm in the 1970s is well within the tradition of American business. This book addresses solutions to this problem in the context of the business firm; the problem is far more difficult (but not impossible) in the government for reasons beyond the scope of this book. In the short run, the growth of government, compounded by inefficiency, is likely to be a severe negative force on business in terms of rising taxes, inadequate services, and continued social and economic distress.

We are predicting a rapid rate of progress in the efficiency of management in a small number of corporations during the next decade—partly in response to the more difficult business environment. We do not see an improvement in business-government relations, in the trend toward a legalistic economy, or in the other environmental problems that were analyzed in this chapter.

It is hoped that, in time, business and government leaders will learn to work together in response to some very serious problems which have been eroding the well-being of the people of the United States. One happy thought is the possibility that management procedures developed in business can be utilized in the government. A whole new way of thinking will be necessary before business and government leaders are able to confront problems as a team rather than as adversaries. A change in thinking and attitudes will take years to make a difference. Thus we do not see in 1980 the kind of prosperity enjoyed by many companies during the long business boom which began with World War II and ended with the 1974–1975 recession. Companies with a Future Firm level of management competence will continue to prosper relative to companies with Present Firm and Prior Firm managements despite the more difficult business environment. A Future Firm will have the management depth and techniques to control costs and to anticipate changes and respond with shifts in resources to expanding market areas while reducing commitments in the markets that are becoming less profitable. Given any extrapolation of the negative trends analyzed in this chapter, most companies with less than a Future Firm level of management competence will be in severe difficulty by 1985.

NOTES AND REFERENCES

1. McGraw-Hill Department of Economics, "The American Economy: Prospects for Growth to 1988," undated pamphlet, p. 2.
2. "Bicentennial Stability," *The Wall Street Journal*, Oct. 23, 1974, p. 16.
3. Hyatt, James C.: "The Anti-Business Bottleneck," *The Wall Street Journal*, Oct. 22, 1974, p. 20.
4. Bacon, Kenneth, and Mitchell Lynch: "Ford Administration May Really Be Serious about Antitrust Drive," *The Wall Street Journal*, Nov. 16, 1974, p. 1.
5. "Autos: Ed Cole's Lament," *Newsweek*, Sept. 9, 1973, pp. 67–68.
6. "Pearl Harbor—1941–1974," *The New York Times*, Dec. 8, 1974, p. 17e.
7. *Boston Globe*, Jan. 3, 1974, p. 30.
8. Weidenbaum, Murray L.: *Government-mandated Price Increases*, Washington, D.C.: American Enterprise Institute, 1975.
9. Ibid., p. 3.
10. Ibid.
11. *Business Week*, "How Companies Fight Soaring Legal Costs," Nov. 16, 1974, p. 104.
12. "A Surfeit of Lawyers," *Newsweek*, Dec. 9, 1974, p. 74.
13. *Statistical Abstract of the United States*, 1973, p. 159.
14. *The Capital Needs and Savings in the U.S. Economy*, New York: New York Stock Exchange, 1974, p. 16.
15. *International Economic Report to the President*, 1974, p. 5.
16. It is not obvious from published reports that the terrible time delays and wildly inflated costs have bought the country a safe nuclear power industry. Data leaked from the AEC and data forced by suits and threats of suits made under the Freedom of Information Act indicate that the AEC has suppressed reports from its own scientists that nuclear reactors were more dangerous than officially acknowledged. (See David Burnham, "A.E.C. Files Show Effort to Conceal Safety Perils," *The New York Times*, Nov. 10, 1974, pp. 1ff.) These findings raise serious doubts about the allocation and management of the huge AEC budget for nuclear energy research. Government management of the country's nuclear energy development program is cast in further doubt by reports that "the Atomic Energy Commission and the industry it nurtured are unable to account for thousands of pounds of nuclear materials that could be fashioned into crude nuclear bombs according to experts in business, universities and the Commission." (David Burnham, "Thousands of Pounds of Materials Used in Nuclear Bombs Are Unaccounted For," *The New York Times*, Dec. 29, 1974, p. 26.)
17. "Advisory Board Comments," in the concluding report of the Ford Foundation Energy Project, *A Time to Choose: America's Energy Future*, Cambridge, Mass.: Ballinger, 1974, p. 36.
18. The President's Materials Policy Commission, *Resources for Freedom*, Washington, D.C.: U.S. Government Printing Office, 1952.
19. National Commission on Materials Policy, *Material Needs and the Environment: Today and Tomorrow*, Washington, D.C.: U.S. Government Printing Office, 1973.
20. "New National Materials Policy: The Key to Achieving Our Resource Needs," paper delivered at the Eco-Technic Recycling Conference IV, New York, Sept. 5, 1974, p. 5.

21. Lewis, Paul, "Getting Even," *The New York Times,* Dec. 14, 1974, p. 13; emphasis added.
22. Rohatyn, Felix G.: "Getting Foreign Cash," *The New York Times,* Apr. 6, 1975, p. 19e.
23. New York: Basic Books, 1971.
24. Ibid., p. 18.
25. Ibid., p. 3.
26. See ibid. and William H. Gruber, Dileep Mehta, and Raymond Vernon, "The R&D Factor in International Trade and International Investment of United States Industries," *Journal of Political Economy,* February 1967, pp. 20–37.
27. Strout, Richard L.: "Hunger: The Global Crisis," *Christian Science Monitor,* Jan. 3, 1975, p. 12.
28. "Aluminum Smelters Are Planned in the Middle East," *The Wall Street Journal,* Apr. 7, 1975, p. 6.
29. "An Economic Program," *The Wall Street Journal,* Dec. 4, 1974, p. 26.
30. "Inflation Swells Cost of Gear Firms Use to Control Pollution," *The Wall Street Journal,* Dec. 9, 1974, p. 16.
31. "The Scenario for Tomorrow," *Business Week,* May 4, 1975, p. 85.
32. Weidenbaum, op. cit., pp. 97–98.

FOURTEEN

Management Innovation in Future Firm

The flow of new-management techniques which will improve corporate performance in Future Firm will be similar in many ways to the new-product innovations which are now achieved each year in research-intensive companies such as IBM, General Electric, Du Pont, Procter & Gamble, and 3M. New products and more efficient production techniques are developed consistently year after year in these companies where executives have learned to manage R&D. Well-managed R&D includes not only the transfer of new technology from the R&D labs into production, but also the ability to direct the efforts of scientists and engineers toward new products for which there is a profitable market.

The R&D productivity in many large companies is a direct result of a planned program of technological innovation. In the past, independent inventors were a primary source of important new discoveries. Early inventions were identified with their inventors, people like Eli Whitney, the Wright brothers, Thomas Edison, and Henry Ford. But who invented the Boeing 747, the IBM 370-158, telecommunication satellites, or the integrated circuit? The technology-based product of today is frequently the result of a massive team effort.

Not all companies win with all R&D projects which are funded. But companies with strong R&D capabilities are able to revolutionize their products every ten to fifteen years through a planned program of R&D.

Imagine, for example, that the products produced by IBM in 1960 were placed next to the IBM products of 1975. Through managed R&D, IBM was able to create a revolutionary group of products and also develop extraordinary improvements in manufacturing productivity.

The R&D management techniques which have built the product lines of the high-technology companies can now be applied to the management of management innovations in all companies. What clearly distinguishes a Future Firm from a Present Firm is the power to produce improvements in the efficiency of management in an organized way resembling the process with which new products are developed in well-managed R&D programs.

FROM PRESENT FIRM TO FUTURE FIRM

One reason for our confidence when we forecast a Future Firm level of management competence is that the characteristics of Future Firm can now be observed in various states of development in Present Firm. We will analyze the following characteristics which will be fully developed in Future Firm but exist only in bits and pieces in the Present Firm of the mid 1970s.

1. Management innovation on request
2. Effective monitoring and planning systems for
   - External environment
   - Internal management
   - Process of management innovation
3. Management-innovation program
   - Plan
   - Resources
   - Management procedures
4. Specialization in management-innovation resources

We will contrast each of these characteristics of Future Firm with the management capabilities of Present Firm.

Management Innovation on Request

Innovations in management do occur in Present Firm, as we indicated with the task-force experiences that were described in Chapter 12. But Future Firm will have a fully developed management innovation program with all the capabilities that were described in Chapters 10 and 11. Management problems will be selected for improvement in Future Firm as technical problems and market opportunities are selected for R&D efforts in Present Firm.

Some management problems will not be subject to innovation on request. A weak company president or a sharp decline in sales because of an economic recession is the kind of problem which will not be improved in the Future Firm management-innovation program. However, a strong management-innovation program will make even a weak company president a less serious problem, because good performance will be institutionalized with procedures. Some companies are able to adapt to recession conditions better than other companies, and Future Firm will have the management capabilities to minimize the impact of a recession on corporate sales and profits. The Future Firm environmental monitoring system to be described below will anticipate the coming of a recession, thereby giving management more time to adjust production and expansion plans.

Present Firm companies produce new product and new production innovations on request through well-conceived procedures for the selection and evaluation of R&D projects. These well-managed R&D programs for new products and processes in Present Firm companies often have many of the procedures for the management of an innovation program which we recommended in Chapters 10 and 11. Incorporating these procedures into programs for improving management, Future Firm will have the capability of producing management innovations on request in the same sense that this can be done for product and process innovations through R&D in Present Firm.

Effective Monitoring and Planning Systems

Future Firm will have a long-range planning capability which will be an order of magnitude more effective than the common practice in Present Firm. Outside consultants are often amazed at the almost total lack of interest in long-range strategic planning that prevails in many companies. As the Boston Consulting Group reported in an issue of *Perspectives:*

> Many companies are unable to think about strategy. Their reports do not even suggest the fundamental strategy issues. When such companies do try to deal with a specific strategy problem, the required information is too costly or takes too long to accumulate. As a consequence, competent managers never achieve their potential because they must rely primarily on intuition. Whether the company is large or small, these defects are common.[1]

Our experience supports these observations. The long-range plans that we have evaluated for clients tend to be mere extrapolations of past trends. When asked to evaluate a corporate long-range plan, we usually find it easy to identify a number of important variables which are not included. This is because our client companies are still in a Present Firm level of management competence, and a good environmental monitoring system is not available.

Once again, as we documented in Chapter 2, there is the historical willingness of corporate management to commit tens or even hundreds of millions of dollars for new plants or R&D for new products without the willingness to commit the relatively small resources needed for effective monitoring systems.

A Future Firm level of management competence will be developed in many companies in direct response to the more difficult business environment that we analyzed in the preceding chapter. One of the most useful (and underutilized) research-based techniques is corporate planning. The wildly unstable conditions in the 1973–1975 economy have led to a dramatic increase in resources committed to planning. This increase in expenditures for planning is occurring in many companies despite the simultaneous cutting of overhead expenses in response to the profits' squeeze of the 1974–1975 recession. *Business Week,* in a cover story special report, described the sudden interest in corporate planning:

> For corporate planners and the top executives who rely on their advice, the world has never looked as hostile or as bewildering as it does today. The very uncertainties, from the clouded economic outlook to the energy crisis, that make sophisticated forward planning more vital than ever before, also make accurate planning that much more difficult.
>
> So the very nature of corporate planning is undergoing a dramatic change, and the companies that fare best in coming years may well be the ones that adapt most quickly to the new styles in planning. Today's changes are most clearly visible in two areas:
>
> *FLEXIBILITY.* Instead of relying on a single corporate plan with perhaps one or two variations, top management at more and more companies is now getting a whole battery of contingency plans and alternative scenarios.
>
> *SPEED.* Companies are reviewing and revising plans more frequently in line with changing conditions. Instead of the old five-year plan that might have been updated annually, plans are often updated quarterly, monthly, or even weekly.
>
> *This is heady stuff for corporate planners, because it was not so long ago that planning was a marginal blue-sky sort of operation that seldom got more than a nod from top management.*[2] But forward planning became a crucial function and the planner a central figure in the company in the complex, fast-changing business world of the 1960's and 1970's. "Planning has become intimately associated with the whole management process," says George A. Steiner, professor of management at UCLA.[3]

In order to achieve planning systems that are flexible and have a rapid response capability when new questions are asked, many companies are developing computer-based planning systems. In companies that are at the frontier of the technology of corporate planning, there are computer-based planning models which link to the corporate budgeting and performance reporting systems.

Future Firm management involves a strong long-range planning capability that is integrated with a continuous monitoring system of external and internal conditions. We are not suggesting the employment of a "futurist" to gaze into the distant future as *The Wall Street Journal* reported is happening.[4] Instead, we recommend a strong long-range planning group that is closely integrated with operations. An understanding of company operations increases a forecaster's ability to discover relevancy in trend analyses. Built-in interactions among the several monitoring systems will be specified in Future Firm. A forecast, no matter how accurate, does little good if corporate management does not make decisions which reflect the information in the forecast.

Charles de Gaulle in 1936 forecasted the need for mobility in warfare. De Gaulle was only a colonel in a tank regiment when he made his analysis. His writing on modern warfare was ignored by the leaders of France. Israel's intelligence group warned of the pending Arab attack in the 1973 war, but the country's leadership did not take action in response to this information. It is easier to see these breakdowns between forecasts and action in the history of war than it is to observe failures in the practices of business. Our experience in assisting clients with planning indicates that the failure to integrate planning with operating decisions is, if anything, more prevalent in business than in warfare. This historic failure to integrate planning with operations is an important reason for forecasting the use in Future Firm of three kinds of monitoring systems which will be integrated under the responsibility of one senior-level corporate planning officer.

The *Business Week* survey of corporate planning reports on the integration of planning and operations supports our recommendations as follows: "Forcing managers, not just planners, to look at 'where they want to end up' is basic to most corporate planning. The idea is that the doers in the company should also be the planners, with the planning department acting as a kind of staff group."[5] This integration of planning and operations is facilitated by a corporate strategy which clearly specifies the following three categories of monitoring in support of planning:

External environment There are a large number of important variables in the external environment which will be monitored in a Future Firm corporate planning system. These variables include macroeconomic conditions, prices, actions of competition, costs, and regulatory actions. Computer storage of information and the flexible retrieval of computer-based information today costs less than 1 percent of the costs of twenty years ago. It is now technically possible to have a cost-effective computer-based planning system which maintains a record over a number of years of the activity in the external environment which bears on the decisions of corporate management.

This formal computer-based monitoring and planning system for external environment variables will provide answers to questions which are now frequently answered by intuition and anecdotal stories. Experience is becoming obsolete too rapidly today for it to be used as the basis for decisions. When patterns of activity in the external environment change, it is critical that corporate management perceive that the old rules for decisions are no longer relevant. The Future Firm environmental monitoring system will identify deviation from historical trends and deviations from the assumptions on which management has based its operating plans.

Internal management The measurement of performance has increased in complexity during the last ten to fifteen years. It is now necessary to add to the traditional performance measures of growth in sales and profits and return on investment such new variables as adaptation to changing demand-and-supply conditions, compliance with OSHA, EEOC, EPA, and other new regulations, and the development and utilization of research-based management techniques.

The short time horizon of the traditional performance measures worked very well during the period of stable prosperity which was enjoyed by business in the United States during the twenty-five-year period which ended in 1973. This short-run maximization of business profitability and growth is now a very high-risk strategy which frequently results in counterproductive decisions.

Senior executives in many of the better-managed companies have become aware of the limitations of the traditional short-run measures of performance. One result of this awareness of the changed environment of business is the initiation of more complex measures for the evaluation of internal management.[6]

Research-based management information systems for the evaluation of internal management in Future Firm will become a critical resource for the monitoring of performance. One function of internal management which is now woefully undeveloped is the capability to innovate in management. This function will be monitored closely in Future Firm.

Management innovation It is more difficult to monitor and plan the management-innovation function than the more traditional business activities such as sales and production. The longer the time before performance can be observed and the less clear the desired outputs, the more difficult it is to measure performance.

The improvement of the practice of management as an important task of management adds a whole new dimension to performance-appraisal systems. During this next decade when there will be a surge of interest in innovation in management, it will be particularly important to support this historically neglected responsibility of management with strong monitoring and planning systems.

The history of the growth in R&D for new products and processes is useful for understanding the management practices which will be implemented to manage programs of management innovation. In the days when R&D was a relatively small activity in most companies, the planning and evaluation of the R&D function was not taken seriously by corporate management. This casualness has been replaced by a serious effort to plan R&D, and significant progress has been achieved in the better-managed companies in the evaluation of R&D performance. Progress similar to what has been achieved in the management of R&D will be experienced during the next decade in the improvement in the effectiveness of planning and evaluation systems for the management of programs of management innovation.

Management-Innovation Program

Future Firm will have a management-innovation program with procedures for funding and management which are similar to what is now considered to be good practice in the large R&D programs. Management-innovation efforts which follow the procedures described in Chapters 10 through 12 are making a significant contribution to performance in a small number of companies. The differences between the management-innovation capabilities in Present and Future Firm management are primarily the size, structure, management procedures, and position in the organization hierarchy of the management-innovation effort.

We find companies able to innovate with new management information systems or with task forces for solving a particular problem that has been recognized. We do not yet find in Present Firm management a well-organized program for bringing together all the kinds of specialists needed to innovate in management. We do not find in Present Firm companies an innovation capability which has a budget and a long-range plan for improving the effectiveness of management. We do not see in Present Firm management an executive vice president whose only responsibility is the management of the management-innovation program.

Structure of Management-Innovation Resources

The organization of an R&D laboratory is frequently analyzed in books and articles on R&D management. In this literature is the recognition of the difficulties that are experienced when attempting to structure a number of kinds of specialists into an R&D program.

There are similar problems in the management of a management-innovation program. Consider the parallel between R&D for new products and R&D for New Management which is presented in Figure 14.1. The four stages in an R&D program for new products have roughly comparable activities in a management-innovation program. Stages I, II, and III in both cases are efforts to improve a given capability or to produce or use new knowledge. Stage IV in both cases is the user of the new capability or new knowledge. Managers are the customers for a management-innovation program and have a similar function to that of customers in a traditional R&D program for new products.

Note that there are three innovation units in our structure of management innovation diagramed in Figure 14.1. This division of responsibility for management innovation will encourage the recognition of the differences in skills that are required in a highly effective management-innovation program in a large company (smaller companies will find it difficult to afford the specialization of resources that is specified in our structuring of a Future Firm management-innovation program).

After the responsibilities for each of the three specialized units in a management-innovation group are defined, we will then suggest a strategy for the development of a management-innovation capability.

1. *Management-science research* would have the responsibility of keeping current in the disciplines of management science and other bodies of knowledge that are relevant to management. It would be staffed by specialists in such disciplines as mathematics, economics, and behavioral science. Without particular regard for immediate applications in the firm

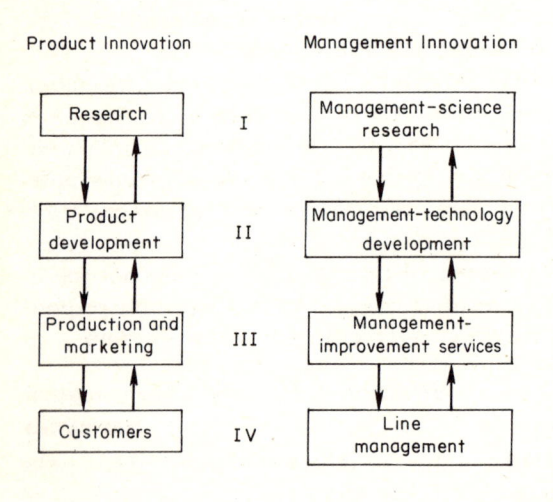

FIG. 14.1 *Parallel structures for product and management innovation.*

for which they work, these specialists would be knowledgeable in the current literature in their fields and contribute to it through research projects of their own which would have potential utility to the firm.

2. *Management-technology development* would keep management-science research apprised of what "discoveries" would be useful. The primary focus of management-technology development would be the development of practical managerial procedures and scientific tools for use by the management of the firm. Since management technologists have to recognize the organizational realities of limited data, time constraints, and financial budgets, personnel in management-technology development would necessarily have very different interests and skills from those of the more theoretical management scientists.

3. *The management-improvement–services* staff would have responsibility for working closely with line management in efforts to define projects for improving the efficiency of management. This staff would also have primary responsibility for assisting line management in the implementation of the management innovations.

FROM PRACTICE TO SCIENCE

Let us imagine a typical Present Firm with some efforts to improve the efficiency of management but without the well-organized management-innovation program that will be functioning in every Future Firm. How should this Present Firm management plan the development of a Future Firm management-innovation capability?

We recommend to clients a strategy for developing a management-innovation program which moves from practice to science. The first action should be the staffing of the management-improvement services resource. Given that line executives are fully programmed with daily responsibilities, they do not have the resources to even look at how they are managing (or coping), let alone work on innovations which will increase their effectiveness. The management-improvement function provides the staff for assisting line executives to define projects which will increase their performance. This is Stage II in the management-innovation cycle (see Figure 10.1).

It has been our experience in working with clients that many management-innovation projects have the following characteristics: low cost, low risk, low technical complexity, and fast payback. Projects with these characteristics should be the first ones initiated in a management-innovation program, as we indicated in Chapters 10 and 11. The critical variable for the successful implementation of this kind of project is the availability of line and staff time which is not fully programmed with the responsibilities of daily operations. The management-improvement–services staff is a valuable source of this needed time that can be assigned to efforts which will improve management performance.

The management-improvement–services staff should be close to the experience-based management end of the research-to-experience continuum that we described in Chapter 5. In Figure 14.2 we diagram the skills and attitudes for each of the three functional units in a management-improvement program. The truly critical shortage in business today is personnel with the time and skill needed to assist experience-based executives to improve their performance. The skill needed is sufficient knowledge of research-based techniques that it becomes possible to communicate with the professional staffs who are specialized in the various kinds of research-based techniques.

Present Firm management has employed large numbers of specialized staff professionals. The specialized professional in one functional area (such as data processing) will frequently have little contact with specialized professionals in other functions (such as organizational development). A first task of a newly formed management-improvement unit is to inventory the resources of specialized skills which will be needed in efforts to innovate in management.

The development of the management-technology and management-science research units will flow logically from the progress achieved in the first efforts of management-improvement services. The size of management-improvement services will increase as more and more management problems are made less serious through the efforts of the management-improvement staff working with line executives.

As the resources of the management-improvement specialists are increased, it will become possible to make investments in management-technology development, and eventually a group of more heavily research-oriented specialists (see Figure 14.2) will spin off into their own group, management-technology development. As experience builds in

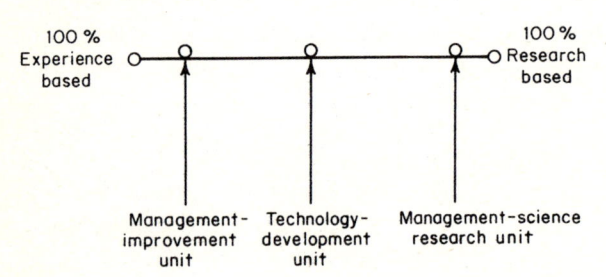

FIG. 14.2 *Skill and attitude in the three functional services of a management-innovation program.*

feeding management technology to the applications people, a spin-off may well occur again, this time creating a theory-oriented group, the management-science research unit.

When all three specialized units in a management-improvement program are functioning, it will be possible to assign problems to those specialists who are most qualified to do the work. The management-improvement unit will be working on defining projects and implementing solutions. The technology development unit will be working on building the systems, collecting the data, and other projects which have been approved by the project selection and evaluation committee. The management-science research unit will be working on more speculative efforts to improve the effectiveness of management, such as a model of the world economy or research on strategies to change consumer opinions of company products.

This depth of resources for the management-improvement program will permit the asking of questions which have historically not been asked. Consider the need for senior managers to examine the quality and usefulness of the feedback that they have been receiving. What is the level of agreement between performance and the rewards, sanctions, standards, and instructions given by management? How accurately do lower-level people seem to understand the information inputs from higher-level management? Is there harmony between the understanding of the performance/standards ratio as seen by various levels in the organization? How do any differences in this understanding affect the response of the operating personnel to the rewards/performance ratio?

The findings described by Lawrence Ferguson[7] may help to illustrate the nature of the research-based work which might follow from these questions. In a study of managerial career patterns, he found that out of a population of managers ranked by performance after five years of service, 83 percent of the managers who ranked in the top 10 percent had left the company by the end of twenty years of service while only 43 percent of the managers ranked in the bottom 50 percent had left the company. This is the kind of information that should be generated in order to develop the understanding of operations needed by top management.

If Ferguson had been working with the close participation of top management on a long-range development program, his findings could have been related to such other systems information as (1) the relationship between salary level and managerial performance, (2) the speed with which managers with high potential are recognized, (3) the reward structure for management development (that is, does it pay managers to hide good people in order to keep them for their own operations?),[8] and (4) the communication channel upward for new ideas and the degree of facility with which the organization is able to accept innovation. One would expect that Ferguson's findings would be relevant to all these other questions on which information should be available.

Just as there are now procedures for checking out physical systems, in time there will be a set of research-based programs for checking on the health of an organization. Some of these will be continuous; others will be in the form of an annual physical; and still others will be ad hoc problem-solving procedures designed to cope with specific situations.

Improvements over time occur because of the learning curve produced when feedback from the work of management-improvement programs is utilized. Each stage of work in the development of a systems understanding of an organization leads to the next stage of analysis. Just as a total system is factored into subsystems for analysis, the development work done in the management-improvement program will likewise be factored into stages of effort and fields of specialization. A systems perspective first permits this factoring of activity to be divided into manageable units, and then allows for the accumulation and integration of the research findings that result from this development work.

Collecting and analyzing information and developing an understanding of a system will be only the first stages of the work of the management-improvement program. Successful systems development *requires* the cooperation of the managers involved in the operations that are being studied. An effort by the technology-development and management-science research units will not be one short, quick look at a problem. Continuing programs provide adaptive models that better reflect the actual operations as the models are tested and altered by experience.

The differentiation of the management-innovation group program into research, development, and application categories reflects differences in the psychological makeup of people who will fill these roles. Good scientists are not necessarily good managers.[9] Management-improvement personnel should be very thoroughly oriented to the principles of line–staff cooperation. They should furthermore recognize the importance of "protecting" line managers from overzealous management-science personnel who do not thoroughly understand what is important for line management. The experience and skill of line managers must be recognized. Research untempered with experience can be dangerous, for many of the factors in a research-based decision are understood only through experience. Professionals with skills in operations research, econometrics, behavioral science, and information systems are relevant to an organization only if they can apply their knowledge to maintaining and improving corporate performance. The firm is not in the business of doing management research for its own sake; the research viewpoint must aid the mission of the firm.

As new *managerial* techniques are developed with increasing rapidity, the *educational* facet of the work of the management-innovation staff will be of great importance in the diffusion of new knowledge. The success of this new staff will depend as much on the ability to educate as it will on the ability to analyze and develop systems. The combination of an analysis function with an education responsibility should result in better communication between the managers and the research-based staff. Later innovation projects should be selected partly on educational grounds for the benefit of the team members and other personnel in the division. This education can be in specific methodologies of the New Management or in important concepts. The techniques used in a project should be allowed and encouraged to diffuse widely throughout the division. When management innovation becomes more widely understood and accepted, the case for a larger share of resources flowing toward the effort can be made. Lower-level managers who initially misunderstand the idea or view it suspiciously can be brought into the picture and assisted. The very important and very difficult problems of the division can be attacked. Experimentation in new methods of problem solving and innovation can be attempted once there is an acceptance of the idea of management innovation.

Eventually the idea of innovation will be so widely diffused throughout the division that the evaluation system for personnel will recognize and reward the innovative managers. Today, short-term optimization seems to be the goal toward which most business managers are oriented. The reason lies in the fact that rewards are based on the short term. Therefore, a crucial aspect of a research-responsive Future Firm would be a reward system which recognizes contribution to longer-run performance.

A commitment to understanding and improving the operations of a corporation or of an operating division is necessary to successfully utilize the New Management. Corporate self-analysis on a continuing basis requires that managers at all levels be willing to continue their education, to improve their managerial capabilities, and to increase their understanding of the operations for which they are responsible. The development of a management-innovation group also creates the ability and commitment to measure and evaluate the progress of the operating divisions. And the present economy, with its rapid change and intense competition, requires precisely this commitment to improvement and attainment of rapid rates of progress.

FUTURE FIRM PERFORMANCE

Future Firm levels of performance can be discovered in most Present Firms. Here and there, in this project and that system, it is possible to observe examples of what will be the standard of management performance in Future Firm. And, as we will indicate in our analysis of the achievements at Anheuser-Busch, these early efforts to innovate in mangement were difficult and exploratory because the management technology for implementing this kind of increase in the effectiveness of management was not well developed. Management-innovation efforts in the 1975–1985 decade are building on pioneering efforts such as those we are about to describe.

Advertising Effectiveness at Anheuser-Busch

Russell Ackoff and James Emshoff, management-science professors at the University of Pennsylvania, began consulting with Anheuser-Busch in 1959. During the 1959–1975 period, several articles[10] were published about what was accomplished, but it was only in the Winter 1975 issue of M.I.T.'s *Sloan Management Review* that a first case study was published.[11] The lag between the start of a consulting relationship in 1959 and the first published case study in 1975 is another example of how it is only in the last few years that published reports have appeared on improvements in company performance which have resulted from the utilization of research-based techniques. Thus proof of the usefulness of research-based techniques has been available for only a few years.

The Ackoff-Emshoff effort to improve the efficiency with which advertising expenditures were managed was a history of rejections and tentative steps forward. Ackoff and Emshoff were first employed as consultants on production-related questions. A research-based effort to study marketing expenditures was initiated, according to Ackoff and Emshoff, with the following sequence of events:

> Production operations involving scheduling and allocation of demand to breweries already had been studied and modified to yield much of the potential savings. Marketing, which involved a major share of the company's expenditures, had not yet been analyzed. An initial examination into this area revealed that the largest category of marketing cost involved advertising. Therefore, in 1961 we first recommended research into it. The proposal was turned down because of the widespread satisfaction with the company's advertising. Responsible managers were unwilling to evaluate and modify a successful program. Research turned instead to distribution and inventories. Just before mid 1961 August A. Busch, Jr., then president and chairman of the board, asked us if we would evaluate an advertising decision he was about to make. In that year Budweiser was budgeted to receive about $15,000,000 worth of advertising. Mr. Busch had been approached by the vice president of marketing with a request for an additional $1,200,000 to be spent on advertising in twelve of the 198 areas into which the company divided its

national market. The vice president had defended his proposal on the basis of the projected increase in sales that he believed would result. Mr. Busch explained that he was confronted with such a proposal every year and that he always had accepted it. He intended to do the same again, but he asked, "Is there any way I can find out at the end of the year whether I got what I paid for?" We said we would think about it and make some suggestions.

The proposal we presented to Mr. Busch shortly thereafter consisted of allowing the Marketing Department to select any six of the twelve areas initially proposed and giving it $600,000 for additional advertising. The remaining six areas would not be touched and would be used as controls. This biased selection procedure was intended to overcome some of the opposition that the Marketing Department felt toward any effort to evaluate its proposal.

Earlier we had developed an equation for forecasting monthly sales in each market area. Our plan now was to measure the deviation of actual monthly sales from the forecast for each market area in the test. Using the statistical characteristics of the forecasts we estimated that we had a 95 percent chance of detecting a 4 percent increase in sales in the areas with additional advertising. Since the increase predicted by the Marketing Department was in excess of this amount, Mr. Busch authorized the test and it was initiated.[12]

Note that Ackoff and Emshoff proposed a research project on advertising that was intended to "overcome some of the opposition that the Marketing Department felt toward any effort to evaluate its proposal."[13] It is also useful to observe that it was August A. Busch, Jr., president and chairman of the board, who authorized the research-based study of advertising effectiveness.

Ackoff and Emshoff report again and again in their case study on the opposition that they experienced in their efforts to build a research-based capability for analyzing Anheuser-Busch advertising expenditures. They also report on their lack of knowledge and experience in doing this kind of work. Note the state of the art in the early 1960s:

> Our commitment to experimentation derived from a determination to find a causal connection between advertising and sales, not merely an association between them, and to develop an ability to manipulate advertising so as to produce desired effects on sales that could be observed.
>
> Since we knew of no tested theory, we fabricated our own. Our hunch was that advertising could be considered to be a stimulus and sales a response to it.
>
> We had nothing to go on but our intuition in selecting experimental treatment levels: a 50 percent reduction, and 50 and 100 percent increases in budgeted levels of advertising.[14]

The Anheuser-Busch research-based program to improve the effectiveness of advertising was a major factor in the increase in their market share from 8.1 to 12.9 percent and a reduction of advertising expenditures from $1.89 to $0.80 per barrel, a 58 percent reduction.[15] Several major findings about the impact of advertising on consumer beer-buying decisions resulted from this effort. Contrary to the folklore of the advertising profession, it was discovered that too much advertising can result in a decrease in sales. In other words, an increase in advertising expenditures can lead to a decrease in sales. A second finding was that pulse advertising using an on-and-off pattern could be used to reduce advertising costs below the level of a program of continuous advertising.

The Ackoff-Emshoff description of the process of spending advertising funds at Anheuser-Busch prior to the research-based effort to understand the relationship between advertising and changes in sales is entirely consistent with our own experiences in evaluating client company advertising programs. Our experience indicates that frequently little effort is made to relate sales performance with expenditures for advertising and for other major categories of expenditures. As we indicated in Chapter 2, research-based management efforts should be invested to increase the performance from large expenditures in proportion to the magnitude of expenditures.

Management Information Systems at Campbell Taggart[16]

In this, the concluding chapter of this book, we will present some very convincing evidence that Future Firm levels of management competence will be achieved in companies because of the greater difficulties that will be experienced by business in the next decade. The performance of Campbell Taggart in coping with the 1973–1974 inflation, which devastated the baking industry, provides further evidence of the usefulness of research-based management techniques.

The baking industry had been hit very hard in 1973–1974 by rapid price increases in key ingredients. Prices paid in 1974 compared with 1971 were up over 400 percent for sugar, 40 percent for flour, and 300 percent for lard. Most of the baking companies found it difficult to make profits in this inflationary environment. *Business Week* cited Campbell Taggart as the exception to the general decline in the profits of the large bakers:

	1973	1974 (9 months)
Continental Baking (ITT Subsidiary)		
Sales	$956,281,000	$823,623,000
Net	125,000	3,529,000
Margin	.01%	.43%
Campbell Taggart		
Sales	$456,515,000	$441,255,000

Net	14,769,000	14,511,000
Margin	3.2%	3.3%
American Bakeries		
Sales	$345,574,000	$303,551,000
Net	(2,019,000)*	748,000
Margin	—	.25%
Interstate Brands		
Sales	$308,020,879	$296,069,878
Net	99,626	3,231,748
Margin	.03%	1.1%

*Loss

How did Campbell Taggart perform so well in comparison with competition? Through the utilization of research-based management techniques! "The key ingredient of these increased profits," reports *Business Week,* "is a control system that monitors costs and pricing so precisely that Campbell Taggart can instantaneously pass on cost increases to its consumers—something that its competitors often cannot do." As Chief Executive Officer Bill O. Mead boasted: "It takes other companies a month or more to get the figures. By that time you may be dead and not know it." This *Business Week* article reports on the imitation by competitors, one of the factors which spurs the coming of Future Firm: "Other national baking companies concede that Campbell Taggart is the industry leader in developing computer control systems, and some are frankly trying to copy parts of it." The control system at Campbell Taggart is linked to management procedures:

> The controls system monitors more than pricing, which was particularly important during price controls. *If a bad profit trend develops over two or three weeks at a plant, the manager can expect a visit from a team of specialists* who analyze sales figures, inspect production facilities and search for inefficiencies.
>
> They may find poorly maintained equipment damaging thousands of units of baked goods or an employee productivity fall off because of inadequate supervision. Key efficiency indicators revealed by the computer, such as the number of product pounds sold per sales route and the amount of bread returned to the plant stale, often alert the inspection team to problem areas even before they arrive. [Italics added.]

This Campbell Taggart experience is typical of the evolution of management in many companies. The first application of computers at Campbell Taggart occurred about fifteen years ago (1959–1960) and was an effort to eliminate paperwork for route salespersons in Houston. The computers now provide each salesperson with a record of sales on 200 products—saving an estimated one hour per day for each Campbell Taggart salesperson. Computer capacity will be expanded in 1975 by minicomputers in twenty plants, bringing the total computer hardware investment to $3.5 million. The linking of effective computer processing of management information with a corporate staff of problem solvers provides Campbell Taggart with the research-based–management capability that has enabled it to maintain profit margins during a period of rapid inflation. Our experience in working with client companies indicates that the new-management capabilities developed by Campbell Taggart can be implemented system by system with relatively low risks and a high rate of return on investment from each new stage of improved systems capability that is developed. Future Firm management systems are not a wildly theoretical pie-in-the-sky concept of the dreamers of the 1950s. There is now very strong evidence that the research-based management capabilities of Future Firm have been working effectively to solve the problems created by the inflation and recession of the 1970–1975 economy.

Equal Employment Compliance System

Another example of research-based management is the equal employment compliance system and management procedures which have been implemented in one of the largest manufacturing companies in the country. This system compares company employment by category of workers (women, blacks, Spanish surname, etc.) with the population in each of 200 plant locations. The system maintains a record of affirmative action efforts by category of worker for a number of activities such as job applicant interviews, job offers, promotions, and training. Each company location has equal employment objectives, and actual performance compared with objectives is monitored in this management information system. The corporate employee relations group gives seminars for management in order to create an understanding of the compliance standards of the Equal Employment Opportunity Commission. This company has been hit with a relatively small number of EEOC suits and has not suffered serious penalties from litigation with the government.

This research-based equal employment compliance program is typical of the kinds of systems which will be standard practice in Future Firm's management response to the large number of government regulations which have been initiated in the last decade. As we described in Chapter 13, the government has created a regulatory environment in which only firms with a strong research-based management capability will be able to survive. The evidence in this chapter and in Chapter 12 indicates that the research-based–management capabilities of Future Firm are a cost-effective strategy for coping with the business problems of the 1970s and 1980s.

Cost Reduction at Emerson Electric[17]

Given the importance of innovation in management, it is surprising that executives do not report on their accomplishments in increasing the efficiency of management in corporate annual reports. There has been a significant increase during the last decade in disclosures about R&D accomplishments in annual reports, and we expect that improvements in the efficiency of management will increasingly be a topic that is covered in annual reports during this next decade.

Senior management at Emerson Electric is justly proud of its management performance, and the 1974 annual report includes a chart of how cost-reduction targets have been met. The extraordinary growth in sales, profits, profits over sales, and profits over equity in this company (presented in Table 14.1) has been achieved in large part by the program of cost cutting that was initiated by W. R. Persons in 1954 when he became chief executive officer. In *The Wall Street Journal* report of how Persons initiated the cost-reduction program, it was observed that "while Emerson used a good, standard cost system for manufacturing, there wasn't much relationship between factory costs and total costs, particularly including sales costs. 'We found a basketful of products we were actually selling for a loss and didn't know it,' he [Persons] says."[18]

Note the discovery in 1954 that the management of Emerson Electric did not know the true costs of products and did not know when losses were experienced. The accountants were producing information which

TABLE 14.1 Performance of Emerson Electric, 1954–1974

	1954	1974	1974/1954
Emerson Electric sales ($000)	80,560	1,137,771	14.1
Net profit after taxes ($000)	1,885	77,303	41.0
Profits as a percent of sales	2.3	6.8	3.0
Position in sales ranking on *Fortune* 500 list	345	172	
Percentage of profits over equity			
Emerson Electric		17.2	
All *Fortune* 500 companies*		12.4	

*Median performance.
SOURCE: *Fortune* 500 lists, 1955 and 1975.

was not useful for the evaluation of performance. Accountants have not been trained to produce information that is needed for many decisions (note our discussion of the work of accountants in Chapter 9) and management in most companies tends not to have a plan for the production, distribution and utilization of critically important information from either external or internal sources.

Emerson Electric has programmed improvement in the effectiveness of management with procedures that are similar to our recommendations in Chapters 10 and 11. Each of Emerson's thirty divisions has an employee assigned responsibility for cost cutting. As *The Wall Street Journal* notes: "Each individual project is charted, and an executive is assigned to monitor its progress.... Not only are projects followed carefully at the division level, but also each month top management monitors the progress. If there is a lag, Mr. Fox [corporate vice president in charge of the cost reduction program] or some member of his staff seeks to remedy the situation."

There are some who question the bottom-line benefits of investments to improve management performance. The bottom-line effects of the Emerson Electric cost-cutting program are very evident in Table 14.1. The Emerson Electric cost-cutting program represents an investment in improved performance that is managed like R&D for new products in companies with cost-effective R&D programs. This *Wall Street Journal* article noted that for seventeen successive years Emerson Electric has experienced record earnings. Profits increased even in periods of recession. In 1970, for example, the average profits decline in manufacturing was 10 percent, while Emerson showed a 9.7 percent increase. We wonder how many of the company presidents who read this front-page *Wall Street Journal* story of June 4, 1975, initiated a similar cost-cutting program in their operations. Of the company presidents (or other managers) who were inspired by this story, we wonder how many recognized that a similar program to increase performance requires a long-run commitment to the encouragement and management of the process of innovation.

A FINAL WORD

As we look ahead toward 1980, we see a *small number of firms in which an extraordinary level of management competence has been developed.* In response to a wildly unstable world, the management in these firms will have developed the capability to cope with difficult conditions. We do not see in 1980 the kind of prosperity enjoyed by many companies during the long business boom which began with World War II and ended with the 1974–1975 recession. Companies with a Future Firm level of management competence, however, will prosper despite the more difficult business environment. A Future Firm will have the management depth and techniques to anticipate changes and respond with shifts in resources to expanding market areas while reducing commitments in the markets that are becoming less profitable.

It has been our experience in working with companies during the growth in the utilization of research-based management techniques that each stage of progress has been cost-effective. That is, the return on investment in efforts to improve the practice of management has been very satisfactory in companies with executives who understand how to innovate in management. The data base becomes more useful with each year that additional information is put into computer storage. Response time becomes shorter as minicomputers are diffused throughout the company. Data are sent from remote terminals to the corporate computer by telecommunications. Computers send information back and forth between corporate headquarters and plants and offices throughout the world. Management at corporate headquarters is informed of divisional performance within the first week after the close of business in a month. Management becomes more experienced in the utilization of research-based techniques to analyze the information in the data base. Year-to-date and historical analyses provide the information that initiates corporate actions when divisional management appears to be in trouble. New-management practices are introduced to improve performance when difficulties are discovered.

When American business sees a new opportunity, it is able to move very quickly. We have presented ways around the roadblocks delaying the adoption of research-based management techniques. There is now ample evidence of the effectiveness of new research-based management. Even the more conservatively managed companies are beginning to make progress toward the adoption of new-management technology. As we watch the development and utilization of research-based management techniques in a number of companies, we find it difficult to be pessimistic about the longer-run future of American business.

NOTES AND REFERENCES

1. Tilles, Seymour: "Strategy and Information," *Perspective*, No. 163, Boston: Boston Consulting Group, 1975.
2. Emphasis added.
3. "Corporate Planning: Piercing Future Fog in the Executive Suite," *Business Week*, Apr. 28, 1975, p. 46.
4. Gallese, Liz R.: "More Companies Use Futurists to Discern What Is Lying Ahead," *The Wall Street Journal*, Mar. 31, 1975, p.1.
5. "Corporate Planning," loc. cit., p. 50.
6. A clear portrayal of the linkage between long-run planning and short-term monitoring

is given in P. Lorange and M. S. Scott Morton, "A Framework for Management Control Systems," *Sloan Management Review,* Fall, 1974, pp. 41–56.
7. Ferguson, L. L.: "Better Management of Managers' Careers," *Harvard Business Review,* March–April 1966, pp. 139–152.
8. Alfred, T. M.: "Checkers or Choice in Manpower Management," *Harvard Business Review,* January–February 1967, pp. 157–169.
9. McClelland, David C.: "The Role of Achievement Orientation in the Transfer of Technology," in William H. Gruber and Donald G. Marquis (eds.), *Factors in the Transfer of Technology,* Cambridge, Mass.: M.I.T., 1969, p. 61.
10. See A. A. Busch, III, "The Essentials of Corporate Growth," address given to Charles Coolidge Parlin Marketing Award Banquet, May 9, 1973; E. H. Vogel, Jr., "Creative Marketing and Management Science," *Management Decision,* Spring 1969, pp. 21–25; "Wharton Analyzes the Beer Drinker," *Business Week,* Mar. 24, 1973, p. 44; "While Big Brewers Quaff, the Little Ones Thirst," *Fortune,* November 1972, pp. 103ff.
11. Ackoff, Russell L., and James R. Emshoff: "Advertising Research at Anheuser-Busch, Inc. (1936–68)," *Sloan Management Review,* Winter 1975, pp. 1–15.
12. Ibid., p. 2.
13. Ibid.
14. Ibid., pp. 3–4.
15. Ibid., p. 12.
16. Based on *Business Week,* "A Price Monitor Keeps the Dough Rising," Dec. 7, 1974, p. 72.
17. Garino, David P.: "How a Big Company Controls Its Costs in Good Times and Bad," *The Wall Street Journal,* June 4, 1975, pp. 1, 20.
18. Ibid. p. 20.

Index

Accountants and accounting, 100, 118, 137
    achievements of, 139
    challenges to, 143
    CPA exam, 141–143
    education for, 141–143
    information, losing control of, 139–143
    management-innovation program and, 155–156
    MIS, relationship to, 140–141
    problems with, 12, 20
    reports, increase in, 130–131
        figure, 131
    (*See also* Audits and auditing)
Ackoff, Russell L., 135, 145, 226–228, 234
Acquisitions (*see* Diversification)
Advertising, 23, 26–27
    effectiveness of, 226–228
    (*See also* Marketing; Sales)
Albrook, Robert C., 91, 95
Alexander, Sydney, 20
Alexander, T., 133, 145
Alfred, T. M., 234
Alibrandi, Joseph F., 48
Allen, S., 115
Allied Products, 106
Allied Stores, 15
Aluminum Company of America, 58
American Bakeries, 229
American Enterprise Institute, 197, 211
American Management Associations, Presidents Association of the, 178, 186
American Telephone and Telegraph, 194–195
Anheuser-Busch, 226–228
Ansoff, I. H., 54
Anthony, Robert, 71, 72, 75, 81
Ash Council Report, 197
Atomic Energy Commission, 211
Audits and auditing, 98
    discovering losses, 28, 108–109
    as integration technique, 108–109
    (*See also* Accountants and accounting)
Auto industry, 31–32, 101, 113, 161, 194
Automation of management, 73–75
    (*See also* Computer-based systems; Computers)

Bacon, Kenneth, 211
Baking industry, 17, 228–230
Ball, Robert, 116
Banks and banking, 4, 108–109, 150
    changing environment of, 4
    competition in, 17
    computers in, 120–124, 132–133
    increased specialization in, 77
    M.B.A.'s utilized by, 83–85
    performance in, 108, 120–124
Beckhard, Richard, 81
Behavioral view of management, 70–71
Berlew, D. F., 162
Boisseau, H. J., 66
Borch, Fred T., 33, 35
Boston Consulting Group, 215, 233
Boston Globe, 211
Bradish, Richard D., 67, 81
Brainstorming, 157
Brandenburg, R. G., 54
Brooks, Harvey, 201
Brownlow Commission, 196–197
Budgets:
    integration and, 105, 117, 120, 121, 126
    performance and, 117, 120–121, 126
    systems for, 12–13
Burgen, Carl G., 208
Burger Chef, 28
Burnham, David, 211
Busch, August A., Jr., 226, 227
Business schools:
    accounting curriculum, 141–143
    careers in relationship to, 1, 43
    Carnegie Foundation report, 1, 42–43, 67–68
    case method, 68–69, 75–76
    emphasis of, 55–58, 69, 75–76
    faculty, 43–44, 55–58, 76
    Ford Foundation report, 1, 42–43, 67–68
    managerial success, relationship to, 69
    in 1950's, 1, 42–44, 67–68
    salaries of graduates from, 88–89
    skills of graduates from, 69, 76
    specialization in, 86–87

235

236 / Index

Business schools (Cont.):
  student differences at, 85–87
  weaknesses of, 42–44, 69, 75–76

Cabot Corporation, 2, 179–182
Camp, Charles B., 115
Campbell Taggart, 17, 228–230
Capital:
  invested in management, 25
  shortage of, 199–201
Careers:
  business schools and, 43
  managerial performance and, 223
Carnegie-Mellon University, 57, 95
Cerro Company, 89
Chandler, Alfred D., 5–7, 19
Charpie, Robert A., 2, 179–182, 184
Chase Manhattan Bank, 83, 108–109
China, 202, 204
Chirac, Jacques, 204
Christensen, A. Sherman, 115
Chrysler Corporation, table, 189
Churchman, C. West, 3–4, 19, 63, 66
Clean Air Act of 1965, 194
Cole, Edward M., 194, 211
Communication:
  barriers to, 110–111
  integration and, 121–126
  in organizations, 26, 109–111
  performance and, 121–126
  specialists hindering, 103
  (See also Organizational structure)
Competition, 7, 134
  foreign, 31–32, 204
  improved management caused by, 15, 17, 229
Computer-based systems:
  corporate planning, 11, 218
  data bases, 45
  in Future Firm, 15, 217–218
  in Present Firm, 11–14
  (See also Computers; Management information systems)
Computer industry, 34, 44
Computers, 44–49
  accounting and, 140–141
  in banking, 120–124
  cost monitoring, 228–230
  EDP, performance of, 48, 120–124
  evolution of, 45–47
  growth in value, 177
  increase in, graph, 43
  information and, 132–133, 138–140
  management-science implementation, 62
  software capability, 12
  specialists in, need for, 123–124
  (See also Computer-based systems; Management information systems)
Conrady, W. N., 131
Continental Baking, 228
Continental Corporation (Diners Club), 28
Copperweld Steel, 106
Cordiner, Ralph, 33, 96–97, 115
Corfam, 28

Cost:
  computerized monitoring of, 228–230
  control systems, 11–13, 228–232
  of information, 136
    graph, 137
  of management, 24–26
  of M.B.A.'s, 87–90
  (See also Profitability)
Council of Economic Advisors, 192
CPA (certified public accountant) exam, 141–143
Cresap, Mark, 130
Crisis management, 147–148

Data:
  collection and analysis of, 137–138
  data bases, 45
  vs. information, 133–136
  overload of, 129–130
  (See also Information)
Davidson, H. Justin, 145
Decentralization:
  evolution of business, 6
  General Electric, 33–34, 96–97
  specialization and, 96–97
Decision making:
  in changing environment of business, 1–5
  by consensus, 169–170
  decentralization and, 6, 97
  information for, 130–138
  in pricing, 3
  in sales force management, 21–22
  specialization in, 97
  as a view of management, 71–73
    table, 72
Demand pull, 49–52
Differentiation, 118–119
  (See also Specialists and specialization)
Digital Equipment Corporation, 196
Diners Club, 28
Discretionary time, 148
Diversification, 28–30, 78
Dougherty, William, Jr., 77, 179
Drucker, Peter F., 39, 54, 102–103, 115, 148, 162, 169–170, 176
Dukakis, Michael, 195–196
Du Pont, 6, 28, 96, 213

Economy, United States, 188–191, 205–207
Eco-Technic Recycling Conference IV, 211
Egypt, 205
Eisenhower administration, 1, 197
Electric utilities, 74–75
Electronic data processing (see Computers)
Emerson Electric, 231–232
Emery, James C., 81
Emshoff, James, 226–228, 234
Energy, 2, 193, 201, 216
Engineers, role of, 52
Engman, Lewis A., 193–194
Environment, 2
  auto industry neglect of, 31–32

Environment (Cont.):
  government regulations about, 194
    table, 197
  (See also Environment of business)
Environment of business, 187–211
  capital shortages, 199–201
  discontinuity in, 1–2
  dysfunctional government relations, 191–195, 207–208
  foreign attitudes, 202–205
  government growth, 195–198
  improvement in management because of, 209–211
  inflation, 1–2, 206
  information needs because of, 130–131
  legalistic, 198–199
  natural resources, 201–203
  need for planning because of, 216
  need for specialization because of, 77, 97
  (See also Environment)
Equal Employment Opportunity Commission, 77, 98, 192–193, 230
Estes, F. M., 101
Europe (see specific country)
Evolution of business, 5–6
  table, 7
Evolution of management information needs, 137–139
Ewing, David W., 41, 54
Experience-based management, 2–5, 67–69
  definition of, 2
  diversification failures, causing, 29–30, 78
  emotional outlook, 79–80
  inadequacy of, 4–5
  need for, 69, 73–76
  research-based staff support of, 2–5, 25–26
  specialization of, 77–78, 101
  thinking process of, 79–80
  (See also Line management)
Exxon, table, 189

Federal Trade Commission, 193–194, 198
Federated Stores, 15
Feedback:
  in decision making, 3
  integration, 118, 127–128
  management improvement, 223–224
  marketing expenditures, 27
  performance and, 118, 127–128
  in systems, 109
Ferguson, Lawrence L., 223–224, 234
Finance, 23, 87, 119, 131–133, 139–141
Financial Accounting Standards Board, 198
Financial Executives Institute, 133–134, 140–141
Firestone Rubber Company, 113
First National Bank of Boston, xii, 150
First National City Bank, 83
Ford, Gerald, 193
Ford administration, 196–198, 211
Ford Foundation:
  business schools, report on, 1, 42–43, 67–68
  Energy Project Report, 211
Ford Motor Company, 138
  table, 189

Forecasting, 3–4, 11–12, 217
Foreign competition, 2, 204
  in auto industry, 31–32
Forrester, Jay, 39, 54
Fortune 500 list of large corporations, 9, 16, 106
Fouraker, Lawrence E., 19
Fowler, J. B., 179
Fox, John A., 179, 180, 184
France, 200, 202, 204, 217
Frohman, Alan L., 170–171, 176
Full Employment Act of 1946, 206
Future Firm:
  characteristics of, 214
  definition of, 8
  effect of environment on, 187–188, 209–211
  General Electric, 34–35
  management of, example, 14–15
  management-innovation capability, 214–215, 219–221
  management science in, 220–221
  management technology in, 221
  monitoring and planning systems, 215–219
  performance of, examples, 225–232
  Sears Roebuck, 14–15, 17
  specialists in, 222–225

Galbraith, Jay, 81, 130, 145
Gallese, Liz B., 233
Garino, David P., 231, 234n
General Electric, 32–35, 96–99, 105
  table, 189
General Foods, 28
General Motors, 6, 31–32, 161
  table, 189
Generalists, 77–78, 113
Gilgore, Sheldon G., 179, 181–182, 184
GNP (gross national product):
  forecasts of, 189–191
  government share of, 195
  growth in, 188–190
Goal orientation, 118
Goodyear Tire and Rubber Company, 113
Gordon, Robert A., 19, 81
Government:
  foreign, 208–209
  United States: control of resources, 201
    debt, 195–196
    inefficiency of, 195–198
    relationship with business, 207–209
    unheeded commissions, 196–197
Government regulations:
  accounting reports required by, 130
  antitrust, 193–195
  auto industry, 32, 194
  business response to, 105–106, 181–182, 208–209
  equal employment, 192–193, 230–231
  negative effects of, 191–192
  partial list of, table, 197
  "real" cost of, 197–198, 200–201
  task forces to respond to, 181–182
Grace, W. R., 28
Grayson, L. Jackson, Jr., 58, 66
Gregg, Charles L., 81
Gross national product (see GNP)

238 / Index

Growth, 188–190
Gruber, William H., 31, 36, 95, 126, 128, 142, 145, 162, 178, 186, 212, 233, 234
Guinea, 205
Gulf Oil Company, table, 189

Haagen-Smit, A., 36
Hammond, John, 103
Harbridge House, 196
Harness, Edward, 169
Harper, John D., 58, 66
Harvard Business School:
    case method, 68–69
    recruitment at, 83
    salary of graduates, 89
    specialization at, 86–87
Harvard University, Center for International Affairs, 203–204
Hekemian, J. S., 36, 95
Hertz, David B., 75, 81
Honda, 31
Honeywell, 34, 196
Hood, H. P., 179, 180
Hoover Commissions, 197
Howell, James E., 19, 81
Hughes, G. M. K., xii
Human resources:
    development of specialized, 98
    M.B.A.'s, 82–95
    needs of, 127
    value of, 25
    (See also Organizational development)
Hyatt, James C., 192, 211

IBM (International Business Machines):
    antitrust suit, 101–102, 115
    research capability, 213–214
    sales in 1940 and 1973, 188–189
        table, 189
    strategic planning, 35–36
Improvement (see Management innovation)
Industrial engineers, 52
Inflation, 1–2
    government policy for, 206–207
    research-based management and, 228–230
Information, 129–144
    control of, 139–144
    cost and profitability of, 136
        graph, 137
    crisis in, 129–134
    for decision making, 130–132, 134–136, 138
    evolution of management, 137–139
    handling of, 129–131
    inadequacy of, 131–133
    for model building, 135–138
    production of, 129–130
    strategy for, 143–144
    systems for, 132–134, 136
    (See also Data; Management information systems)
Innovation:
    in management (see Management innovation)
    technological: auto industry, 31–32
        diffusion of, 8–9, 49–51

Institute of Management Sciences (TIMS), 60–61, 66
Integration:
    amount needed, 105–107
    in banking, 120–124
    budgets to promote, 105–106, 117, 120–121
    communication to further, 121–126
    defined, 97
    differentiation and, 118–119
    of EDP, 120–124
    integrators and, 112
    performance and, 117–127
    planning and, 120–121, 125–126
    in plastics firms, 118–119
    of R&D, 125–126
    specialization and, 97–100, 104–105
    techniques of, 106–111
        formal systems, 107–109
        management actions, 110–111
        organization, 109–110
Interstate Brands, 229
Investment in management:
    to avoid losses, 27–29
    at General Electric, 32–35
    management competence and, 24–27
    management-investment ratio, 24
    in recessionary period, 21
    ROI calculation, 24–27
    (See also Management innovation)
Israel, 217
ITT (International Telephone and Telegraph), table, 189

Jacobson's, 179
Japan, 194–195, 200–201, 208–209
Jones, Curtis H., 36, 95
Jones, Reginald H., 33–37
Justice Department, U.S., 193–194

Kahn, R., 145
Katz, D., 145
Kaysen, Carl, 201
Keen, Peter G. W., 79, 81
Kennedy, D. W., 107, 115, 145
Knowledge:
    economic importance of, 38–39
    for management (see Management knowledge)
Kolb, David A., 162, 170–171, 176
Kuwait, 205

Landis Commission, 197
Laubach, Gerald D., xi–xii, 106, 179
Lawrence, Paul, 107, 112, 115, 118–119, 128
Lawsuits, increase in, table, 198
Lawyers:
    in antitrust work, 101, 115
    cost of, 199
    demand for, 198–199
    management of, 101–102, 104
    performance evaluation of, 102
    selection of, 104
    specialization of, 77, 104
    in Washington, D.C., 199

Index / 239

Learning curve, 224
Lewis, Paul, 202, 212
Libya, 205
Line management:
  analytic competence of, 40
  division performance and, 25
  management-innovation effort by, 147–152
  problem solution by, 80–81
  shortage of, 35
  specialists, involvement with, 80–81
  specialization of, 101
  in task forces, 179–180
  time constraints on, 147–148
  (See also Experience-based management)
Little, Arthur D., Inc., 196
Little, John D. C., 61–63, 66
Litton Industries, 28
Livingston, J. Sterling, 43, 54, 69, 81
Lodish, Leonard M., 61–63, 66
Logan, Louis L., 142, 145
Lorange, Peter, 233
Lorsch, Jay, 107, 112, 115, 118–119, 128
Losses, corporate, 27–29
LTV, Inc., 28
Lynch, Mitchell, 211

McClelland, David C., 234
McCracken, Paul W., 192
McGraw-Hill, Inc., 191, 211
Machlup, Fritz, 38–39, 54
McKenney, James L., 79, 81
Mackler, Robert J., 41, 54
Management:
  behavioral view of, 70–71
  changing activities of, 73–75
  cost of, 24–27
  decision-making view of, 71–73
  improvement of, 7–10
Management competence:
  availability of resources for, 29–30
  investment needed for, 24–27
  measurement of, 9–10, 32
  range of, 9–10, 16
    graph, 10
Management consultants:
  in advertising, 226–228
  Harbridge House, 196
  Arthur D. Little, Inc., 196
Management information systems (MIS):
  for accounting, 131–132, 139–143
  computer-based, 12–15
  control of, 140–141
  coordination of, 131–132
  definition of, 133–134
  evaluation of, 136
  improvement in management based on, 11–15, 233
  integration and, 106–107
  model building in, 135–138
  to monitor costs, 228–230
  overdesign of, 132–133
  specialist problems caused by, 18
  staff needs to develop, 151
  (See also Computer-based systems; Computers)

Management innovation:
  acceptance of, 160
  budgets, 149–150, 161
  demand pull, caused by, 49–52
  evaluation of, 218–219
  failures in, 153, 164, 167–168
  funding of, 155, 160
  in Future Firm, 214–215, 219–225
  future structure of, 219–221
  line management involvement with, 147–152
  line-staff relationship during, 150–151
  managerial freedom to do, 146
  program for, 155–162
    initiation of, 155–156
    planning of, 158–159
  project selection, 159–160
  project visibility, 161
  in recessions, 149, 155
  resources for, 158
  staff selection, 150–151, 156
  strategy for, 152–155, 161–162
  structural development of, 221–225
  success factors in, 147
  (See also Investment in management)
Management-innovation project:
  diagnosis and solution, 168–170
  documentation of, 172
  evaluation of, 172–173
  failures of, 164, 167–168
  flowchart of, figure, 165
  implementation, 170–171
  problem finding, 165–166
  selection of, 166
  specification and justification, 166–168
  stages of, 164, 174
  termination of, 173–174
  unanticipated consequences of, 170–171
Management knowledge:
  availability of, 39–42, 53
  change in management activities, 75
  demand pull, 49–51
  diffusion of, 225
  specialists in, 38–42
  supply push, 49–51, 53
  (See also Knowledge; Management science;
    Management technology)
Management practices:
  improvement in, 7–10
  integration and, 127–128
  monitoring of, 6–7
  performance and, 127–128
Management problems:
  brainstorming, 157
  finding, 22–23, 156–158, 165–166
  management depth, 29–30
  research-based solution of, 23–24
Management science, 56–65
  application of, example, 61–63
  applying, 52–53, 61–63
  attitudes toward, 55–56
  definition of, 41
  demand pull on, 56
  in Future Firm, 220–221
  manager interaction with, 57–58, 63–65
  publications, 59–60, 64

240 / Index

Management science (Cont.):
  return on investment from, 63–65
  utilization problems, 56–61
    inventory of, table, 59
    literature on, 59–60
    scientists concern for, 58–60
  (See also Management knowledge; Management technology)
Management technologists, 51–53
  definition of, 52
Management technology:
  changing management activity, 75
  definition of, 61
  in Future Firm, 221
  (See also Management knowledge; Management science)
Managers, 70–73
  as assets, 25
  career patterns, 223
  freedom of action, 73, 146
Mansfield, Edwin, 8–9, 19, 51, 54
Manufacturing, 30
  cost control in, 11, 231–232
  integration and differentiation, relation to, 118–119
  management-innovation project in, 164–167
March, J. G., 95
Marcor, 15
Marketing, 24–27
  advertising: effectiveness of, 226–228
    media-selection model, 61–63
  customer control system, 12
  information for, 135
  integration and differentiation, relation to, 118–119
  model building for, 135
  in Present Firm, 11–12
  in Prior Firm, 11
  sales-force management, 21–22
  sales forecasting, 3–4, 11–12
  (See also Advertising; Sales)
Marquis, Donald G., xii, 234
Massachusetts, Commonwealth of, 194–195
Massachusetts Institute of Technology, 57, 86, 88–89, 91, 95
M.B.A.'s (master's degrees in management), 42–44, 82–95
  in banking, 83–85
  costs of, 87–90
  defined, 42
  increase in, graph, 42–43
  job satisfaction of, 92–93
  organizational socialization of, 92
  personal characteristics of, 93–94
  quality differences in, 83, 85–87, 100
  recruitment of, 83, 87–88
  research skills of, 69, 85–86
  retention of, 91–94
  return on investment in, 90–91
  salary expectations of, 83, 88–89
  specialization of, 85–87
  strategy for utilization, 84–85
  work experience, 87
Mead, William O., 229
MEDIAC (media-selection model), 61–63

Mehta, Dileep, 212
Michelin, 113–114
Miles, Raymond E., 95
Mills, Ted, 54
Mintzberg, Henry, 145, 162
MIS (see Management information systems)
M.I.T. Sloan School of Management, xii, 88–89
Mobil Oil, table, 189
Model building:
  accounting information for, 137
  increase in, 41–42
  information and, 135–138
  (See also Computers; Management science)
Monitoring systems:
  in Future Firm, 215–219
  for surprise reduction, 26
  (See also Computer-based systems; Computers; Management information systems)
Montgomery Ward, 15
Moody's Industrials, table, 189
Moore, Geoffrey, 206
Moore, Leo B., 168, 176
Multinational corporations, 6, 203–205
Murphy, Thomas A., 101
Myers, Sumner, 50, 54

National Bureau of Economic Research, 206
National Commission on Materials Policy, 211
National Industrial Conference Board, 140
Natural resources shortages, 201, 203
NCNB Corporation, 77, 179
New Management:
  defined, 17–18
  (See also Research-based management)
New York Stock Exchange, 30–31, 199–200
Niles, J. S., 95
Nolan, Richard L., 54, 145
North Carolina National Bank, 17, 77, 179
Northeastern University, 141–142

OPEC nations (see Organization of Petroleum Exporting Countries)
Operations research (see Management science)
Operations Research Society of America (ORSA), 60
Opinion Research Corporation, 192
Organization of Petroleum Exporting Countries (OPEC), 201–203, 205
Organizational development, 106, 174
  in division management, 25
  evolution of, 40–41
  management development, 26
  management interest in, 41
  New Management, inputs of, 18
Organizational socialization, 92
Organizational structure:
  communication, 109–111
  decentralization, 5–6, 96–100
  differentiation, 118–119
  evolution of, 5–7
  integration, 109–110, 118–119, 122–125
  of management innovation in Future Firm, 219–221
  of multinational corporations, 6

Penney, J. C., 15
Pension Reform Act, 198
Performance:
  budgets and, 117, 120–121, 126
  communication and, 121–126
  divisional, 25
  economic conditions, limited by, 188–190
  feedback on, 118, 127–128
  of Future Firm, examples, 225–232
  improvement in management, 7, 9–10
  integration and, 117–127
  of management-innovation projects, 172–173
  management practices related to, 127–128
  in managerial careers, 223
  measures of, 32, 218
    banking, 120–123
    EDP, 120–123
    plastics firms, 119
    R&D, 125–126
  organizational structure and, 6
  planning and, 120–121, 125–126
  of specialists, 102
  of top management, 122, 126
  (*See also* Profitability)
Personnel function, 40–41
Persons, W. R., 231
Peterson, C., 179
Pfizer, Inc., xi, 106–107, 179, 182–183
Pharmaceutical industry, 31
Pierson, Frank C., 19
Planning, 41, 71–73
  computer-based systems, 11
  flexibility in, 216
  in Future Firm, 215–219
  incentives for, 106
  integration and, 106, 120–121, 125–126
  integration with operations, 217
  management-innovation, 158–159
  performance and, 120–121, 125–126
  production and inventory, 13
  rapid response, 216–217
  reducing surprises, 26
  (*See also* Strategic planning)
Plastics industry, integration and performance in, 118–119
Poensgen, O. H., 31, 36, 126, 128
Pounds, William F., 162
Prakke, F., 31, 36, 126, 128
Present Firm:
  definition of, 8
  management of, example, 11–14
President's Materials Policy Commission, 211
Price, D. J. de S., 64, 66
Price-Waterhouse and Company, 142–143
Pricing decisions, 3
Prior Firm:
  definition of, 8
  management of, example, 10–11
Problem finding, 23, 156–158, 165–166
Procter and Gamble, 169, 176, 213
Production (*see* Manufacturing)
Productivity, 188–190
Profitability:
  General Electric, 35–36

Profitability (*Cont.*):
  of information, 136
    graph, 137
  management competence, 30–32
  research-based management, 15, 17, 32
  retailing, 15
  short-run vs. long-run, 30–32, 218
  (*See also* Performance)
Project management (*see* Management-innovation project)
Public opinion of business, 192–193

Quantitative techniques, 39–41

Rappaport, Alfred, 145
RCA (Radio Corporation of America), 28, 34
Recruitment of M.B.A.'s, 83, 87–88
Research and development (R&D):
  funding increase, 177
  in industry, 51
  integration of, 125–126
  management depth, 30
  performance of, 125–126
  time orientation, 126
Research-based management:
  case studies, 14–15, 226–232
  defined, 17
  in government, 196
  increase in utilization of, 6–10, 15
  inputs and outputs, 17–18
  as line-management support, 3–5, 25–26
  as response to change, 3–5
  staff work, 2–5, 17–18
    definition of, 2
  task forces, 181–183
  thinking process of, 79–80
  (*See also* Specialists and specialization)
Retailing, 15
Return on investment (ROI):
  of improvement in management, 24–27, 35–36
  of management innovation, 171
  of management science, 63–65
  of marketing management, 26–27
  of M.B.A.'s, 90–91
  (*See also* Performance; Profitability)
Risk, 160, 218
Rix (fast-food chain), 28
Roark, Rayford L., 138
Rockwell, George B., 179
Rohatyn, Felix G., 202–203, 212

Salary structure, M.B.A.'s, 83, 88–89
Sales:
  management innovation in, 156
  (*See also* Marketing)
Sales catalogue, 15
Sales-force management, 21–22
Sales forecasting, 3–4, 11–12
Saudi Arabia, 205
Saxbe, William B., 193–194
Sayles, Leonard B., 70, 75, 76, 81, 162
Schainblatt, A. H., 63, 66

242 / Index

Schein, Edgar, 91, 92, 95
Schellhardt, Timothy D., 19
Scott Morton, Michael S., 233
Sears Roebuck, 14–15, 17, 96
Securities and Exchange Commission, 31
Seed, Allen H., III, 78, 81
Servan-Schreiber, Jean-Jacques, 116
Silk, Leonard, 42–43, 54
Simon, Herbert A., 95, 144
Smith, James, 4
SofTech, Inc., 128, 179
South Africa, 202
Specialists and specialization:
    classification of, 100
    communication problem, 103
    in computers, graph, 43
    in experience-based management, 78, 101
    in Future Firm, 222–225
    increase in, 42, 77
    integration and, 97–100, 104–105
    inventory of, 98
    management of, 101–104
    M.B.A.'s, 85–87
    monitoring of, 98
    myopia problem, 18, 77, 109–110
    need for, 77
    performance evaluation, 102
    personnel development, 98
    problems of, 101–104
    selection of, 77
    strategy for use, 79–80, 98–99
    task forces, 181–183
    traditional professionals, 101–102
    use of, 18
    (See also Research-based management)
Stanford University, 86, 91, 95
State Street Financial Corporation, 179
Steiner, George A., 216
Stieglitz, H., 140, 145
Stopford, John M., 19
Strategic planning:
    definition of, 71
    General Electric, 33–34, 37
    IBM, 35
    lack of, 215
    (See also Planning)
Strauss, George, 54
Strout, Richard L., 204, 212
Supply and demand (see Demand pull; Supply push)
Supply push, 49–51
Sweden, 208
Synnott, William R., xii
Systems analysis:
    increase in, 42–43
    as new-management input, 18
    (See also Management information systems)

Task forces, 177–186
    government regulations, responding to, 181–182
    vs. innovation project, 183–184

Task forces (Cont.):
    integration and, 185
    line management in, 179–180
    role of president, 180–181
    specialists in, 179–180
Technology:
    changes in, 6
    diffusion of: demand pull, 49–52
        lag in, 8–9
        table, 9
        supply push, 49–51
    forecasting, 6
    information processing, 130
    integration and, 105, 107
    transfer of economic value, 65
Telex, 35, 115
Terrell, Richard L., 101
Texaco, table, 189
Thin management, 22, 29–30, 33, 35
3M Company, 213
Tilles, Seymour, 233
Time logs, 148
Time orientation, 118–119, 126
Tire industry, 113–114
Top management:
    education of, 67–68
    integration and, 122, 126
    lack of time to solve problems, 30
    on task forces, 178–181
Trueblood, Robert M., 145
Truman administration, 197, 201

United Kingdom, 202
University of California at Los Angeles, 216
University of Chicago, 40, 88, 95
    table, 86
University of Pennsylvania (Wharton School of Business), 57, 95, 226
Urban, Glen L., 56, 66
U.S.S.R., 202–204

Vanderwicken, Peter, 176
Vernon, Raymond, 203–204, 212

Wankel engine, 31
Washington, D.C., population per lawyer, 199
Weidenbaum, Murray L., 197–198, 209, 211
Wellemeyer, Marilyn, 95
West Germany, 194–195, 200, 208–209
Westinghouse, 130
White House Council on Environmental Quality, 207
Whittaker Corporation, 48
Wilkerson, C. D., 140, 145
Winter, S. K., 162
Withington, F. G., 45–47, 54, 144
Wolfley, Alan, 89
Wood, Arthur M., 14